Unless P...

NEWCOMERS TO OLD TOWNS

Sonya Salamon

NEWCOMERS TO

WITH THE COLLABORATION OF
*Karen Davis-Brown, Patricia A. Howard, Consolata Kabonesa,
Bret Kloos, Cynthia Loula, Matteo B. Marini, Stephanie Schaefer,
Jane B. Tornatore, and Stacey Williams*

OLD TOWNS

Suburbanization of the Heartland

THE UNIVERSITY OF CHICAGO PRESS • CHICAGO AND LONDON

Sonya Salamon is professor of community studies and director of the Community and Rural Studies Concentration in the Department of Human and Community Development at the University of Illinois at Urbana-Champaign. She is the author of *Prairie Patrimony: Family, Farming, and Community in the Midwest*.

The University of Chicago Press, Chicago 60637
The University of Chicago Press, Ltd., London
© 2003 by The University of Chicago
All rights reserved. Published 2003
Printed in the United States of America

12 11 10 09 08 07 06 05 04 03   1 2 3 4 5

ISBN: 0-226-73412-9 (cloth)

Library of Congress Cataloging-in-Publication Data

Salamon, Sonya.
    Newcomers to old towns : suburbanization of the heartland / Sonya Salamon with the collaboration of Karen Davis-Brown . . . [et al.].
        p. cm.
    Includes bibliographical references and index.
    ISBN 0-226-73412-9 (cloth : alk. paper)
        1. Urban-rural migration—Middle West. 2. Urban-rural migration—Illinois—Case studies. 3. Sociology, Rural—Middle West. 4. Sociology, Rural—Illinois. 5. Middle West—Rural conditions. 6. Illinois—Rural conditions. I. Title.

HT384.M629 S35 2003
307.72′0977—dc21
                                                                    2002067527

♾ The paper used in this publication meets the minimum requirements of the American National Standard for Information Sciences—Permanence of Paper for Printed Library Materials, ANSI Z39.48-1992.

To Myron

CONTENTS

ILLUSTRATIONS

Figures

Photographs follow page 92.

PREFACE

I began to think about this book as I drove around Illinois to interview farmers. My research took me to small towns in all parts of the state, where I stayed three or four nights in each town. It was clear as I surveyed the landscape on those long drives that changes were under way in the countryside. In towns and along the highways I could see subdivisions sprouting up. Some small towns were making improvements to their main streets in hopes of attracting tourists. New faces were evident even in remote towns. The town doctors, according to the farmers I talked to, were Pakistani, Filipino, or Indian, and they and their families lived and worked in the small towns. Staying at a motel in one town, I answered a knock on the door and found three generations of Indian women and their numerous children inquiring when I was going to stop typing and check out.

Farmers' lives, too, had changed since I first studied them almost thirty years ago. There were definitely a lot fewer of them. Farm families were sensitive to the implications of their diminishing numbers for schools and communities. Some farmers seemed almost suburban as parents chauffeured their children around for team sports or classes and decorated their homes and gardens. They traveled farther to shop at large stores in the small cities within an hour of home.

My curiosity was piqued by the changes I observed. Thus began my interest in newcomers to old towns and the effects of rapid change on small farming communities. The field studies for the book were carried out over a six-year period, and the writing has consumed another five years. A project of this size involves many collaborators, funding sources, settings, and subjects. My gratitude to everyone who took part is great.

Research efforts such as this multicommunity study must often be collaborative. In this case a number of master's- and doctoral-level students were responsible for the bulk of the fieldwork, and the case studies drew upon class papers or master's theses. Karen Davis-Brown (now at a consulting firm in Sacramento, California, that does research and evaluation for organizations and agencies working with children and families) did the fieldwork for chapter 3. Stephanie Schaefer (now a policy and advocacy specialist with the National Association of Child Advocates in Washington, D.C.), Bret Kloos (now in the Department of Psychology at Yale University), Consolata Kabonesa (now in the Department of Women and Gender, Makerere University, Kampala, Uganda), and Patricia A. Howard (who has recently completed her Ph.D. in anthropology at the University of Illinois at Urbana-Champaign) were all members of a qualitative methods workshop that I taught in the spring of 1995. Chapter 4 uses data produced by these students, who designed, carried out, and analyzed a community survey as a team. Cynthia Loula (a part-time instructor of family studies at Joliet Junior College) did the neighborhood survey for the chapter 5 community study. Stacey Williams (now a social worker in suburban Indianapolis) completed the fieldwork for and wrote her master's thesis on the chapter 6 community. Patricia Howard also did the fieldwork and analyzed data for the community study in chapter 7. Jane B. Tornatore (now a postdoctoral fellow at the Department of Veteran's Affairs, Puget Sound Health Care Services, Seattle, Washington) carried out the fieldwork for and wrote her master's thesis on the community study in chapter 8. These individuals are listed as collaborators on the chapters in which each played a major role; they have all read and commented on the chapters, which I wrote.

Appendix A was written jointly with Matteo B. Marini, an Italian rural development economist from the University of Calabria, while he visited at the University of Illinois during 1996 and 1997 on a Fulbright Fellowship. That appendix proposes a "neighborhood hypothesis" developed inductively from the qualitative community case studies. Marini tested the hypothesis using census and economic data.

I first wish to thank Calvin Beale, a fine and generous colleague who has been an important sounding board and consultant about demographic issues throughout the ten-year development of this book. Critical to the germination of the first draft was spending three months of my 1995–96 sabbatical at the U.S. Department of Agriculture, Economic Research Service (ERS), and eating lunch with Calvin every day. I have also consulted him from time to time since my sabbatical, particularly as the 2000 census data began to appear in 2001. Timothy Parker and Peggy Cook of the ERS generously provided unpublished Illinois data about counties and jobs, respectively. Other colleagues at the ERS who provided intellectual stimulation are John Cromartie, Mark Nord, David McGranahan, Linda Swanson, and Deborah Tootle.

The W. K. Kellogg National Rural Studies Committee is also very important to my work. Regular interaction as a member between 1987 and 1997 contributed to my shift of focus from farmers to rural communities. The multidisciplinary makeup of the committee was especially exciting. In particular I owe a great deal to committee chair Emery Castle, vice chair Gene F. Summers, David L. Brown, Ronald J. Oakerson, Ed Bergman, Julian Wolpert, Bruce A. Weber, Bonnie Thornton Dill, and Carol B. Stack.

Colleagues who generously took precious time to read all or part of the manuscript at various stages include Bill Falk, Ann Reisner, Aaron Ebata, Glen Elder, Jane Adams, and Mike Bell. None of them are responsible for the end product, of course, but their feedback made an enormous difference to my writing.

Numerous other colleagues talked about small towns with me over the years at meetings, via E-mail, and by telephone. I acknowledge with respect and gratitude the late Janet M. Fitchen, Peggy Barlett, Max Pfeffer, Jane Adams, Kate MacTavish, Robin Jarrett, Linda Lobao, Robert Moreno, Maureen Perry-Jenkins, Andrew Sofranko, Tom Lyson, Ben Mueller, Ann Silvis, Cynthia M. Duncan, Paul Eberts, Charles Geisler, and Mildred Warner. Louise Lamphere and Carole Nagengast at the University of New Mexico were kind and stimulating hosts during my 1995–96 sabbatical.

Marla Kibler ably provided out-of-the-ordinary secretarial assistance and access to Chuck Kibler, who prepared the community maps. Peggy L. Currid's and, more importantly, Lois R. Crum's careful editing of the manuscript improved the clarity and accuracy of my prose immeasurably.

My community field studies and the writing process were supported by funding from a variety of sources. The Smallville study was supported during 1988 and 1989 by an Ameritech Research Fellowship. Fieldwork in Splitville, Bunkerton, Corntown, and Arbordale was carried out with funding through the Illinois Agricultural Experiment Station between 1989 and 1995 under Hatch Projects 60-0386 and 60-313. Funding for studies on farming topics in rural Illinois indirectly supported observations that were made in many small towns, observations that I draw on particularly in chapters 1 and 9. Fieldwork for a 1992–94 study that focused on adoption of sustainable farming systems, funded by grant number LWF 62-01-03113 from the North Central Region Sustainable Agriculture Research and Education Program, took me to about a dozen communities all over Illinois. My horizons were broadened considerably by staying in each of them for about five days and interviewing farmers. Similarly, a 1996–98 grant from the Illinois Council for Food and Agricultural Research (C-FAR) Project 97-108 to study the impact of urban sprawl on farmers in Kane County contributed to my understanding of the suburbanization process taking place in the Midwest. Funding during 1999–2001 from the U.S. Department of Agriculture, National Research Initiative Competitive Grants Program number 98-35401-6139, to study rural mobile home parks allowed me to revisit Prairieview and explore changes that had taken place since my class first studied the community three years earlier.

The Economic Research Service of the U.S. Department of Agriculture gave me some support from Cooperative Agreement number 43-3AEN-5-80073; that support included three months as a visiting scholar during my 1995–96 sabbatical, when I first drafted the ideas that became this book. Particularly important was the late-1995 blizzard that shut down Washington, D.C., for about a week, leaving me alone in an apartment with nothing to think about but the book.

The Rural Sociological Society has kindly permitted me to draw heavily on a paper that appeared as "Territory Contested through Property in a Midwestern Post-Agricultural Community" (with Jane B. Tornatore), *Rural Sociology* 59, no. 4 (1994): 636–54. The Associated Press granted permission to reprint an article as figure 8. The photographs are reprinted courtesy of the University of Illinois Extension, College of Agricultural, Consumer and Environmental Sciences, Information Technology and Communication Services. Some of them were selected from the College archive, and others were taken especially for the book by David Riecks of the College.

Finally, I owe a great debt to the more than 250 families and approximately 30 small-town public servants with whom I and my associates talked and who generously shared their lives and work. I cannot thank them by name here, but they know who they are. I am sure not all of them will be happy with the picture drawn of them or their community. My intention was to describe their lives and their towns to show what it means to be ordinary people dealing with rapid change.

My husband, Myron Salamon, has endlessly endured dinner conversations, edited countless versions of chapters 1 and 9, and in other ways too numerous to mention provided support (computer and otherwise) for the research and writing of this book during the decade it required.

PART I

Changes in the Heartland

In the process of modern industrial and political development . . . fewer individuals have the secure interpersonal relations which formerly gave meaning and stability to existence. . . .

The quest for community will not be denied, for it springs from some of the powerful needs of human nature—needs for a clear sense of cultural purpose, membership, status, and continuity.

Robert A. Nisbet, 1953

1 COMMUNITY CONNECTIONS, RESOURCES, AND PEOPLE

Life in a small midwestern town does not evoke, in an outsider, an image of arcadian perfection. Yet for twenty-five years, rural midwesterners have told me proudly about their beloved communities and their preference for life there over life anywhere else. It is not local ambience that binds them, for if the truth be told, most Illinois small towns are not distinguished by scenic locale or fine architecture. Rather, the rural residents equate people—fellow community members—with their sense of a good place to live. Small-town people need not yearn for community, as do many in the United States, because they have it; they know everyone and everyone knows them. Community members have a sense of place, shaped by a shared history and a shared culture derived from continuity of generations. These deep roots give them an awareness of who they are as people. As a citizen of a special place, albeit one with acknowledged warts, a member of a small community is considered a good person—virtuous, loyal, trustworthy, and altruistic. Community serves as a metaphor for their intimately connected lives. Small-town people recognize that they must be committed to shouldering the work required of citizens to produce and sustain an authentic community. They have learned over time that community exists in the doing and redoing.

Now, as the twenty-first century begins, towns in rural Illinois are drifting from their deep-rooted heritage and losing the vestiges of community that connect them with the golden age of small towns at the turn of the twentieth century. Under an onslaught of suburbanization, residents are struggling to preserve what is best about the insular but supportive towns they love. This book explores an unheralded social and physical transformation that is under way in the countryside among agrarian communities. Regional suburbanization processes are reconfiguring the rural Midwest and, in all likelihood, much of rural America (see Bloom 2000; Herbers 1986). Because rural America accounts for most of the geographic area of the United States, it is important to shed light on this transformation process.

Writing this book was a labor of love for this urban transplant to the rural Midwest, who learned after the passage of years to appreciate the workaday charm of its cohesive small communities nestled on the flatlands. My admiration was spurred by observing various communities over twenty-five years of research but also by learning from small-town students in my classes and by regularly combing a regional newspaper. My attraction to the Midwest was sealed by watching Illinoisans deal with the disastrous 1993 flood. Even cynical reporters were motivated to write glowingly about rural communities along the surging Mississippi. Journalists from the *New Yorker* (Stewart 1993) and the *New York Times* (Rimer 1993) contrasted the generosity, selflessness, egalitarianism, and cooperation of Iowans, Missourians, and Illinoisans with the gouging, exploitation, and class-biased reactions observed in Florida after Hurricane Andrew in 1992. These national reporters witnessed the distinctive social fabric of the midwestern agrarian community at its best: a communal response to crisis, woven from customs of cooperation, trust, watchfulness, and volunteerism. They are customs that were honed on the prairie frontier by current midwesterners' ancestors, who learned that the best way to protect their families was to sustain their fledgling communities.

Negative stereotypes abound for midwestern agrarian communities, perhaps rooted in high school reading assignments of such authors as Edgar Lee Masters, Sherwood Anderson, and Sinclair Lewis or in television sitcoms. Puritanical, provincial, nosy, materialistic characters suffocate creative and individualistic heroes and heroines in early-twentieth-century novels about the small towns that then typified much of America. Classical anthropological and sociological midwestern community studies similarly document coercive conformity in which local gossip, criticism, and actions aggressively maintain an egalitarian and homogeneous facade (see Atherton 1954; Billington 1966; Blumenthal 1932; Lynd and Lynd 1929, 1937; Varenne 1977; Vidich and Bensman 1958). Yet midwesterners working the great flood were extolled as the epitome of unselfish cooperation and altruism. Each image contains truths. As we will see, what seemed to early novelists an impervious, rigid social structure appears more fragile and fluid as transformation processes move diverse people into, not out of, small rural towns.

My exploration of rural community change focuses on the meanings people attach to community and how commitment to place is shaped by these meanings. I define a rural place where a sense of community is strongly felt as an *agrarian community* to highlight its origin as a farming community. This definition is forged from ethnographic study of twenty-one Illinois small towns (all under 6,000 population and most under 2,500) since 1975. In agrarian communities families can trace a shared background through multiple generations, since the mid- and late nineteenth century. In many places people also have an ethnic origin in common (Salamon 1992). Such stability means that over generations, community members have shared a history, an identity, and norms associated with the land in a particular place. Thus, I see agrarian communities as cultural systems densely connected by social networks that link families in functional and emotional ways. Outside the Midwest such towns similarly have been defined as having cultures emphasizing place, space, rurality, and a sense of community (Bell 1994).

In midwestern communities functioning according to agrarian norms, the homes are clustered and the streets are narrow enough to promote neighborliness (Kunstler 1993). The communities' ideal is a tight-knit integration of all residents; in reality, differences exist, but they are downplayed by egalitarian norms. Cooperation, trust, and consensus-building lie behind the ideals of self-reliance, continuity, and respectful support for dependent members (Freudenberg 1986; Salamon 1992; Smith 1966). The current social transformation therefore must be gauged against agrarian norms that have altered since frontier days but are still salient to community meaning. A critical point is that agriculture is no longer synonymous with life in a rural small town (Castle 1995). Agrarian communities, once proud, self-contained, insular worlds, are being transformed into places where people only live; they work, shop, and obtain services elsewhere.

The rural transformation is spurred by a combination of economic, social, and technological forces that have reversed a twentieth-century pattern of rural exodus. Between 1990 and 1996, rural America grew by nearly 3 million people (Johnson and Beale 1998). Despite the long-term decline in the numbers of farms and farm families, rural areas experienced a faster rate of job growth than did metropolitan areas in the early 1990s (Beale 1989; Beale and Kalbacher 1989; Johnson and Beale 1998). Even while rural townspeople were relishing these economic benefits, state governments were pressuring rural school districts to consolidate and federal policies forced the centralization of health care delivery systems. A regional concentration of jobs, shopping, and services into nearby small cities was encouraged by these trends, by improved state highway systems, and by the preference of rural people for regional malls and urban services. Together these factors now diminish the likelihood that a small town will maintain a local school or a vibrant main street—institutions that provided a midwestern small town's heart and character. Such regionalization also eroded the relative insularity that helped maintain the unique identity of a small town and create loyalty based on exclusiveness.

The restructuring of rural America is driven by a robust national preference for the safe, friendly, close-to-nature, agreeably scaled, family-focused, peaceful life associated with old, agrarian, small rural towns (Hummon 1990; Kunstler 1993). It has been a preference strong enough to produce a population "deconcentration" (Johnson and Beale 1998). The romanticized appeal of small towns fostered an influx of new residents into rural America in response to specific issues in urban areas. For example, big-city crime produced white flight (Turner 1998). Despite the events of September 11, 2001, and the downturn of the economy, national prosperity remains at a level that ensures that rural places will retain a strong allure for people whose roots are not there but who can afford to live there and work elsewhere. Therein lies my story of how our enduring national vision of Arcadia—a small-town way of life in a rural landscape—has newcomers refashioning agrarian communities into suburban enclaves for nearby small cities.

Clarification of a few critical terms is needed here. Throughout the book I make an artificial distinction by using the term *town* for the physical dimensions of a place that make it a spatial territory— an entity on a map with visible boundaries, a street plan, and public spaces (Gieryn 2000). *Town* is distinguished from *community*, which I use to emphasize the social relationships attached to a place. Clearly the town and community aspects of a place overlap and interact. These components—physical setting and social relationships— together produce over time a town and community greater than the sum of its parts. An organic community is identified by a distinctive culture and identity that provide meaning and a place identity to its members.

In a previous book I described community culture as being ethnically derived; I focused on the culturally conservative family-based beliefs and practices related to intergenerational land transfers, kin relations, and farm succession (Salamon 1992). Each of the ethnic farming communities I described in that book, however, also had a distinctive personality (even if the same ethnicity) that developed from its settlement pattern, stratification, environment, religious leadership, and a history of weathering events together—tornadoes, fires, the Great Depression, or floods. That is, even a community culture that is dominated by ethnicity is also shaped by history, geography (soils and topography), demography, conflicts, and citizenship. Together these dimensions create a unique story line of place that accounts for how and why a particular group does things the way they do. In addition, uniqueness is constantly reinforced by the way a place defines *we* as differing from *they*—the people from neighboring places (Barth 1969). Typically, *we* in one midwestern town are closer-knit, nicer, and better than those folks over there, even if they look just like us.

A community that works as an organic whole is defined by a distinct culture with a sense of permanence, an interconnectedness created by strong connections built from repeated interactions based on shared norms; there is a sense of trust that enables members of the community to mobilize and act in the group's behalf (Coleman 1990; Kunstler 1993; Putnam 1993a; Tilly 1973; Williams 1988). Sharing a sense of community means that residents transcend simple proximity because they act in ways that identify their interests as being connected to the interests of their neighbors (Fowler 1991; Kemmis 1995; Lavenda 1997; Putnam 1993b).

Today, Illinois towns (or towns throughout the rural Midwest) in outward respects are indistinguishable from the suburbs that ring Chicago. A visitor finds in both small town and Chicago suburb the same fast-food restaurants, gas stations, motel chains, and supermarkets. Disk-jockey patter on rural radio stations is identical to the packaged routine that one hears on the city stations. Only when a visitor gets out of the car and interacts with shop owners, supermarket checkers, or motel desk clerks are the distinctive cultural features of a small town clearly discernible.

I found small-town people more open, friendly, and curious about me than those back home in Urbana, not a large place by Chicago standards. Watching as townsfolk joked among themselves in a café, shopping at the local drugstore, and participating in ordinary street and shop interactions provided a window into what is taken for granted about daily small-town life. Rural midwesterners greet strangers with a nod or a hello, strike up a conversation readily, include them in a joke, and in general are eager to be neighborly. Oldtimers (lifelong residents typically born in the place) like where they live and feel confident that others will, too. Newcomers to such towns are different. For example, when my students carried out research in a town where upscale subdivisions have mushroomed (see chapter 4), oldtimers always invited them inside, but newcomers kept them on the front step. Oldtimers observe that customary forms of community hospitality, such as the friendly wave when passing on rural roads or the leisurely chat when getting mail at the post office, are not practiced readily by most newcomers. Newcomers find the neighborly ways of small-town oldtimers quaint, amusing, and inefficient. Mutual respect is not inevitably generated.

Since the 1980s, diverse groups of newcomers, attracted by the authenticity and peacefulness of small towns, have settled in and thereby profoundly changed such places physically and socially. In some cases this influx started as early as the 1960s, before the rural rebound was officially noted (Beale 1990; Johnson and Beale 1998). Some towns recruited newcomers, and others experienced their arrival almost as a hostile takeover. In the latter case, there were newcomers who saw small towns as interchangeable; for these people residences and land are commodities bought, sold, or invested in unsentimentally. Other newcomers respect the special sense of place where they take up residence and value a town's uniqueness. The shift from the oldtimer's concept of community as social relationships to the concept of property and place as commodities is altering the storied agrarian social fabric of the rural Midwest (Davis 1991; Urry 1995). The new communities and the altered rural countryside form what I call a *postagrarian* social fabric. Postagrarian towns are those formed by surbanization; they are located in what remains a productive agricultural landscape but are not socially or economically connected to it. This is a suburban phenomenon that differs from the one that forms rings of suburbs around larger cities, for the focal points are smaller cities and the towns are widely scattered. I describe how this gradually suburbanizing social fabric is being woven in six distinct community transformation case studies that make up the core of this book.

In the six central Illinois town case studies, newcomer and oldtimer encounters illustrate the impact of exurban sprawl (the settling of places outside a suburban ring by urbanites), which is engulfing agrarian communities nationwide (Herbers 1986; Johnson and Beale 1998; Lewis 1995; Luloff and Swanson 1990; Palen 1995). A variety of push and pull factors have lured particular newcomers to particular sleepy small towns that had long suffered deterioration of their main streets and which had surplus housing because of the continual exodus of the young and energetic. Several of the case study towns are being exploited for financial gain by real estate developers for their amenities or ambience. One town has seen rural working-poor families pushed there by the gentrification of other towns in the region. The transformation of rural America mirrors national residential trends—suburbanization, urban sprawl, and uneven development—that generate upscale conditions in some places while leaving other places behind (Bradshaw 1993; Falk and Lyson 1993; Logan and Molotch 1987).

As residents from transformed postagrarian communities commute between small towns and the regional center for work, leisure, and services, their daily routines knit together the countryside and the city. Thus, distinctions between rural and urban places have become fuzzier in the regional commuting zone emerging from postagrarian suburbanization trends. The term *commuting zone* was coined to explain rural labor markets. A commuting zone is one or more counties that make up commuting flows (Killian and Parker 1991). A midwestern rural regional commuting zone may be visualized metaphorically as an archipelago: towns are connected to a small city as an archipelago is linked to the mainland (Alonso 1993). Each postagrarian town lies in the broad expanse of soybean and cornfield landscape as islands dot the sea.

Calvin Beale (personal communication, 1996) has suggested another metaphor for the emerging postagrarian social fabric of this earthbound archipelago. From a regional perspective, the small towns represented by the case studies, as a consequence of the postagrarian transformation, are emerging as neighborhoods for a nearby metro area that is the central magnet for work, shopping, services, and entertainment within the commuting zone. Four of the eleven counties that form a single commuting zone are represented by the six community case studies.

Neighborhood is thus another key term that I employ. Usually neighborhoods are distinctive residential areas within a town or city among which people are sorted by class, lifestyle, and profession through residential choice (or lack of it). Neighborhood enclaves include residents with a common culture or way of life whose ties are more instrumental than primary and intimate (Warren 1978). Ideally, the people living in a neighborhood are marked by a loyalty developed from frequent, regular involvement with one another (Fischer 1982, 1991). Inspired by Beale's suggestion, my argument is that former agrarian towns are being transformed into neighborhood places within a regional commuting zone, for differing categories of newcomers sharing a preference for small-town life. Homogeneous places emerge as newcomers sort themselves among postagrarian towns whose residents most resemble them, particularly by class. Because the newcomers remain attached to the city that anchors the commuting zone for all household functions except residence, these postagrarian towns are essentially urban neighborhoods, but they are distinguished by the rural hallmark of being spatially dispersed. Commuting drives suburbanization and is reinforced by the tendency for newcomer segregation in new subdivisions. Thus, a postagrarian town, in contrast to an agrarian town, is defined more by geographical than social boundaries.

Neighborhoodization, I argue, is the postagrarian community outcome of the rural regional suburbanization process. Suburbanized, homogeneous rural neighborhoods are oriented outward toward the metro area anchoring the region, rather than inward. The emerging postagrarian rural landscape is thus defined by towns functioning as distinctive class-segregated neighborhoods in a small-city commuting zone. The population of suburbanized postagrarian towns exhibits less trust than an agrarian-community population does, avoids neighborly contact and conflict, and focuses on possessions rather than social acts to validate the family reputation (Baumgartner 1988; Kenny 2000). Neighborhoodization means that the logical end of the suburbanization process is a social fabric of postagrarian towns in a monocultural landscape, replacing the more nuanced, subtly distinctive tapestry of cultures in agrarian towns (Gieryn 2000). The place name is the same, but the nontown suburbanized culture is not what oldtimers equate with their formerly authentic hometown.

As early as the 1950s, sociologists were proclaiming the demise of small towns and their distinctive way of life (Gallaher and Padfield 1980; Vidich and Bensman 1958). It is fascinating that we now return to the community questions that drove classical community theorists—Ferdinand Tonnies, Max Weber, Emile Durkheim, and Georg Simmel—as they observed the vast spatial migration shifts from rural to urban areas in the nineteenth century. Today the nation faces the social consequences of another population shift, but in reverse—a vast movement of people from urban to rural areas. I have the same concern as the classical theorists: what happens to a sense of community under conditions of rapid change? Like them, I ask, Does this social transformation entail a loss of community? Is community saved or liberated (Wellman 1979)? Why does one community change in a particular way and another differently? Which type of newcomers is attracted to which community? These questions about community-change processes are first addressed in chapter 2, in a general way. Explored throughout the six town case studies are four community dimension questions used to compare an agrarian town with a transformed postagrarian town:

1. How are social relations in the transformed community reflected in the use and design of public *spaces and* (residents' sense of) *place*?
2. Are there *interconnections* across the community that link all residents through social networks?
3. Is the emergent social system one in which all residents are provided equal access to community *social resources*?
4. What sorts of *cross-age relations* are taken for granted in everyday life, particularly in regard to community youth?

Classic small-town novels evoke claustrophobic midwestern places rather than the affectionate picture painted by agrarian-community oldtimers. The rural good life hawked in real estate advertisements— family togetherness and closeness to nature—convey little sense that these same communities were places from which people fled during much of the twentieth century. That newcomers now choose to live in or at least adjacent to older towns makes such places fascinating material for natural experiments examining social change. The small scale of rural communities provides an ideal setting for studying the dynamics of social life because such communities are more accessible than a complex city or a diffuse suburb. From census and ethnographic data we are able to learn who came and when they came and who was already there. These baseline data and outcomes allow us to ask the specific questions listed above about community social change.

AGRARIAN VERSUS POSTAGRARIAN COMMUNITIES

Because rural small towns have been the wellspring for the nation's leadership and democratic ideals and have served as supportive and resourceful settings for youth development, it is important to examine the extent of "communityness" in the six transformed rural towns in the case studies. Four dimensions that reflect the questions raised above constitute the comparative framework for organizing the community case studies. Each dimension is important both alone and as it interacts in the transformations that typify a community:

spatial attributes of place (home and town) and space; connectedness of place; social resources available to residents; and cross-age relations, primarily those between youth and adults. Following are the factors taken into account by the description of a critical community dimension in each town case study.

Space and Place

With regard to the layout of their streets, midwestern agrarian towns uniformly follow a grid, based on a template adopted by nineteenth-century railroad companies such as the Illinois Central for town development along new rail lines. Throughout the region, the main business street has a grain elevator anchoring one end and residential side streets running perpendicular to it. The pattern is consistent even to the naming of streets for trees (Hudson 1985). Each street is narrow, with a tree-lined sidewalk providing natural cooling in the summer. Houses are oriented to the street, with wide porches. The procession of porches allows neighbors to socialize, but the porch also serves as a mediating zone between the world of family and the world of community (Kunstler 1993). Such a plan encourages interaction, watchfulness over children, and awareness of neighborhood comings and goings. One rainy afternoon while interviewing a retired Irish-American farming couple in a central Illinois village, I experienced this watchfulness firsthand. Soon after my arrival, a neighbor from across the street telephoned to say, "Your visitor left her lights on." Watchfulness by neighbors creates a sense of security for residents, even as it functions as a social control mechanism for families and youth (Gieryn 2000).

The grid pattern imposed a social order that was inherently democratic in that all streets were similar, even if some lots might be larger and some homes grander than others. The traditional midwestern railroad-town plan is being revived by New Urbanist planners and architects in places such as Celebration and Seaside, Florida, and Kentlands, Maryland, to help foster a sense of community (Ross 1999). New Urbanists consider community engagement and attachment related to how space is designed; that is, the building and maintenance of community are supported or undermined by the physical plan of residential and public areas.

Land use at the edge of agrarian towns is now disrupting the egalitarian "square to the road" scheme. Developers are designing rural subdivisions like the suburbs the New Urbanists advocate abandoning. Built outside the original town grid, new rural subdivisions have culs-de-sac or artificial lakes and houses set on a "welcoming diagonal" (Riley 1985). Privacy is maximized by orienting the home to the back and by placing double or triple garages in the front. These plans incorporate newcomer priorities for privately viewing nature as a landscape devoid of people other than one's family (Halle 1993). Conspicuous consumption is evidenced by professionally landscaped, deep lawns surrounding the ostentatious homes. Such displays interrupt the original agrarian landscape; they try to impress rather than to fit unassumingly into the egalitarian order created by the original grid (Urry 1995). When the community balance is tipped toward such display homes, towns transform into places fundamentally based on consumption, intruding on a primarily productive agrarian landscape (Gladwell 2000). The juxtaposition of an agrarian town, still involved in productive activities, and such consumption-based suburbs emphasizes the emergence of two categories of residents divided by occupation or class as well as space.

Rural subdivisions carry names like Rolling Prairie or Woodland Acres, to honor the landscape features that the developer has just obliterated (Lippard 1997). Within the new subdivision neighborhoods, propinquity does not necessarily foster a sense of community, as it did in the agrarian town plan. In fact, these new places build in a residential segregation by class and consumption in towns where previously the classes were mixed together and differences were not emphasized (Gieryn 2000). These physical changes to the rural landscape offer visual clues about the segregation and disconnection emerging within towns. Older grid towns—at least parts of them—are coming to spatially resemble suburbanized America (Palen 1995).

Public spaces are arenas where a sense of community develops that bonds residents to a place (Francaviglia 1996; Low and Altman 1992; Oldenburg 1999). Agrarian towns have public spaces such as a central square or park, a café, a bowling alley, or a library, where community members of all ages gather. Agrarian communities are tolerant of adolescents' use of public space, even if noise is generated by their "dragging main" or hanging out in a parking lot. Oldtimers show forbearance, however reluctantly, because they are aware of the limited recreational alternatives (Childress 1993, 2000; Schwartz 1987; Willits, Crider, and Funk 1988). New subdivisions normally are not designed with communal spaces for recreation, or even with sidewalks. Discontent among suburban youth is related to their lack of spaces comparable to agrarian town public spaces (Childress 2000; Gans 1967).

Located far enough away from agrarian town centers to make neighboring inconvenient, new subdivisions create barriers to the informal interactions basic to community building. Thus, lifestyle consumption patterns for space and home reflect the cultural differences between new and old residents' definitions of the good life and the good community. Newcomers do not speak of class differences directly, but their consumption choices and their avoidance of contact with persons of less obvious wealth reveal a consciousness of class (Ortner 1991).

An adolescent who develops attachment to a place is more likely to stay or, if she or he leaves, to return as an adult to raise a family. When adolescents feel marginalized from local spaces and activities, alienation develops and emotional ties to a place are more tenuous (Chawla 1992; Childress 2000). Emotions associated with a place are related to one's early experiences there (Hummon 1990). If youth and others feel strongly attached to place, they are more likely to share responsibility for it, which will be visible in their use and care of its public spaces (Logan and Molotch 1987, 133). A sense of community expressed in these ways is influenced by the design of town spaces and public arenas.

Interconnectedness

To produce and maintain a sense of community, people must interact in ways that foster it (Kemmis 1995; Williams 1988). Interactions produce connections or social ties that generate social networks among community members (Wuthnow 1998). The strength or looseness of these connections is related to the frequency, specificity, or breadth of tasks; spontaneity or formality of the interactions; and the commitment of actors to one another. Agrarian connections reflect the classical Tonnies concept of *gemeinschaft*, where families and land, stable kin groups, neighborhoods, and friendships were fundamental to social organization and provided enduring, intimate, and supportive ties (Tonnies 1957). Agrarian communities have strong, dense connections; frequent, spontaneous, and informal interactions about broad and specific issues; and a loyalty to place. Even for nineteenth-century towns, Tonnies's concept represented an idealized traditional past, but that idealization retains an allure of authenticity for newcomers, thereby producing the rural revival. The social costs for strong connections are considered high, because such ties limit people's options and constitute barriers to innovation and efficiency in a rapidly changing world (Granovetter 1973).

In agrarian communities, residential stability means that families have multiple generations of kin living nearby (Fischer 1982; Logan and Spitze 1994). Families are connected by a web of kinship in which relatives are seen daily, children are brought up by extended kin as much as by parents, and kin often are close friends (Elder and Conger 2000; Salamon 1992). It is because multiple generations live in proximity that midwestern agrarian communities are gemeinschaft-like places where the elderly function as grandparents to everyone. Interconnectedness is reinforced when a high proportion of families are linked by kinship ties of some sort: "Everyone is related to everyone else somehow" is a common remark heard in agrarian communities. Stable residence also means that neighbors are well acquainted and, moreover, know each other's family history and reputation. Although such knowledge can be used coercively as a social control mechanism, unconditional acceptance of one's idiosyncrasies can free one from acting on pretense.

Households in agrarian communities are linked by social networks with overlapping memberships in which kin and neighbors, as well as work, school, or church groups, constitute "small worlds" (Elder and Conger 2000). These small worlds are the mechanism for interconnecting agrarian communities. Families see kin and neighbors at church. Children encounter a teacher downtown or at Sunday school. Similarly, teachers or the local garage owner play on the town softball team, whose summer evening games are watched by the whole town. When life takes place in these small worlds, people share cultural attitudes, beliefs, and practices that define behavior, and social networks have closure. For a child or a youth, network closure means that multiple adults are connected to one another and the child; the adults can readily confer about the youth and jointly enforce community standards. In such a setting, a child receives consistent reinforcement for good behavior or sanctions for bad, from a variety of adults who are in agreement. Network closure is a positive community attribute for children's development (Coleman 1988, 1990; Elder and Conger 2000). Of course, network closure also effectively regulates adult behavior in agrarian communities. Much research shows that newcomers often reject the agrarian network-connection ideals that oldtimers share (see, e.g., Engel 1984; Fitchen 1991; Salamon and Tornatore 1994; Sokolow 1981; Spain 1993). Nonetheless, these same town ideals probably were an attraction for newcomers. Newcomers tend to romanticize town harmony and benefits and do not fathom the social costs of strong interconnectedness.

Newcomers to small towns carry urban and suburban social baggage honed in a *gesellschaft*, a society in which individualism prevails and governance is more by laws and bureaucracies than by the traditions, morals, and customs of a gemeinschaft (Greenhouse,

Yngvesson, and Engel 1994; Tonnies 1957). Newcomers to small town may have no understanding of the local history and culture. They are not likely to have relatives nearby or in town. Newcomers are therefore not burdened by the need to uphold a family reputation. They also are more mobile than oldtimers, less likely to spend their whole lives in the same place. Having segregated social networks—for work, kinship, school, and leisure—means that newcomers' lives are more fragmented and more diffuse across space than those of oldtimers. Newcomers, although living in the same place as oldtimers, are unlikely to experience the benefits of network closure either as adults or as children. Newcomers, particularly middle-class newcomers, prefer loose connections and porous institutions that maximize autonomy and freedom (Wuthnow 1998).

Newcomers who live in or near a small town may go to church somewhere else. Their choice of church is linked more to theology than to community membership and status; in agrarian towns, however, community and church reinforce each other (Ammerman 1997; Salamon 1992; Vidich and Bensman 1958). Agrarian-community churches are depended on to consistently mobilize on behalf of the community for social support or moral leadership. In the conservative Protestant churches that often attract rootless newcomers, the congregations are focused more inward than outward on secular community-building activities (Ammerman 1997; Wilson and Janoski 1995; Wuthnow 1994).

Developers marketing new rural subdivisions sell quality of life, investment, and nature rather than agrarian community life (see the advertisement at the end of this chapter). In many respects the lives of newcomers resemble life as it has recently been documented for suburbia, even as the layout of their subdivisions mimics that of the suburbs (see, e.g., Baumgartner 1988; Greenhouse 1986; Kenny 2000; Palen 1995). If they choose, newcomers can easily avoid face-to-face interactions with oldtimers, because the new subdivisions effectively segregate them spatially. Residents of the new subdivisions may have scant knowledge even about their neighbors, being more connected to the nearby city than to their neighborhood. Without interaction, no connections are made. If connections are made in the town, they tend to be where newcomers have narrow, vested interests, such as in the local schools or in church (Gans 1961; Wuthnow 1998). Newcomers who buy an older home in the original town are more likely to form connections with oldtimers, because of the street layout and an identification with the old town.

Shunning community connections by avoiding interaction facilitates newcomer-family mobility (Wuthnow 1998). Local issues matter little if a family views itself as sojourners who intend to move on (Siu 1952, 1987). Having come to a small town for the children's sake, parents are free to relocate when the children are launched. A suburban detachment and the associated avoidance of conflict—conflict in old towns over politics and finances being endemic—has been termed *moral minimalism,* and it distinctively characterizes suburban, and perhaps postagrarian, places (Baumgartner 1988; Kenny 2000). Thus, newcomers may live in a small community but not belong to it. They may prefer loose connections to the overlapping small worlds so treasured by oldtimers (Wuthnow 1998). Because they are less connected with their neighbors, newcomers are not as trusting as the oldtimers (Putnam 2000). With time and a robust influx of additional newcomers, their preference for loose connections may overwhelm oldtimer agrarian connections. Loose connectedness, similar to that found in suburbs, may be expected to characterize the postagrarian social fabric.

Social Resources

Embedded in the networks that link people loosely or closely are social resources used to organize and mobilize for activities on behalf of the community. These intangible resources are elemental aspects of the sense of community that people feel. Citizens' interest in the welfare of others is the manifestation of that sense of community (Wuthnow 1998). Furthermore, whether community resources are equally accessible to everyone and whether reciprocity is expected and delivered are issues related to a key aspect of community social resources, the trust felt by people for one another (Putnam 2000). Community resources are drawn upon for constructive, supportive ends, such as to fight the 1993 flood, or they may be used for coercive or destructive purposes such as racism, denying a certain category of people equal access.

Social capital, an attribute of a community's social structure, is a reservoir of social resources that facilitates cooperation for shared goals and activities. These activities in turn enhance community, family, and individual well-being (Coleman 1988; Putnam 2000). Community social capital is generated by citizens' actions to sustain and maintain their town as a good place to live. Active civic engagement ranges from participation as high school boosters or Lions Club members to organizing the annual Fourth of July celebration. These are the volunteer activities that agrarian communities depend on to make them work (Charles 1993). Engagement of the whole town in local school activities is common in agrarian communities—regardless of whether residents have school-aged children. Agrarian communities are horizontally connected by members' participation in a vast array of civic activities. The interactional processes entailed in such activities reinforce norms, define community identity, and help cement members' commitment (Putnam 1993a). Therefore, the greater the vitality of a community's institutions, the greater the ease of community mobilization for activities that generate more social resources, as noted previously regarding the great Mississippi flood of 1993.

When overlapping social network connections link a community, social capital is generated. People who know one another well and know that neighbors can be depended upon to reciprocate support are crucial sources of community trust, a valuable social resource (Coleman 1990). Active civic engagement thus not only makes agrarian communities work; it is what produces trust and responsiveness. While community resources have diminished nationally, midwestern agrarian communities have continued to sustain more civic engagement and higher levels of trust than other communities (Putnam 1993b; 2000). As our national icon for the good community, agrarian communities in the Midwest embody communitarian ideals of commitment to the general welfare (Etzioni 1993).

Recently we have begun to understand that the social resources available in agrarian communities make them exceptional incubators for youth development (Elder and Conger 2000). The accepted wisdom is, of course, that the best and brightest always leave the agrarian towns, taking with them the valuable resources of the community investment in them and their energy and talent, which are of potential benefit to the community. According to Edward Alsworth Ross's famous dictum, Indiana, Michigan, Illinois, and Missouri rural towns had already by the early twentieth century become "communities which remind one of fished-out ponds populated chiefly by bullheads and suckers" (1915, 157). When an agrarian-community identity connects a population, and rich social resources are present, a positive *community effect* is visible in the development of children, who benefit from this strong, caring social environment (Elder and Conger 2000; Schwartz 1987). Despite a continuing exodus of the best and brightest, those (bullheads and suckers) who remain annually produce a new crop of bright youth, whom they bemoan losing.

Transformed postagrarian towns are less likely, once newcomers outnumber oldtimers, to have citizens committed to broad-based community volunteerism. Newcomers may be entirely virtuous people, but if they are not connected to others in the community, they do not contribute to the local store of social resources (Putnam 2000). As recent arrivals, newcomers tend to lack the attachment to place that typically motivates voluntary civic engagement. With dual careers, daily commutes to the city, and the investment required to maintain a high level of domestic comfort, they may have little time or energy for community activities. Furthermore, because many newcomers are essentially sojourners, they do not cultivate lifelong relationships in the town; therefore, the costs outweigh the benefits for the type of civic engagement that oldtimers expect (Wuthnow 1998). Newcomers are likely to be active in the schools, because they value education highly, but they sustain engagement only if a child of theirs is enrolled. Being disconnected from the community, they usually do not place strong trust in neighbors or in norms of reciprocity in the community at large. When social resources are destroyed by neglect or conflict, social erosion occurs more at the community level than at the family level (Coleman, cited in Coontz 1992). That is, newcomer families look after their own steadfastly, but postagrarian community social resources are likely to decline from agrarian levels without consistent effort in activities that maintain them.

Cross-Age Relations

Cross-age relations in a community are connections between generations. Such community relations can be age-segregated and age-stratified or integrated with multiple cross-age ties. Age integration can be viewed as indexing cross-age ties (Glen H. Elder Jr., personal communication, May 15, 2001). Children and youth, because their world is mainly contained within a town's borders, are major producers and carriers of community life (Suttles 1972). How youth are treated by a community through cross-age relations therefore reveals fundamental community priorities and concerns (Schwartz 1987).

When youth have sustained relations with adults outside the family—in the neighborhood, schools, and church—interactions with adults of various ages provide the youth with social resources of support, role modeling, monitoring, and caring that foster successful development. This is a description of integrated cross-age relations. In a community in which the ages are fully integrated, a child grows up in an environment structured by adults of differing ages, not just the child's parents (Riley and Uhlenberg 2000). Children are considered a community or public responsibility; they belong to everyone. Where ages are segregated, isolated by housing patterns, work, and school demands, children tend to be considered private possessions and the responsibility only of the family. Youth in age-segregated communities, such as suburbs, mature in a peer-structured environment and mistrust adults or avoid them. Such children frequently are considered inconvenient problems for the family and the community (Benson 1997; Elder and Conger 2000). Community attitudes are clearly evident in the barriers that are erected for the use of public spaces and places by youth (Childress 2000; Schwartz 1987).

A child's neighborhood environment influences his or her development because adults mediate access to crucial community resources (Bryant 1985). Closure of social networks means that children develop, for example, in a watchful setting where community standards are understood and effectively enforced (Coleman 1990; Freudenberg 1986). Adolescents thrive where they are cherished and tolerated because they are treated as a public possession (Elder and Conger 2000; Schwartz 1987). Social class differences tend to be minimized in agrarian communities. Yet we know that identity in such communities derives from a family's reputation and that children of lower station, in particular, feel stigmatized (Fitchen 1981; MacTavish and Salamon 2001). Small-town youth decry the nosiness that the watchfulness of age integration creates. Adults in every agrarian community, recalling their childhood or youth, commented, "When I got in trouble, my parents would know about it before I got home from school." Such a process is indicative of the entire community's taking responsibility for raising "our children." Actions are rarely anonymous in these contexts.

Agrarian-community adults are tolerant of youth, for the place has no future if all the youth leave. Where community tolerance operates, adolescents are accorded personal dignity and acceptance, unless their behavior impinges on the rights of other age groups (Schwartz 1987). A norm of tolerance seems to be strongly associated with cross-age relations of respect born of age integration; adults feel that their actions make a real difference in teenagers' lives. Community public spaces, for example, are considered to belong to all, and youth are entitled to use them (Childress 2000). Elderly residents in tolerant agrarian communities see adolescents as "basically good kids," and this respect inspires consideration by youth toward the elderly. The status of youth, then, provides an index of community priorities and the nature of the local social resources being produced (Coleman 1988; Putnam 1993b).

Cross-age contacts tend to be absent in suburban subdivisions, if for no other reason than that the settlement pattern tends toward

age segregation (Riley and Uhlenberg 2000). In contrast to agrarian communities, where adults structure youths' lives, suburban
communities are likely to have a peer-structured environment, because of age-group segregation. Suburban communities with peer-
structured youth cultures have produced negative to disastrous developmental outcomes, as demonstrated in Columbine High School,
where Colorado youth attacked their peers and teachers (Elder and
Conger 2000).

As newcomers settle in agrarian towns, if they differ by class or
culture from the oldtimers, the belief that all children belong to the
whole community potentially erodes. Upscale residents especially favor segregation of children, not only by residence but also according
to academic achievement in school, a high priority for them (Kenny
2000). Newcomers with a suburban culture, which is ahistorical, may
allow less latitude in rule enforcement or performance for youth
than oldtimers who act on the basis of firm knowledge about a family
reputation or a child's history (Schwartz 1987). When individualism
is emphasized in a community, the generations tend to be more segregated and, as a consequence of these cross-age relations, less tolerant of one another. Such differentiation has tended to reinforce class
position and make less likely the social mobility through educational
investment that was nurtured by agrarian communities, even though
it spurred an exodus of the youth (Ross 1915). Whether the watchfulness over children practiced by oldtimers is extended to children
of newcomers and whether newcomers really want such monitoring are open questions. Evidence from suburban studies shows that
when people of different backgrounds are thrown together, conflict
emerges because of the different meanings attached to children and
socialization practices (Baumgartner 1988; Gans 1967).

Whether adolescents are treated uniformly by community authorities may be linked to family status or reputation (Hollingshead
1949; Schwartz 1987). Behavior condoned for middle-class adolescents, for example, may be considered deviant when performed by
a poor (or a newcomer) adolescent. Such adolescents, although born
in the community, may be defined as outsiders and stigmatized by
insiders (Becker 1963). We do not know whether postagrarian communities will consistently treat youth as everyone's responsibility
or view them according to the family financial status.

The strengths of agrarian communities derive from rich connections across age groups—young and old benefit from the behavioral
tolerance fostered by social contacts. We can see these strengths
when youth shovel the sidewalks of the elderly after a snow, when

adults monitor youths' politeness, and when they report deviance to the parents. But tolerance and watchfulness require personal involvement. Newcomers may be unwilling to commit that much of themselves to the community (Baumgartner 1988). Whether cross-age linkages prevail as newcomers increase in numbers is a critical gauge of which postagrarian community form will emerge as a town is transformed. Midwestern old towns have been crucibles for launching successful and resilient youth; their transformation into anonymous nontowns raises concern for our democratic icon and the youth produced there.

COMMUNITY CULTURE

A basic assumption for the case studies presented here is that a distinctive culture permeates community life. Culture functions as the glue that holds the community together by determining the members' connections to one another—what those connections are, how and where they occur, and what meaning is assigned to them. Community culture is that abstract quality that people allude to when they acknowledge attachment to a place that has a unique identity. It shapes what people think or do or feel and believe, but it also constrains options, by inhibiting alternative practices of doing, thinking, or feeling; people are not highly conscious of this function (Ortner 1984, 1990). Learning the culture and helping to reproduce it are not accomplished rapidly; that is why forming an attachment to community takes time and repeated experiences (see Kasarda and Janowitz 1974; Williams 1988).

What are the sources of community culture? I wrote previously that communities dominated by an ethnic group had a culture derived from ethnic origin, the settling of a place by a group with a single ethnic background (Salamon 1992). My bottom-up approach focused on families, a conservative cultural force whose intergenerational land transfer and kinship customs accounted for local land tenure patterns and, indirectly, community vitality. In this book I again take a family-focused approach to community, but I shift the focus outside the household to the community context. Each case study town has a cultural identity that has arisen from its settlement pattern, its ethnicity, its history (experiencing events together, such as tornadoes, the depression, or floods), its geography, and its demography. Life is constructed within a shared geographically bounded space identified with the community—including the buildings, the open spaces, and the taken-for-granted practices linked to place. Culture is reproduced in customary, regular, repetitive, frequent, and ordinary life events (Arensberg 1972, 1981). Redundant interactions in local public spaces build the horizontal ties that connect a community identity with a specific place (Low and Altman 1992; Oldenburg 1999; Tolbert, Lyson, and Irwin 1998; Williams 1988). Together these dimensions create a community story line that accounts for norms and rituals.

How does one see culture in action? Culture is not revealed by asking people about it directly. Rather, culture is discerned from learning about and observing a place by interacting with all generations, classes, and genders to capture the range of beliefs and practices. Community culture is visible in (1) a distinctive style and vocabulary for joining in interaction; (2) the numbers and variety of local institutions such as businesses, voluntary organizations, churches, newspapers, and schools; (3) the presence of public spaces, where people interact on a regular basis, and their manner of interaction; and (4) whether regular festivals or rituals are produced (Lavenda 1997; Oldenburg 1999; Prosterman 1995; Salamon 1992; Tolbert, Lyson, and Irwin 1998). These cultural elements, environmental and social, are the context and the vehicles for celebrating, maintaining, and thereby reinforcing community.

Observing an agrarian community in the company of an oldtimer, as she or he goes about daily errands or eats at the local café, has allowed me occasionally to sample the vivid, detailed, interwoven, and textured culture that binds residents. The experience is unlike my efficient errand-running in the city: the pace is stately, and each stop downtown is spent chatting with a business owner or, at the post office, with other neighbors. The weather is discussed, of course, but the conversation often takes the form of jokes about my companion's reputation or persona. My presence made the University of Illinois's current athletic success or failure, or my status as a professor, grist for the lively conversation mill. Sizing up of the stranger and deciding whether that person is to be trusted takes place while seemingly idle talk goes on.

I became fascinated, when interviewing farmers all over Illinois, by the fact that the act of having lunch together involved extensive impression management by my companion, according to his local status. If the farmer wishes, for example, to polish his reputation as a rogue, he introduces no one to the strange woman with him. If he would like to burnish his family prestige, he might play up my professional interest in him and his family. The farmer to whom I dedicated my previous book always introduced me as an Illinois professor and commented, "She's writing a book about me." I could imagine the event of my visit as material for banter in the months ahead.

These farmers' deliberately chosen actions toward a person new to the community's textured, colorful, and distinctive world are based on their history and experiences in that world (Williams 1988). For me to cross from newcomer status to incorporation into the community culture would require my regular interactions over a long period to prove loyalty by dealing locally. Gradually, through positive, routine interactions, I would build a reputation and gain a history, and so would my family. Through such repetitive interactions, community is maintained and reproduced. Local culture is what newcomers must learn about a place and its people and act upon unthinkingly before finding acceptance.

Community does not exist abstractly or in a void, to be activated in an emergency for efficient mobilization. Oldtimers know that community culture is deep and thick, although the daily interactions themselves may seem superficial and repetitive. But if community has been built, it is there to be mobilized when cooperation is needed (Tilly 1973). A community is a living thing to its citizens, an organism that requires nourishment and vigilant protection if it is to reciprocate with support and caring (Fowler 1991). But if newcomers in sufficient numbers fail to make the social investment that acceptance requires and scorn the local culture, that organic social system can wither and degenerate over time.

THE CASE STUDY COMMUNITIES

Each small-town case study shows change being experienced differently. (All place names used are pseudonyms to protect confidentiality, as we promised the informants.) Smallville (chapter 3) is an aging western Illinois town still organized around agrarian cultural beliefs of cooperation, trust, and robust civic engagement. These traits make Smallville an appropriate agrarian benchmark town with which post-agrarian change in the remaining five case studies can be compared. The other five towns are in the same regional commuting zone of a central Illinois small metro center that I call Central City. Prairieview (chapter 4) in the past several decades has rapidly boomed into an upscale suburban place with numerous subdivisions built adjacent to the town. Bunkerton (chapter 5), a county seat, was declining because of the loss of several industries and a nearby military base. Its Chamber of Commerce organized a successful initiative to attract buyers for its stock of surplus housing. Newcomers to Bunkerton are not as upscale as those in Prairieview. The lower-middle-class and blue-collar newcomers live in the original town and thus are more firmly integrated in community life.

Corntown (chapter 6) and Arbordale (chapter 7) are both recipients of newcomers of Mexican background; a phenomenon of immigration or migration of such persons is now found throughout rural America in conjunction with food processing and industrial animal production and meat processing. This ethnic group began settling in both Illinois towns before such a change was on the national radar screen. As early as the 1960s, Mexican Americans from Texas began to settle—out of the migrant pathway that annually streams through Illinois and up to Michigan. In each town a high seasonal labor demand lured migrants, especially after World War II. Corntown was a vegetable-growing and -canning center, and in smaller Arbordale family-owned nursery businesses have predominated over the past century. I employ the term *Mexicanos* for people of Mexican background, whether citizens of the United States or immigrants from Mexico, although demographic data adhere to the term *Hispanic,* employed in the U.S. census (see appendix B).

Splitville (chapter 8) is a town like Smallville that has an aging population but a surplus of shabby housing. Working-poor newcomers were attracted to Splitville for affordable rental housing or the opportunity for home ownership by a contract purchase.

Each of these community transformation case studies represents trends found elsewhere in the Midwest and, no doubt, in much of rural America that lies within commuting distance of second- and third-tier small cities. Individually, each case study captures a snapshot view of a stage of oldtimer resistance to, acceptance of, engulfment by, or embracement of a postagrarian transformation that is ongoing in the Midwest.

The reader should note that although the actual community studies were completed before 1995, the present tense is typically employed throughout to convey immediacy. Census data from the 1990s are those mainly cited and are the most relevant to describe the context that existed when the field studies were done (see appendix B). Where possible, however, 2000 census data are provided. On the whole, town size and ethnicity proportions reported in the 2000 census confirm the trends that I describe. The six towns are too small to risk providing the real town name while disguising the community members. I felt particularly free to describe those contested events that were public enough to be reported in the regional newspaper. The names of newspapers, of course, are not given. For the same purpose of confidentiality, several other sources are referred to in either abbreviated or generic form. School statistics in most cases come from the Illinois State Board of Education's publications. I cite those but omit the name of the town. Two published histories and publications by a village board and a festival committee are cited generically.

Nonetheless, residents are likely to recognize their towns. I prefer the risks involved with that recognition, viewing it as part of my obligation to respectfully tell the town's story. I am aware that townspeople may not like everything that I write about their community. I learned this at a conference in Iowa, where I presented preliminary findings about the Splitville community conflict (chapter 8). An audience member recognized the town, and afterward he angrily confronted me. As a close friend of some oldtimer residents, he was furious about my representation of the newcomers, a group he despised. His strong reaction caused me to rethink all my representations of community members so as not to show bias toward or against one category. The Splitville situation is so contentious, however, that it would be difficult not to offend someone. I try throughout the book to maintain the perspective of a bystander who knows the place well but is not a part of the social system. Such a stance encourages people to talk about their community candidly, but they expect that confidentiality will be maintained.

If I have any bias, it is sympathy for oldtimers trying to sustain old towns in the midst of a newcomer influx. Of course, the representation of each community is obviously one selected and digested first by the field researchers and then through my writing (see Clifford and Marcus 1986; Naples 1997; Van Maanen 1995). One strategy I employed as a researcher was to make a conscientious effort to interview a cross section of community residents. I drew on a variety of data—newspapers, local histories, and the census—to examine the same issue, so that my case would not rely solely on participant observation and interviews (see appendix B). The technical term for this research strategy is *data triangulation* (Denzin 1989).

An example of triangulation is to juxtapose two news items about Prairieview, the upscaled suburbanized town, which represents the fundamental transformation of community culture taking place as a new and multithreaded postagrarian rural social fabric evolves. Each item appeared about the same time in the Central City newspaper (it was Central City's commuters who spurred Prairieview's doubling in population between 1980 and 1990). Reflected in the news items are the taken-for-granted perceptions about community culture held by oldtimers and newcomers, who are now uneasily contesting the space in this rapidly changing postagrarian place. The letter appeared after oldtimers who ran the town were ousted in a local election by relative newcomers.

To the editor:
As I read the article [previous week, postelection edition], titled "Old guard gives way to the young as voters speak," my thoughts were "just the way it should be." It's nice to see young people take an active interest in their local government.

Being a part of the Old Guard, I wanted to reflect back over some accomplishments of this Old Guard for the past 10 years. This Old Guard gave you an administration building at a cost of $325,000, a water treatment plant at $670,000, a new sewer plant at $1.7 million, water wells at $250,000 and a dressed-up Main Street at $85,000, just to name a few. We also garnered grant money of more than $4 million and enough annexations to take care of the village growth for the next 10 to 20 years . . . without any increases in the village taxes.

So, the Old Guard leaves you with a community that has doubled its population in 10 years.

We leave you with modern up-to-date facilities. . . . Yes, the Old Guard leaves this to the Young Guard stamped "paid in full." We leave you debt free, so guard it well.

Prairieview is a great community. I say to the Young Guard: Treat her well and give her lots of tender loving care, and I'm sure she will give to you many good feelings as you lead Prairieview. (Central City newspaper, April 1997)

This letter writer embodies attachment to an agrarian hometown community and culture. Prairieview, as the self-described Old Guard (oldtimer) writer indicates, is undergoing rapid change, in the form of an authentic invasion by upscale newcomers. He is gracious about ceding power. The invasion has forced him to think about community culture and what it contributes to how he thinks about himself (Campion and Fine 1998). The qualities that gave the community a special character and culture are being engulfed by the tidal wave of newcomers.

Prairieview as a unique rural place is not likely to be what attracts newcomers. Described in the advertisement below is what newcomers seek in rural Illinois. Run for many weeks around the time the oldtimer penned his letter, the advertisement appeals to different concerns than those that aroused him as a village board member. The features to which newcomers are likely to form an attachment could be found anywhere, unlike the rich texture of social relationships that our letter writer infers. The advertisement had a map locating the new subdivision adjacent to Prairieview.

> Welcome to the Lakes at Riverview: [county]'s Newest Residential Development
> If You're Looking For . . .
> • Quality of Life
> • Country Living Just Minutes from the City
> • A Valuable Investment
> Imagine living in this peaceful and unique 700 acre community surrounding 3 lakes and along the [river]. 300 acres of common area, including 170 acres of spring-fed lakes, 3 miles of shoreline, 8 miles of recreational greenbelt for walking/biking/bird watching/ or cross country skiing. (Central City newspaper, Sunday real estate section, various dates in 1997)

The fundamentally different cultures underlying the two forms of community account for the emphases revealed by the two clippings. These two forms of community exist side by side in Prairieview, but the transformation is moving toward the eclipse of the agrarian town by the upscale postagrarian suburban nontown.

Residents of the Lakes at Riverview are not likely to respond sentimentally or even with familiarity to the community culture assumed by a list I recently received via E-mail from a farm magazine reporter. The list is salient for the agrarian community cultural assumptions it evokes. Here are selected comments from the forty-two-item list.

> *You Might Be from a Small Town If . . .*
> You can name everyone you graduated with.
> You ever went to parties at a pasture, barn, or in the middle of a dirt road.
> You said the "f" word and your parents knew within the hour.
> You could never buy cigarettes because all the store clerks know how old you were and if you were old enough, they would still tell your folks.
> You schedule parties around the schedule of different police officers, since you know which ones would bust you and which ones wouldn't.
> The town next to you is considered "trashy" or "snooty" but is actually just like your town.

Anyone you want can be found at either the Dairy Queen or
the feed store.

You refer to anyone with a house newer than 1980 as "rich"
people.

The city council meets at the coffee shop.

You decide to walk somewhere for exercise and 5 people pull
over and ask you if you need a ride.

Your teachers call you by your older sibling's name.

Your teachers remember when they taught your parents.

People from Smallville would instantly identify with the agrarian
cultural themes of the list and roar with a laughter born of community experience.

The selection of the six communities for study between 1988 and
1995 was not guided by a grand research design to explore the transformation of the rural Midwest. Rather, each community was chosen
because the population influx it experienced was intrinsically interesting. All the communities are small, with populations under 6,000,
and have been in existence more than a century. Originally, all six
were relatively self-contained, with jobs, schools, banking, and shopping available locally. At the outset I did not see events in any one
community as related to changes in any other of the communities.
Chapter 2 describes how during the past two decades, the six communities were wrenched by a regional restructuring that centralized services in their commuting zone. The social and economic community
interrelationships emerged as seemingly unrelated trends, but linkages became apparent when I compared population, housing, landscape, transportation, institutional, and neighborhood changes. As
much as the data allow, what was and what is now are contrasted to
outline the process of change that members of each community must
ignore, accommodate, or attempt to alter.

The impact of a newcomer influx on small, central Illinois postagrarian communities is described in the five case studies constituting chapters 4–8. The social processes alluded to in the E-mail list
about small-town life—watchfulness, gossip, overlapping social networks, stability, continuity, and an affectionate recognition—reflect
the four community dimensions used to frame the six case studies. Except for the agrarian benchmark, Smallville (chapter 3), the
towns share two crucial, common elements: newcomers have become
residents, and the towns are located within the same commuting
zone. Smallville alone escaped a newcomer influx that substantively
changes the physical landscape, community organization, and social

relationships of a town. In each case study, demographic changes are shown to alter some social relationships. In several communities, continuity is maintained with past agrarian norms. That is, the social change has proceeded unevenly in the set of towns (Kottak 1999).

Eventually I came to see that regional trends explained why one community was changed by upscale newcomers and another down-scaled by lower-income newcomers. Chapter 9 considers the implications of the ongoing rural social transformation described by the community case studies for the future of democracy, trust, and youth development in the new regional social fabric.

Each community is introduced with a brief history, which is followed by a description of the agent of change that altered established spaces, social connections, resources, and cross-age relations. The nature of community connections rests on whether a store of social resources exists, generated by actions of its leadership and levels of civic engagement. Which social resources are present helps explain the attitude of the community authority figures toward children—the attitudes of both oldtimers and newcomers. What a group values culturally about where they live—nature, face-to-face interactions, security, or history—causes them to act in specific ways toward their and others' children. How youth are treated, therefore, provides an analytical window for tracing both change and the enduring structure of meaning in a given cultural system (Ohnuki-Tierney 1990; Fernandez 1990). To a certain extent, youth are the product of the social connections and the social resources of a community. Their lives are the laboratories in which change is played out. In turn, the commitment of the populace to the future that children represent also shapes what type of citizens youth become. Thus, a civic society is played out in the community socialization of youth.

In appendix A a neighborhood hypothesis is proposed, based on the qualitative community case studies, and is tested using census and economic data. Patterns of changing income and occupational trends identified qualitatively in the case studies are compared with quantitative data. Thus, triangulation with several data sources underlines the validity of the described emerging patterns in the postagrarian social fabric of the Midwest. The community sample is described and the methods used in the six field studies are reported in appendix B.

In a time when so many people search for community—for integration in a strongly connected social group where one can feel rooted but yet be free because one is known—case studies of townspeople coping with sudden and radical changes are illuminating. People in these small places show us what it takes to be part of a real, organic community and what occurs when people new to it face shouldering the costs as well as the benefits of what was a seamless agrarian form of community life in old towns.

2 DYNAMICS OF SMALL-TOWN CHANGE

Despite the impression of insularity and stagnation of the Midwest conveyed by novelists, towns almost from their founding were embedded firmly in the wider society (Barron 1997; Cayton and Onuf 1990; Cronon 1991; Warren 1978). They are constantly buffeted by events that cause them to boom or decline, triggering reaction or proactive measures. Economic or technological events altering a region as a whole are external factors driving change. Other factors that shape change are internally generated, such as a booster campaign. In this chapter I examine from a regional perspective why and how rural places are transformed (or not). As noted previously, I draw artificial distinctions between *town*, indicating the structural dimensions of place, and *community*, indicating the social relationships. Both concepts also are explored singly and interactively through the six case studies in the following chapters.

Boosterism is a uniquely American tradition for touting a small town. It expresses a historical midwestern dedication on the part of towns to achieve "progress" through commercial development and population growth (Atherton 1954; Charles 1993; Curti 1959) or to maintain local pride and middle-class esteem (Hatch 1979). Through boosterism, one town's economy or institutions tended to prosper at the expense of neighboring towns. For example, when the frontier moved west beyond the Mississippi, "county seat wars" erupted, sometimes violently, among towns competing to become the site of county government (Schellenberg 1981). These conflicts developed primarily in the Midwest, where a county seat was selected popularly rather than by state mandate. Even after the county-seat honor was awarded, rivalries festered and soured intercommunity cooperation. Another expression of boosterism is the "growth machine," in which the business elite harnesses a town's real estate for development by touting population growth as progress (Logan and Molotch 1987). A town committed to economic development through booster activities theoretically welcomes newcomers, growth being equated with progress. It is assumed that recruited newcomers can easily be incorporated because they will be similar to the white, middle-class boosters.

Commitment to progress and prosperity by midwestern towns reflects a region settled and developed in the era during which commercial capitalism was established nationally (Cayton and Onuf 1990). Illinois is home to Rotary Club, the quintessential businessmen's service and booster club. Rotary was founded in Chicago, and its imitators, Kiwanis Club and Lions Club, also are based in Chicago. Illinois had the highest number of midwestern local club chapters by the late 1920s—the golden age of club expansion (Charles 1993). Through much of the twentieth century, these clubs, until relatively recently male-only, used booster mechanisms to respond publicly and cooperatively to external economic pressures. Women also contributed to the cause, but they did so behind the scenes as facilitators of community activities. Boosterism requires community cohesion, orchestrated by service clubs, to undertake activities that promote the middle-class ideals that are believed to be for a town's benefit. By making their town grow bigger, wealthier, or grander, boosters aim to achieve superiority over nearby towns, an all-American cultural goal. Since the early settlement of the Midwest, booster activities have mobilized competition among towns to win the power and resources considered necessary for economic progress. Service clubs, which combine social, business, and civic concerns, now are given credit for helping to integrate towns into a regional economy (Charles 1993).

Service club charters equated service with community. Clubs traditionally supported community integration by sponsoring annual celebrations such as the Fourth of July parade or by improving town facilities such as the ball field or a park. It took a broad spectrum of civically engaged citizens to bring off these activities. Service clubs also have been committed to activities such as sponsorship of Boy Scout troops and sports leagues for youth (e.g., Little League) that foster community identification. Their intensive support of youth activities was and is viewed as a commitment to strengthening a town by creating youth loyalty, while instilling agrarian values or protecting the youth from urban problems (Charles 1993). The clubs' dedication to commercial ends built horizontal linkages via integration of local social networks and generation of social capital as a community social resource (Lavenda 1997; Putnam 2000).

Rural communities were characterized by tension between farmers in the countryside and boosters who were owners of main-street businesses. Farmers at the turn of the twentieth century often were immigrants struggling on small farms (Adams 1994; Fink 1986). The native-born business elite of small towns looked down on the peasantlike farm families, who spoke poor English, whose women and children worked in the fields, and who were organized socially by kinship and ethnic traditions (Salamon 1992). And farmers felt badly used by towns: they complained that they were taxed without representation, that their school concerns were ignored, or that their business was taken for granted (Brunner, Hughes, and Patten 1927). After World War II the farm population declined, and the business elite diminished in power as main streets withered. By the 1970s, when the regional transformation on which I focus began, typical Illinois farm operations probably generated greater cash flow than did town businesses. The service clubs, in order to survive, had to be open to anyone, including farmers and women, who was willing to do community service (Salamon 1995). Indeed, the cooperation of diverse citizens in community booster activities promotes the horizontal ties that foster trust (Flora and Flora 1990; Flora, Sharp, and Flora 1997). Trust then is available as a resource for facilitating other community activities (Putnam 2000; Tolbert, Lyson, and Irwin 1998).

Whether boosterism strives to bring in new business, obtain a consolidated school, or triumph in school sports, it generates regional competition that spawns a town hierarchy measured by size and actual or perceived winners and losers in the unrelenting struggle for resources. A new competitive pattern emerged among towns, characterized by hostility toward higher-order places and a sense of superiority over those places deemed of lower order (Hatch 1979). Long-term rivalries reinforced internal community identity and cohesion, but at the expense of cooperation among towns near one another. Such rivalries are annually symbolized on high school football fields and basketball courts. The decline in rural population prompted school consolidation initiatives, in which state-level professionals attempted to seize control from locally dominated school boards and in many states succeeded (Fuller 1982; Reynolds 1995). Here was yet another arena for competition among towns: having failed in the struggle to retain their schools, towns began competing to become *the* regional center, this effort paralleling their booster activities for economic growth.

The attributes of wealth, ethnicity, size, or geography shape a town's strategies in regional rivalries (Salamon 1992). Over the long term, larger size has generally guaranteed higher placement in the regional order. Businesses, services, schools, and jobs have tended toward centralization, usually in the county seat (Johansen and Fuguitt 1984). An aid to winning rivalries is the location of a town relative to good transportation. In the nineteenth century, prosperity or decline depended on whether or not a town was a stop on a major rail line, such as the Illinois Central. After the federal interstate highway initiative during the 1950s and 1960s, it was location relative to an interstate that affected a town's prosperity. Towns with an interstate exit acquired costs as well as benefits, however. Roads once eagerly awaited became, for some small towns, only an easier way for residents to go elsewhere for shopping, work, and leisure activities (Sofranko 1992). Interstate rest stops are used as drug drops or prostitution settings, often offsetting the economic benefits of attracting tourists or an outlet mall. Nonetheless, interstate location today is pivotal to the transformation of a rural countryside dominated by a commuting population.

State policies also favored larger towns (more than 2,500 pop.) over smaller ones. The economic rationale is that a critical mass is required for survival. Triage (favoring those towns most likely to thrive over all others) is an extreme regional strategy proposed by planners to save the more viable towns (Daniels and Lapping 1987). In the recent past, economic processes not controlled by state governments have favored locational factors over size: land, rural amenities, and distance from small cities where jobs are located (Herbers 1986). Land in the postagrarian countryside thus became economically important in ways distinct from the productivity of its soils, the measure used when "rural" was equated with "agriculture" (Castle 1995). Land transformed into real estate is appropriated for new forms of booster activities (outlined below) that attract urban migrants new to the rural countryside, distinguished from oldtimers by their firm attachment to a nearby small city.

SMALL CITIES REACH OUT TO SMALL TOWNS

Small-city economic growth is driving the emergence of the Illinois postagrarian rural landscape. Central Illinois has five urbanized areas, which consist of a central city or cities and the surrounding closely settled territory or fringe area, ranging from 95,000 to about 150,000 in population: Bloomington-Normal, Champaign-Urbana, Decatur, Danville, and the state capital, Springfield (see fig. 1). Each small city is the center of an archipelago-like commuting zone of sixty miles, incorporating numerous small island towns. In the evolving rural landscape, some towns have been upscaled while others have become equivalent to a rural slum through a newcomer influx. Which push and pull factors explain this? Are agrarian communities changing according to some logic, or are population shifts occurring randomly in the rural Midwest? A regional analysis of the area surrounding Central City provides an explanation for the differential fates of archipelago island-towns in this Illinois postagrarian landscape, a transformed landscape emerging in the Midwest and probably in many other rural regions of the United States.

Our six Illinois communities stand where farming visually dominates the countryside; the landscape looks like a productive one. Yet not all newcomers to the small towns are there for involvement in production. Some newcomers, particularly those of Mexican background, are involved in rural productive activities and chose a town originally for a good job in a local agribusiness factory. Others, the middle- or upper-middle-class newcomers, are consumers of rurality and are truly postagrarian residents. The regional postagrarian archipelago is simultaneously a landscape of consumption and a landscape of production, corresponding to the class position of the town population (Gieryn 2000). Agrarian towns are no longer home to many farmers, and those who do live there are retired and aging in place.

Although agricultural production may control the central Illinois landscape, in the rural economy agriculture is only one among diverse manufacturing, service, or residential economic activities. Illinois is economically dependent on agriculture, but the number of farms dropped almost 30% from 107,000 in 1980 to 76,000 by 1996 (Illinois Department of Agriculture 1996). Table 1 shows all counties (represented by the six towns) losing many family farms during the 1980s and the 1990s. Central City's county lost land to commercial and suburban sprawl around it and Prairieview. Between 1982 and 1997 it lost 5.4% of its land in farms. Counties adjacent to Central City's county actually gained land in farms between 1992 and 1997, after government policies changed.

Through the 1970s and early 1980s, most town main streets were devastated by rural regional malls. In the 1990s Central City (and other regional small cities shown in fig. 1) experienced a business

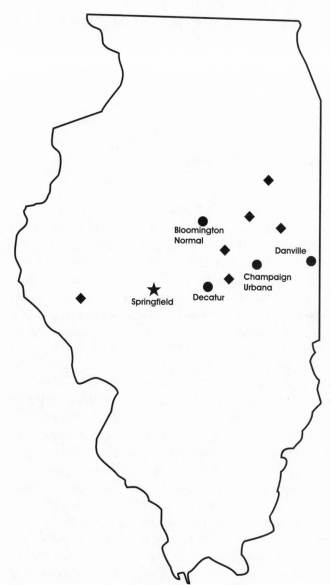

Figure 1 Location of central Illinois small cities and case study towns

restructuring, which involved an explosion of superstores that con-
spicuously altered the rural landscape. Annexed to the city, adjacent
to a shopping mall, and at an interstate intersection, these huge
stores line four-lane roads where cornfields once stood. Traffic is
jammed daily in late afternoon as archipelago commuters stop after
work to shop at Target, Home Depot, Best Buy, Pier One, Circuit

Table 1 Farm Loss at County Level Where Six Case Study Towns Are
Located

	NUMBER OF FARMS		NET CHANGE IN NUMBER OF FARMS (%)
COUNTY	1982	1997	
County 1 (Prairieview, Splitville)	1,871	1,371	−27
County 2 (Bunkerton)	804	550	−32
County 3 (Corntown)	1,390	984	−29
County 4 (Arbordale)	1,899	1,393	−27
County 5 (Smallville)	1,291	1,028	−20

Sources: USDA 1982, 1997.

City, Sam's Club, Wal-Mart, or Meijer's supermarket—the same
megastores that line Chicago suburban strips. Shoppers then zip
home to small towns via the interstate. Among the crowds in the
mall and the megastores are adolescent "mall rats" wearing sweat-
shirts and Future Farmers of America jackets with names of towns
as far as 60 to 75 miles away. These megastores and the mall sounded
the final death knell for the small-town businesses remaining. Few
new retail businesses opened in small towns except antique shops or
Casey's gasoline-convenience stores, ubiquitous on the edges of
small towns. The expansion of service-sector jobs, associated with
mall and strip developments, corresponded with the regional decline
in manufacturing jobs and a military base closure. Central City now
offers more jobs (see appendix A).

Medical services also were consolidated from the countryside into
the small central Illinois cities starting in the late 1980s. Two medical
institutions in Central City, for example, began to compete for small-
town health business as HMOs became powerful. Together, these
Central City medical clinics and clinics in other counterpart cities
shown in figure 1 serve an eleven-county area. The regional trauma
center, governed by federal health policy, is run by a Central City
clinic. Small hospitals, one in Bunkerton, for example, closed as residents chose to travel to where the specialists and the latest medical
equipment were located. Prairieview's rapid growth, however, recently spawned a new satellite clinic affiliated with a Central City
clinic.

A chief push factor for upscale rural home buyers to leave the
five small central Illinois cities was the arrival of crack cocaine. "In
1990," said the Central City Police Department's crime analyst,
"crack came down in full force from Chicago. Suddenly robberies
and burglaries went way up because everyone needed money for

crack." By 1991 Central City robberies had increased by nearly 50% and motor vehicle theft by 151%. Drive-by shootings occurred for the first time. The numbers of juvenile cases, especially for violent crimes, also skyrocketed. When compared with seventy-five rural counties in downstate Illinois, Central City's county had more violent crime than other counties with a small city, but the adjacent rural counties (where three of the towns in this study lie) remained well below the rate for all rural counties (Central City newspaper, Oct. 1996). Thus, the central Illinois small cities became more threatening, and the adjacent rural counties looked much safer to the urban middle class. Similar events helped fuel white flight to Chicago's suburbs several decades earlier (Palen 1995).

These external factors (the economy, population shifts, the crime rate, and retail/service restructuring) seriously influenced the towns composing the Central City rural commuting zone. Table 2 charts the major economic activity of the five relevant counties during our critical time frame (the 1980s through the mid-1990s). County shifts in job types typically held are reflected in the diminished importance of agriculture and the increase in service jobs. This employment shift normally requires commuting to places such as Central City. Most important, these changes show that small cities and the hinterlands became more inextricably interdependent. Newspapers represent a hallmark of that interdependence. Marketing strategies by the city newspaper exploit the commuting zone to absorb readers who work in Central City but live in the towns within a sixty-mile radius. Central City's newspaper now regularly covers regional village board meetings, weddings and funeral announcements, and political developments (except for those in Smallville, located in western Illinois, outside the region). Supplementing the daily Central City newspaper are weekly, locally owned newspapers barely surviving in three of the five towns. The weeklies are published by women, in another departure from the past domination of core business activities by males.

Historical events and contextual factors such as natural amenities, highways, or industries account for specific internal attributes that influence which newcomers are attracted to a small town and which stakeholders make decisions about changes. Interactions between external and internal factors underlie the logic of the regional transformation trajectory. Our set of Illinois communities represents specific town types in the regional social fabric emerging as a consequence of the transformation. Town attributes are best understood by being

Table 2 Primary Economic Activity for Five Central Illinois Counties, with Index
of Rurality

COUNTY	1979	1986	1994	RURAL-URBAN CONTINUUM CODE 1994[a]
County 1 (Prairieview/Splitville)	Metro	Metro	Metro	3
County 2 (Bunkerton)	Agricultural	Agricultural	Service	6
County 3 (Corntown)	Manufacturing	Manufacturing	Manufacturing	4
County 4 (Arbordale)	Agricultural	Agricultural	Service	6
County 5 (Smallville)	Agricultural	Unclassified	Service	7

Sources: Peggy J. Cook, personal communication, 1995–96; Cook and Mizer 1994; Butler and Beale 1994.

[a] This code designates rurality by placing a county on a rural/urban continuum of 1–10. Designation of 3 is for a metro area of fewer than 250,000 residents. 4 or higher designates nonmetro counties: 4 is a county with an urban population of 20,000 or more adjacent to a metro area; 6 designates an urban population of between 2,500 and 19,999 adjacent to a metro area; 7 designates an urban population of between 2,500 and 19,999 not adjacent to a metro area.

Table 3 1990 National Characteristics of Nonmetro Places with Populations
between 2,500 and 9,999

Median age	33.9 years
Percent completing high school or higher	68.9%
Percent residing in same town 5 years ago	53.6%
Median household income	$21,365
Median value of owned homes	$46,500
Percent below the poverty level	18.4%
Percent over 16 years of age in the labor force	58.3%
Percent of labor force in agriculture	2.5%
Percent of labor force in manufacturing	20.2%
Percent of labor force in professional services	23.8%
Mean travel time to work	15.8 minutes
Percent receiving Social Security income	35%
Percent receiving public assistance	10%

Sources: Bureau of the Census 1990a; 1990c, table 2.

Notes: Communities under 2,500 have a somewhat older population, which would have less education, a lower labor force participation, and a higher poverty level, and would receive higher levels of Social Security. Data for places with populations between 2,500 and 9,999 are not readily available for 1980.

measured against national averages for rural (nonmetro) places with populations ranging from 2,500 to 9,999, based on the 1990 census, which reflects conditions at the time of the community studies (see table 3). Such national data unfortunately are not available for 1980, nor for towns of populations less than 2,500 (Calvin L. Beale, personal communication, 1996).

A REGIONAL SMALL-TOWN ECONOMIC TYPOLOGY

Internal attributes linked to macrosocietal forces account for the community distinctions captured in the typology of towns that I arrived at inductively from the case studies (see tables 4 and 5). Four general categories of places emerged from the agrarian midwestern town form that typified the twentieth century. This economic typology best captures the rural Midwest east of the Mississippi (but including eastern Iowa), which, compared to the corn belt west of the Mississippi, is more urbanized (with major, midsized, and small cities), has more small towns, and throughout its history has had a more diversified economy (Cronon 1991). The typology does not capture, for the most part, rural areas of the western corn belt or the thinly populated Great Plains. It is, however, representative of the reconfigured landscape within sixty-mile commuting zones surrounding small cities (pop. 50,000–150,000) in the central Midwest. The four town types, named according to the distinctive economic characteristic, are *agrarian, affluent residential, mixed economy,* and *shabby residential.* Excluding the mixed economy type, they are essentially residential variations on bedroom communities or sleeper towns, as residents term them.

Agrarian

Midwestern agrarian towns have had a consistent set of demographic and economic traits since World War II: a population dwindling and aging in place, declining or stagnant home values, and a deteriorating local economy (loss of jobs, businesses, and services) (Fuguitt, Brown, and Beale 1989). Agrarian towns are hamlets typically found at the periphery of a commuting zone or in a farming-dependent county (Cook and Mizer 1994). These were never grand places with a wealthy elite, even in the heyday of agriculture. Modest houses are clustered densely along tree-lined streets that follow the rectangular grid of the original platting (Johnson 1976). There may still be several stores on the main street, and perhaps a café that is open for breakfast and lunch. Farmers still move into town when they retire and are involved in civic activities. These communities have grown somewhat smaller and older in recent decades, yet socially they bear more resemblance to towns of the golden age than to the newer, postagrarian types. What distinguishes agrarian communities in the typology is the lack of a substantial newcomer population. To a certain extent, such communities remain agrarian because residents struggle to keep them that way. They resemble the "yeoman" communities I describe elsewhere; they share an agrarian covenant, are highly cohesive, and retain some younger families, even those that leave farming (Salamon 1992). These places remain agrarian primarily in culture, for even here farming employs only a handful of local people because of a decline in farm numbers (see table 1).

Owing to a lack of local jobs, agrarian communities are likely to

Table 4 Characteristics of Six Case Study Towns, 1980–1990

ECONOMIC TYPOLOGY TYPE (TOWN)	YEAR	POPULATION	MEDIAN AGE	PERCENT RESIDING IN SAME HOUSE AS IN 1985
Agrarian	1980	487	41.7	62.8
(Smallville)	1990	495	40.2	70.6
Affluent residential	1980	1,986	29.9	46.6
(Prairieview)	1990	3,100	32.4	47.7
Mixed service	1980	4,250	32.8	62.0
& residential	1990	4,290	33.4	57.0
(Bunkerton)				
Mixed	1980	6,411	31.0	54.2
manufacturing &	1990	5,880	35.7	62.5
agriculture				
(Corntown)				
Mixed	1980	1,269	33.3	57.2
agriculture &	1990	1,280	33.4	64.9
manufacturing				
(Arbordale)				
Shabby residential	1980	207	32.2	71.8
Splitville)	1990	180	35.9	69.1

Sources: Bureau of the Census 1980a, 1980c, 1990a, 1990b.

Table 5 Household Characteristics of Six Case Study Towns, 1980–1990

ECONOMIC TYPOLOGY TYPE (TOWN)	YEAR	PERCENT COMPLETING HIGH SCHOOL OR HIGHER	MEAN TRAVEL TIME TO WORK (MINUTES)
Agrarian	1980	57.7	16.7
(Smallville)	1990	77.7	20.5
Affluent residential	1980	51.8	18.0
(Prairieview)	1990	89.5	18.9
Mixed service	1980	69.2	14.0
& residential	1990	74.1	15.8
(Bunkerton)			
Mixed	1980	54.4	11.8
manufacturing &	1990	68.7	15.5
agriculture			
(Corntown)			
Mixed	1980	41.5	15.1
agriculture &	1990	63.5	15.1
manufacturing			
(Arbordale)			
Shabby residential	1980	41.5	31.8
(Splitville)	1990	54.4	29.1

Sources: Bureau of the Census 1980a, 1980c, 1990a.

MEDIAN VALUE OF OWNED HOME ($)	MEDIAN HOUSEHOLD INCOME ($)	PERCENT BELOW POVERTY LEVEL	PERCENT FEMALE-HEADED HOUSEHOLDS	PERCENT HISPANIC
21,600	12,450	11.7	27.7	1.0
21,200	16,635	19.8	6.4	0.2
52,900	20,723	5.2	20.6	.03
75,000	39,085	4.3	8.2	0
35,900	15,935	7.0	11.9	0.1
45,600	23,770	10.5	6.6	0.5
30,500	14,992	10.8	11.0	4.7
33,000	22,266	14.2	9.4	5.0
25,500	13,393	12.8	27.4	18.5
27,500	22,365	14.6	10.9	24.7
19,500	15,625	21.6	20.7	0
27,500	22,083	10.5	7.1	3.3

PERCENT OVER 16 IN LABOR FORCE	PERCENT EMPLOYED IN AGRICULTURE	PERCENT EMPLOYED IN PROFESSIONAL SERVICES	PERCENT EMPLOYED IN MANUFACTURING
48.2	8.2	13.8	18.9
52.2	9.3	19.2	26.0
52.0	1.3	25.4	13.3
77.6	1.9	32.8	12.9
62.4	2.6	18.7	26.5
64.9	1.2	24.0	19.3
62.7	1.9	13.5	43.7
63.3	1.1	12.9	37.7
76.2	12.0	18.7	29.2
64.2	17.5	14.9	24.9
42.7	10.5	19.7	10.5
57.7	2.7	16.0	11.0

have fewer than 1,000 people and be located on secondary or worse roads, at the farthest reaches of a county or commuting zone. Location precludes an easy commute to metro centers. The agrarian culture means that citizens view their community metaphorically as a family (Tonnies 1957). People may have conflicts, and some inequality exists, but community members feel a moral responsibility for one another, based on norms of reciprocity (Tauxe 1993, 169). The dense connections among the residents and their civic involvement foster the attachment of young people (especially those from farm and business families), some of whom are willing to commute long distances in order to live near family and reap the advantages of being embedded in strong social and kin networks.

Agrarian customs of community concern prevent the emergence of deteriorated or empty houses that attract newcomers who are undesirable from the oldtimers' point of view. Furthermore, inclusive community norms function to embrace newcomers. When incorporated into the social system, newcomers are subject to social pressures that reinforce conformity to community behavioral and property norms (Salamon 1996; Salamon and Davis-Brown 1990). An agrarian community thereby resists becoming a shabby residential town, although the two types share many attributes.

Smallville, the agrarian town studied in chapter 3, suffered a distinctive deterioration of economic indicators throughout the 1980s. Median home values stayed about the same ($21,000), which, given inflation, means that homes actually lost value. Median 1990 household income is the lowest among the six towns and almost 25% below the national average for small towns (table 3). Furthermore, the poverty rate almost doubled during the decade (11.7% in 1980, 19.8% by 1990) despite increases in educational levels (in 1980, 57.7% completed high school or higher; in 1990, 77.7%) and number in the workforce (rising from 48.2% in 1980 to 52.2% by 1990). The town is stable, for in 1990 a high 70% of residents live in the same home as they did five years before. To maintain their rural residence, however, people are traveling farther to work (mean travel time in 1990 is almost 4 minutes more than in 1980) (see tables 6 and 7 in chapter 3, below). Demographic trends for the agrarian community augur a gloomy future.

Affluent Residential

This town type transformed rapidly from an agrarian to an affluent bedroom community. Its demography resembles that of the suburban collar-ring of Chicago where it is penetrating the rural hinterlands (Palen 1995). Such transitional places have a bifurcated social structure, meaning that development essentially produces parallel communities of oldtimers in the original town and newcomers in upscale subdivisions built adjacent to the town (Bradshaw 1993). Presumably, the parallel structure is transitional and will disappear as oldtimers from the agrarian era die off and newcomers continue to arrive. The newcomers have a suburbanite profile—young, well-educated, high-income professionals. They own housing valued higher than the national rural average (see table 3) (Palen 1995). The oldtimers are older, not as well educated, and are retired from agricultural or blue-collar jobs.

The landscape reflects the bifurcated social structure. Oldtimers reside where the town is laid out on a grid, evidence of its agrarian past. The streets there are designed for walking, and housing is clustered in an urbanlike density (Fishman 1987). Front porches orient the homes to the street, so neighborhood watchfulness is maximized. In contrast, a new subdivision stands typically on what was recently a cornfield, bordering the old town. Lots are larger and homes are grander than in the old town. New subdivisions are designed for car rather than foot traffic. The streets seldom have sidewalks, and they form culs-de-sac, which maximize privacy. Homes are oriented toward the backyard or the patio, to focus on the family and nature, rather than toward the street and the community. Garages dominate the front exposure, allowing a quick getaway to activities in the nearby city and avoiding interaction with neighbors. Subdivision residents have lives focused on the nearby small city, where they commute for work, services, shopping, and entertainment. Their connections with the community are narrowly defined by church membership or school activities.

Striking growth for this town type occurred in Prairieview, reflecting the national rural rebound trend (Johnson and Beale 1998). Prairieview has grown at a similar rate over the last three decades: in the 1970s (starting at the 1970 size of 1,300) its growth was 53%; in the 1980s, 56%; and in the 1990s, 57% (town documents; Bureau of the Census 1970, 1980a, 1990a, 2001). Thus, the suburbanization process began even before the rural rebound. Rapid growth by newcomers is evidenced by the fact that fewer than half of 1990 residents live in the same house that they lived in five years ago (table 8, in chapter 4, below). That the newcomers are affluent is seen in the increase in median home values by almost 50% between 1980 and 1990 (from $52,900 to $75,000). The median income has also nearly doubled (from $20,723 to $39,085), and the poverty rate has fallen by a full percentage point, from 5.2% to an exceedingly low 4.3%, between 1980 and 1990. Evidence of the transformation from an agrarian to a suburban town is shown in table 9 (chapter 4, below) by the large gain in persons with high school or higher education (up by 30%, from 51.8% to 89.5%), the drop in female-headed households (from 20.6% down to 8.2%, table 8), and the steep increase in persons employed in professional services from an already high 25.4% in 1980 to 32.8% of the workforce by 1990, compared with the national average of 23.8% (tables 3 and 9).

To transform into an upscale bedroom town, a town requires attributes that attract affluent home buyers—a fine school system, good roads for commuting ease, and scenic qualities such as woods or water near ample land available for development. Something that is not necessary but is helpful is a main street fit for gentrification. (Prairieview lacked grand old homes suitable for renovation.) When such attributes (the more the better) are present, the affluent are willing and even eager to commute from where they can build lavish, imposing homes on large lots with expensive landscaping. A town like this provides upscale families a countryside lifestyle and the advantages of a city (urban medical and other services, cultural activities, and shopping) nearby. Affluent small-town newcomers, like suburbanites, say this combination delivers them "the best of both worlds" (Palen 1995). Good schools and ambience in particular are critical to emergence as *the* affluent neighborhood in an exurban archipelago.

When a residence is considered primarily as a financial investment, property is bought and sold more readily to use accumulated equity for buying a better home. Towns that become affluent bedroom towns thus have populations that are more mobile than the original residents, again resembling affluent suburbanites (Jackson 1985). Upper-income professionals also are transferred frequently. Affluent small-town newcomers, like suburbanites, resemble sojourners who live in a place but never are of it. They remain by choice relatively unassimilated, always ready to move (Siu 1952). They do not think of a home purchase as a lifetime commitment, nor do they expect to live in the same place forever. A community is chosen, for example, as a good place to bring up children. When a specific life task, such as the children's schooling, is accomplished, the rationale for residence in that place ends. A return to the city or a move to a more exurban locale may be the life plan. When a postagrarian town becomes more homogeneously affluent, it attracts more and similar newcomers, and the town becomes thoroughly suburban.

Mixed Economy

The mixed category includes towns with economies based on combinations of agriculture, manufacturing, service, or residential elements. A town that won the nineteenth-century county-seat war and is the site of county government has an economy diversified by public services, another variation. A mixed-economy town is distinguished by providing jobs to residents, rather than solely serving as a bedroom place for a city elsewhere. Larger Illinois towns (pop. 2,500–10,000) historically were sustained by an economy diversified by manufacturing or services and agriculture (Cronon 1991). In a dynamic regional economy, diversification gives a town more options than its housing stock or land to sustain it. It is important to note that business-friendly attitudes and continual dedication to active boosterism are used to sustain a mixed-economy town. Three of our communities possess mixed economies: Bunkerton, Corntown, and Arbordale.

Mixed-economy towns that are blue-collar in population remain on the original grid plan. Those towns, where the housing stock has been used as a growth machine, have a residential atmosphere. The town plan is likely to show alterations of the landscape. A recent physical change in such towns is that plant managers or other elite community members choose to live in newer subdivisions on the edge of town, away from the original grid, where everyone else lives.

Residents of a mixed-economy town are more likely to work in factories than in professional or service occupations. For small manufacturing companies, a midwestern town offers a good infrastructure and a relatively well-educated workforce with a strong work ethic (Cronon 1991; Salamon 1995). Mixed-economy towns are comparable to the affluent residential type in having a higher-than-national average (58.3%) of residents sixteen years of age and older in the workforce (tables 3 and 5). Compared to affluent residential towns, these towns present advantages for blue-collar families, a workforce with a preference for small-town life: the housing is cheaper, the cost of living is lower, and their strong inclination to live near kin can therefore be realized (Perry-Jenkins and Salamon 2002). A benefit of a convenient commuting-zone location is that women, who have entered the workforce in increasing numbers from rural areas, are able to easily commute to work (Tickamyer and Bokemeier 1988). Women can no longer rely on their mothers for child care, however; grandmothers, too, are in the workforce.

Corntown and its county (table 2), derive a mixed economy from a few stable factories. Although some Corntown manufacturing activities were lost or changed character in the past twenty years, its small-scale manufacturing plants and a local value-added agribusiness have, over the long term, provided good jobs for residents not involved with farming. Towns like Corntown may experience some population loss when one or more of the mainstay employers downsize or close. Agriculture, manufacturing, and unique employers such as military bases in rural areas all have undergone radical restructuring in the past several decades. Vital communities either mobilize to obtain replacement industries or grow their own as a consequence of local initiatives (Flora, Sharp, and Flora 1997).

Newcomers to a mixed-economy town are able to find jobs locally and are attracted by this opportunity. Over time, newcomers come to resemble oldtimers in these towns: they hold jobs that pay decent wages, are working-class, and own modest homes located within the original town grid. Oldtimers and newcomers may work side by side in manufacturing plants, agribusinesses, or service jobs. Because a town like Bunkerton has a stable economic base as a county seat, it historically was home to a small professional elite. As a consequence of having an elite, such a town may possess large, high-quality homes that attract middle-class or skilled blue-collar families who prefer older homes to new. Among our mixed-economy towns, only Bunkerton attracts newcomer-commuters by residential factors such as ambience or housing.

In the more industrialized mixed-economy towns of Corntown and Arbordale, blue-collar newcomers are able to purchase desirable housing at affordable prices because of a population decline related to economic restructuring. Like blue-collar workers or first-time home buyers in larger blue-collar towns, the newcomers share enough features and values with the oldtimers that they change the town but do not transform it entirely. Despite an influx of newcomers, the mixed-economy towns maintain continuity with the old town population, landscape, and culture.

Shabby Residential

Towns transformed by lower-income newcomers into shabby residential places resemble agrarian towns demographically, because the population of these towns peaked early in the twentieth century, and physically, because the town housing stock is old and modest. Further, such communities possess little scenic or architectural ambience. Splitville, like agrarian Smallville, is marginalized by location at the edge of the county and is served by secondary roads. The homes are on the original grid, and no new homes have been built in the past twenty or thirty years, although some have been renovated. Shabby towns develop from agrarian towns that lack social resources, such as a strong ethnic identity or cohesion indicative of a store of social capital like Smallville has, to deal with an influx of newcomers (Salamon 1992). Surplus deteriorated housing, affordable to poor people, is Splitville's major economic resource. Unlike Smallville, Splitville experienced a newcomer influx.

Like the residents of the agrarian town, the population of the shabby residential town has aged because the young have left. When community loyalty is weak, youth are less willing to stay or return. Thus, after elderly home owners die, heirs usually are absent, and the inherited low-value property is difficult to sell. Inherited homes are sometimes abandoned by heirs. The county takes abandoned properties for back taxes. Gradually property rentals increase in these towns. Former factories and closed schools or stores may be converted to apartments.

A rural midwestern small town typically lacks the basic services of a drugstore and a grocery store—which the poorest of the poor require because of a lack of personal or public transportation (Fitchen 1995). Instead of that group, a shabby midwestern town attracts young, working-poor rural people who can afford personal transportation but have only limited funds for housing. When newcomers become numerous, such towns essentially turn into the rural lower-income neighborhood for the regional commuting zone, as Splitville has done.

When compared with oldtimers, who usually have lived all their lives in the town, poor newcomers, like wealthy newcomers, live differently. As a rule they are not mobile by choice, as are wealthy newcomers. High residential mobility is a hallmark of poor rural people, a consequence of displacement from rural places that become more upscale through new subdivisions, gentrification of deteriorated housing that they occupied, high urban rents, or income irregularities (Fitchen 1994). Lower-income newcomers use their homes for self-employment activities, such as car repairs. Relative to oldtimers, the newcomers pay less attention to property upkeep. Housing values may not have actually changed much (when inflation is taken into account) as a consequence of the newcomer influx (Splitville had median home values $19,500 in 1980 and $27,500 in 1990), but oldtimers are convinced that the property values have eroded owing to the newcomer influx (Fitchen 1991; Salamon and Tornatore 1994).

If we compare the extent to which the current town resembles the same place ten or twenty years ago, those towns that transformed from agrarian to bedroom towns have changed more drastically overall than the other types (see appendix A). The agrarian and mixed-economy towns show more continuity with past characteristics. A clear distinction is evident between town growth based on creating jobs versus residential growth as a bedroom place for a small city. Our community case studies flesh out these differences.

Taken as a whole, the changes described in this chapter give clues about regional change in the rural countryside. Because the towns (with the exception of agrarian Smallville in western Illinois) lie within the Central City commuting zone, it is reasonable to assume that change among them will be interrelated. Some places in the same zone are bound to be winners and others losers in economic and population terms. A rural commuting zone is unlikely to produce more than a single affluent residential commuting town, because only a limited number of doctors, lawyers, and other professionals desire rural ambience and can be absorbed within the zone. Similarly, when lower-income families are forced to move away from an affluent town by high rents or high home values, a more affordable town is sought nearby (Fitchen 1995). For similar reasons, then, a regional suburbanization transformation produces limited numbers of affluent residential towns (probably only one) and shabby towns (perhaps a few) in a single commuting zone.

CHANGE INITIATED WITH A RURAL GROWTH MACHINE

Three towns that experienced population flux with great social consequences for a sense of community—Prairieview (upscale residential), Bunkerton (mixed economy) and Splitville (shabby residential)—have in common that buildings or land was exploited to create financial gain for a few. Developers, local business boosters, or real estate agents in these towns capitalized on the housing demand created by the powerful rural rebound (Johnson and Beale 1998).

The rural growth machines described here did not meet local resistance in any organized way, except in Splitville, where newcomers were deemed undesirable because they were working-poor rather than middle-class households. The accepted wisdom of small-town boosterism reincarnated as a rural growth machine seems to lull old-timers into believing that the initiative will bring progress that will benefit the town. Oldtimers could not foresee a third great transformation of the rural Midwest, one in which growth-machine accommodation brought engulfment by suburbanization or "neighborhoodization" of their agrarian towns (Barron 1997).

Agrarian community identity, norms, cohesion, and social capital—the uniqueness of the community as a place—are forever altered when a town changes into a rural regional commuting-zone neighborhood. When farmland or housing stock is used as a growth machine, developers manipulate the town attributes and location to achieve economic gain. The land developers of agrarian towns initially are local farmers or relatives of farmers, but if development accelerates (as in Prairieview), outsider developers soon replace them (Rudel 1989). These processes produce growth with distinct winners and losers (Logan and Molotch 1987). Towns targeted by a growth machine are likely to experience "spillover effects," such as higher property taxes or farmland taken for new public demands such as parks (Daniels and Bowers 1997).

Because the rural growth machines described below are different from urban growth machines in size and residential emphasis, and because the rural rebound enhances the potential for change, the various scenarios our towns represent are described briefly here and further in the specific case studies.

Rural Growth Machine Scenario One

Towns transformed into upscale sleeper towns, like Prairieview, exemplify a transformation orchestrated by local or nearby city developers. The use of a town as a suburbanization growth machine requires a place with attributes attractive to upscale commuters. The first areas to be developed are farmland tracts contiguous to the original town; sometimes these are obtained from heirs not committed to agriculture (Rudel 1989). Once several upscale subdivisions are in place, with affluent buyers, further development is attracted, along with land speculation. Developers and newcomers both favor residential development (which increases property values) but are likely to oppose industrial development that creates jobs for the less affluent, because rural amenities are their selling point. Established residents tend to experience higher taxes to provide the upscale newcomers the level of services they demand, yet they often receive fewer services than the newcomers. Oldtimers may be denied access to settings that have customarily been used over the course of generations for recreation or hunting (Daniels and Bowers 1997; Sokolow 1981; Spain 1993). Rural residential development typically takes place under county jurisdiction, with codes notoriously more lenient than urban codes (Daniels and Bowers 1997). Home buyers, however, naively assume that city building codes will be enforced.

Central Illinois was originally wetland; it was drained in the nineteenth century to create farm fields. Before towns became more experienced with oversight, early developers largely ignored drainage issues and destroyed the tile laid by farmers to drain fields. In the western suburbs of Chicago, flooding has become a real problem: subdivisions have even been built in wetlands and floodplains. In Prairieview, riverfront subdivision buyers were told they were buying in a 50- to 100-year floodplain. When the river flooded 10 years later, they felt cheated and spoke of suing the town: to them, 50 years meant 50 years from when they purchased the home.

Developers may attempt to circumvent even lenient zoning laws or shift the burden of certain costs (road development or school construction) to the town residents. Oldtimers, especially if they are retired and on fixed incomes, receive few benefits from growth but are called on to financially support both developers' profits and newcomers' increased demands for urbanlike services (Daniels and Bowers 1997; Sorensen and Esseks 1998).

Rural Growth Machine Scenario Two

A business elite mobilized by boosterism goals can employ existing town real estate as a growth machine. This scenario in central Illinois operated in several towns that served as county seats. As a result, each town has fine old homes built in the early twentieth century by professionals and businesspeople before the towns declined as agricultural and manufacturing centers. As population also declined, the fine housing stock deteriorated but was available for exploitation as an untapped resource. Because mixed-economy towns tend to be larger than towns of other types (see table 4), small numbers of newcomers can be absorbed without a profound social impact. If a mixed-economy town has small manufacturing plants within its boundaries, as, for example, Corntown has, pollution or noise are likely to be involved. Such a setting is not suitable for a growth-machine strategy that depends on attracting upscale or middle-class home buyers. Thus, not all mixed-economy towns are amenable to growth-machine dynamics.

This scenario is exemplified by the transformation of Bunkerton, a mixed-economy town. Bunkerton, besides serving as the site of county government, also has some small manufacturing plants, whose blue-collar workers dominate the town. By virtue of a population exodus after a nearby military base closed, Bunkerton possessed surplus housing stock in good condition. Because Bunkerton had housed the civilian employees of the military base, the school system was also of good quality. If more home buyers were lured from the nearby small city, argued local boosters, main-street business would be revitalized. The newcomers who arrived were upper-working-class and lower-middle-class commuter families seeking small-town life or affordable housing for a first home purchase. Oldtimers soon found that town priorities veered away from them and toward the demands of business or newer residents. For example, tax breaks given to new businesses necessitated higher property taxes for home owners (Daniels and Bowers 1997). As a consequence of the growth-machine dynamics, business profits and growth, more than family and community social issues, drive the Bunkerton town agenda.

Rural Growth Machine Scenario Three

A particular sort of real estate entrepreneur can find opportunity where others have dismissed profit potential. This scenario, employed in Splitville, superficially resembles a growth machine, but what occurs is not a manipulation of space to achieve growth, as in the other scenarios (Logan and Molotch 1987). Rather than profiting from converting farmland by housing construction, the entrepreneur in this scenario exploits an existing deteriorated housing stock. The strategy is to extract maximum profits with minimal investment in improvements on existing homes. Property is bought up cheaply, either houses that their owners are unable to sell because of the location or the condition of the homes or abandoned structures seized by the county for back taxes. The homes are rented as is or sold on contract to families without the resources to obtain mortgages on their own.

Targeted as the market for these homes are people with incomes too irregular to obtain credit or whose reputation makes them unwelcome in other towns. The entrepreneur is fundamentally an absentee rural slum landlord. By residing elsewhere, the entrepreneur experiences no local social pressure or financial burden by using this growth-machine strategy. Oldtimers are the losers in this scenario, as they are under the first scenario. They have difficulty selling their property once the newcomers are readily visible to potential buyers, and they receive the brunt of property and social violations if they mobilize to assert newcomers' conformity to town upkeep norms. Because a town with such housing resources is already marginalized, the county is not eager to cite the entrepreneur for code violations or to make regular inspections. "Village busting," as Calvin Beale terms the process (personal communication, 1996), is essentially the result: oldtimers flee in reaction to the transformation.

For this growth-machine entrepreneur to operate in a rural location, some town conditions seem to be prerequisites. Uninhabited storefronts, deteriorated houses, and empty warehouses, schools, or factories attract such entrepreneurs. If the local economy or population is relatively stable, few such buildings are available. A cohesive agrarian community, like Smallville, without ambience or a location favorable for commuting, is not a plausible candidate for entrepreneurial exploitation using any of the scenarios. Its high level of social capital enables mobilization against building-code violations, for example, militating against a rural slum landlord's operating freely.

When towns with a prior purely residential economy, whether upscale or poor, are transformed by newcomers, they attract mobile people who make the population more fluid than it is likely to be in towns having a stable mixed economy. High mobility affects the social fabric of small towns. Newcomers (whether affluent or working-poor) are unlikely to invest time and energy in a community if they expect their residence to be temporary. Class differences between newcomers and oldtimers have implications for the community connections and the social resources that maintain a sense of community. Key to the transformation of the countryside is that half of the set of communities deviate little from what each was before the restructuring. As the case studies outline, these latter towns remain relatively consistent physically and socially, despite the arrival of newcomers. Town transformations thus differ under similar regional suburbanization processes.

REFLECTIONS

Today, midwestern small towns face the decline of their population, small businesses, tax base, services, and, of course, family farms (Fuguitt, Brown, and Beale 1989; Johansen and Fuguitt 1984; Luloff and Swanson 1990). Farmers and main-street business owners, including, more recently, women, now join publicly to maintain what they value about their small community; yet none of these groups have enough numbers to act effectively alone (Aronoff 1993; Elder and Conger 2000; Salamon, Farnsworth and Rendziak 1998). All fear that the closing of a school, a church, or critical businesses will result in losing the heart of the community. It is becoming more and more evident that small towns that sustain a vibrant main street and greater numbers of family farms in the surrounding countryside benefit from committed volunteerism by a broad cross section of engaged citizens (Putnam 2000; Tolbert, Lyson, and Irwin 1998). Viable main-street businesses, churches, and schools provide communities with the public spaces known as "third places," where locals subtly work at building community (Oldenburg 1999).

In the six community case studies that constitute part 2 of this volume, demographic transformations are explained—which community features change and which features sustain continuity with the past. Each community is introduced with a brief history, which is followed by a description of the internal or external agent of change. Visible evidence of change is sought in the town layout or public spaces and in the processes of community connectedness, the availability of social resources, and cross-age relations. I argue that a town's physical plan and its use of and access to public spaces symbolize community social priorities. Similarly, the interconnections in a community are indicative of whether a cross section of people know one another and are linked by the overlapping social networks. Such networks are fundamental to relationships that are underlain by trust and to rich community social resources. If newcomers avoid contact with oldtimers, it is difficult to build community together (Kenny 2000).

Finally, the accessibility of town public spaces, the availability of social resources, and the density of cross-age interconnections explain town actions taken toward youth—actions both of oldtimers and of newcomers. The treatment of youth highlights the fundamental organizing principles that underlie a community and symbolizes whether a place retains its agrarian culture or is transformed into a postagrarian suburban nontown, *in* but not *of* the surrounding rural countryside.

PART II

Newcomers, Old Towns

You live differently in a small place. I had been a city person all my life: my homes had been in the dense urban tangles of Sydney, New York, Cairo and London. Though each of those cities is different, I was much the same in all of them. People say cities breed acceptance of diversity, but I didn't learn that lesson there. It took a village to teach me tolerance and a measure of tact.

If you meet a person who lives near you in a big city and you don't like her, that's fine: you can conduct your life so that you never have to speak with that person again. But in a village of 250, you don't have that luxury. You will see each other, day following day. You will sit side by side at town meetings or at other people's dinner tables. You will work together on school committees or at the annual fair. You're stuck with each other. . . .

In urban neighborhoods like finds like: the wealthy gather at the leafy end of town, the impoverished struggle on elsewhere, often invisible to the afflu- ent. But all of our village's half dozen streets are leafy: all share wide, glori- ous views of pastures and hillsides. Millionaire or minimum-wage worker, we cluster in the enforced coziness of our 18th century townscape.

Geraldine Brooks, *New York Times*, July 2, 2001

3 A PERSISTENT AGRARIAN TOWN: SMALLVILLE

In collaboration with Karen Davis-Brown

Smallville lies in a remote corner of a relatively sparsely settled western Illinois rural county (pop. 18,000, according to the 1990 census). Acknowledging that its peripheral location and size preclude growth, Smallville citizens work together simply to sustain what they value about their modest community. Their town may look undistinguished, but to Smallville citizens it is a little paradise worth defending. Smallville is remarkably successful at surviving, according to people in Bigville (pop. 1,500), its nearest neighbor, whose school consolidation bid was thwarted by Smallville during the 1980s when the county was reeling from the farm crisis. Smallville is envied by Bigville for its resiliency, which derives from community strengths of connectedness and trust. Life in Smallville is framed by constant mobilization to sustain the village by defying the regional postagrarian trends of consolidation and centralization. For example, people in Smallville resist what they view as the county seat's strategies for absorbing all county schools, businesses, and services.

The village was established in the early 1830s, laid out by Kentuckian settlers followed soon after by Tennesseans. The southerners, however, were quickly outnumbered by easterners from New England and Middle Atlantic states and by Germans migrating one family at a time from elsewhere in Illinois and from Iowa. Thus, no ethnic group dominates Smallville, although many cite some German heritage, a possible source of its tight-knit community culture (Salamon 1992). Located at the county's edge, Smallville never benefited financially from either a railroad or a major highway. Farm families today raise corn, soybeans, and hogs on the surrounding landscape of marginal-to-good soils. Farming dominated the village economy

Table 6 Smallville Demographic Profile

YEAR	POPU-LATION	MEDIAN AGE	PERCENT RESIDING IN SAME HOUSE AS 5 YEARS BEFORE	MEDIAN VALUE OF OWNED HOMES ($)	MEDIAN HOUSEHOLD INCOME ($)	PERCENT BELOW POVERTY LEVEL	PERCENT FEMALE-HEADED HOUSE-HOLDS[a]
1980	487	41.7	62.8	21,600	12,450	11.7	1.9
1990	495	40.2	70.6	21,200	16,635	19.8	3.2
2000	437	43.5	68.6	41,200	26,458	24.4	2.7

Sources: Bureau of the Census 1980a, 1990a, 2001, 2002.
[a] With own children under 18.

from the start, despite the early presence of several small factories and mills. When mineral springs were discovered on Smallville's outskirts, a health resort was developed, but it closed when the new automobiles could not navigate the roads (Settler Days Festival committee, 1984). None of these businesses today diversify Smallville's economy, and the old secondary roads remain unimproved. "We're out here in the boonies. . . . If the electricity goes out, Smallville is the last town to get it back," related a woman resident. Emphasizing its uniqueness, Smallville alone in the county consistently votes Republican. Locals refer to themselves as "conservative farmers."

At the turn of the century, the village population peaked at 800. By 2000 it had declined to less than 450, but the 200 to 300 countryside residents must be included to arrive at the community's true size (table 6). The approximately 700 residents of town and country combined surprisingly sustain three churches, a restaurant, three garages, a meat locker, a branch bank, a bowling alley, a Masonic Lodge, and a lumber yard. In addition, Smallville takes pride in supporting the smallest elementary and high school districts in the state. When studied in 1988, the high school had only fifty students.

Smallville represents the profile of a rural community typically considered to be in decline (Fuguitt, Brown, and Beale 1989). "The town population has stayed the same, but the school population has gone down. When I was in high school, there were 100 students; now there are only about 50," said a retired school teacher. The large elderly population (25.5% over 65, according to the 1990 census) includes farmers who still move into town when they retire. Smallville's mayor, for example, is a semiretired farmer living in town and commuting out to the farm to help his son. The mayor's wife holds no title but serves as the town secretary. By the kitchen telephone hangs a schedule that she uses to book the town hall for 4-H meetings or cheerleader practices.

In addition to retired farmers, Smallville has welcomed a few retirees who moved back after completing careers elsewhere. "They want to live in a small town," explained the mayor. "What those retirees really want is cheap housing," commented a local cynic. One returnee was a "big shot" for a multinational food corporation: "They traveled all over the world, but they decided to come here," said the mayor. The former executive, according to the mayor, attempted to streamline the way Smallville worked. "When he first came, he tried to make a lot of changes in the town, to make it better. . . . He got pretty frustrated. He asked me what was wrong and I told him 'you can't expect to come in here and expect people to change just like that.' . . . he slowed down quite a bit. So now he gets along better and people like him more." What the returnee from the corporate world experienced in his boyhood home was the power of shared community norms in operation.

COMMUNITY CHANGE
Space and Place

The village layout closely follows the original midwestern grid. All local businesses are clustered within two blocks on the wide main street, which, on a typical day, is lined by diagonally parked pickup trucks. One church is on the main street, and two others are tucked away on streets that parallel the main street to the east and the west (fig. 2). Modest clapboard homes that declined in value between 1980 and 1990 (table 6) are set close to one another on the tree-lined narrow side streets. From their front porches on summer evenings, people visit with mothers pushing strollers or other neighbors walking by on the sidewalks. Behind their homes many residents cultivate kitchen gardens. At one end of the main street stands a large implement dealership and some new duplexes, labeled "federal housing" by locals. Residents of this Title 8 housing vary from a retired schoolteacher to a poor family paying almost nothing toward housing rented for $400 to $500 per month. The federal housing development, a few new mobile homes, and a high proportion of the population older than sixty-five account for the increase in the number of town residents living below the poverty line and the low median income relative to the national median between 1980 and 1990 (tables 3 and 6). The location of these few new types of housing along the main street means that even elderly people can easily walk to local businesses and regularly see other residents.

Smallville sits in what is categorized as a service county (table 2),

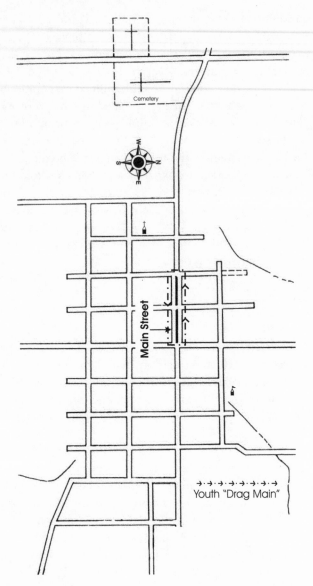

Figure 2 Smallville town map

a rural county deeply affected by the 1980s farm crisis (Bender 1985; Cook and Mizer 1994). During the 1980s half of the fourteen county villages lost half of their local retail businesses. The county extension adviser attributed these losses to the weak farm economy, the population decline, small plant closings, and the opening of a Wal-Mart in the county seat (Wright 1988). Yet, in contrast to the empty storefronts lining bleak main streets in the other county towns, Small-

Table 7 Smallville Employment Profile

YEAR	PERCENT COMPLETING HIGH SCHOOL OR HIGHER	MEAN TRAVEL TIME TO WORK (MINUTES)	PERCENT OVER 16 IN LABOR FORCE	PERCENT EMPLOYED IN AGRICULTURE	PERCENT EMPLOYED IN PROFESSIONAL SERVICES	PERCENT EMPLOYED IN MANUFACTURING
1980	57.7	16.7	48.2	8.2	13.8	18.9
1990	77.7	20.5	52.2	9.3	19.2	26.0
2000	81.1	22.2	50.6	10.3[a]	38.7[a]	9.0[a]

Sources: Bureau of the Census 1980a, 1990a, 2002.

[a] Due to major revisions in the 2000 census classification of jobs by industry, these data are not exactly comparable with the 1980 and 1990 data.

ville's main-street businesses survived, as a result of community actions taken by local leaders. For example, when the village café was in danger of folding, a group of citizen investors took it over because they agreed that a main-street restaurant was necessary to sustain the town. The Coffee House now functions as the community center. It is "just packed" when the men gather at the "Liars' Table" for coffee at six in the morning, the women at half past nine, and both groups between three and four in the afternoon. People bring new babies to show off; teenagers hang out and visit with the older folks and the young families who stop by. Older men constantly tease the young waitresses as they might tease their own daughters. Twice a week, senior citizens from several nearby towns are served a hot meal at noon, adding to the main-street bustle the café creates. Smallville as a town has worked to provide the public arenas where community is built.

Except for persons related to a farmer or a local business family, Smallville's workforce must commute elsewhere (note the rise in commuting time over the 1980s, table 7). Smallville generates few jobs aside from those associated with the few farms and family businesses that remain in and around town. Therein lies the central dilemma for Smallville: people love the community, but it is difficult to earn a living there or nearby, given the rurality of the entire sparsely populated county. The town is becoming a bedroom community, albeit a lively one, and that is a concern for the residents.

Interconnectedness

Smallville citizens describe their community as a friendly one, functioning with a tolerant and open social structure despite its small size and relative insularity. One minister, a recent arrival to his wife's hometown, agrees: "I judge a town by if people wave. To me that's a sign of how friendly a town is. Smallville people are wavers." How newcomers are treated reflects whether a friendly community tries to be inclusive. Two families, one low-income and the other middle-class, moved from neighboring Bigville to Smallville and reported identical warm experiences: A family of lifelong low-income Bigville residents moved after losing their home to fire, expecting to return when housing became available. "By the time there was an opening, I said, 'No way,' I felt like I was right at home in Smallville. People here are so friendly right away, saying how glad they was we were in town," related the wife. Similarly, a middle-class businesswoman said, "We lived in Bigville a few years, but it was too cliquish. We finally gave up and moved to Smallville and noticed the difference right away. People told us they were glad we were there, offered to help out any way they could. We've made more friends in the short time we've lived here than the whole time we lived in Bigville."

People from various walks of life agree that Smallville is a more inclusive community than others in the county, and they take pride in their uniqueness. The low-income woman reflected, "One thing about Smallville, the people who have money in this town look out for the community. They're all for Smallville. . . . Everybody here just neighbors like family." As a poor person sensitive to status differences, she compared the "outdoing" her children experienced in the Bigville school with the tolerance the family discovered in Smallville. "There all the kids with money were in a clique and they'd throw it up in the other kids' faces. . . . But in Smallville it doesn't seem to matter as much. Even the kids from the richer families don't look down on the poorer kids." A member of Smallville's town board also described the village as egalitarian: "We're definitely a closer-knit community than most. Nobody's better than us, but we're not snobby like they are in other parts of the county." This democratic sentiment was echoed by a prominent local businessman: "We belonged to the country club in [the county seat] for a while, but people would ask us where we were from, and like roll their eyes or make snide comments about being from our end of the county. Never mind that we could've bought any of them three or four times over. . . . We quit going." A farmer agreed: "The people in [Bigville] seem to have a lot more time to belong to the country club, to play golf. . . . Any free time we have goes to community projects. We don't have free time or money to belong to the country club."

A strong track record of effective community mobilization and an ability to cooperate on behalf of the greater good are evidence of the density of network connections among Smallville residents. For instance, Smallville experienced more than a 50% increase in low-income households during the 1980s, including some living in the new mobile homes scattered throughout the town (table 6). Smallville's mobile homes resulted from the personal initiative of a local wealthy farmer. He bought various empty town lots and used the land to entice low-income families from elsewhere in the county to move in. Opinions are mixed about the farmer's actions, but all agree about his motives. "He wasn't bringing in mobile homes just to be ornery. . . . He was trying to bring in families with kids to raise the enrollment of the school. But, then, those kind of people they move on and somebody else comes in. . . . some have 'hoodlums' now." To guard against future problems, Smallville adopted a zoning ordinance that permits the town to tear down deteriorated homes, the ones most likely to attract the undesirable tenants. "People come in because of cheap housing. . . . that's why we're trying to get rid of it," said the mayor. Smallville, unlike many small communities, overcame opposition to a zoning ordinance by reaching consensus that it would help maintain the residential standards preferred by the community.

The village infrastructure is completely supported by volunteer labor, from the mayor's office to the ambulance service. "Smallville is so small, everybody's in everything," said a farm woman whose commitment is representative. In addition to her regular farm work, she has for years been "in charge of the chicken dinner" for Pioneer Days. Pioneer Days is an annual village homecoming celebration in August, complete with a parade, a fair, and a community feast. Preparing the chicken dinner involves coordinating the women of the church groups, who cook vast quantities of food to be consumed over the two days of the festival. She can count on the Smallville churches to be as committed to putting on the festival as she is.

This farm woman's volunteerism also includes coordinating the ambulance service and working as a trained ambulance volunteer. She is frustrated, however, because it has become more difficult to find enough volunteers to make the huge commitment that staffing the ambulance requires: "We're having the hardest time. People just don't seem to care. There's a few of us, but we can't get people to take time to go for the training. We're afraid we're going to lose it." A Smallville pattern, however, is that when the town is in danger of losing something valuable to maintaining its autonomy, the tight-knit community readily mobilizes to save the endangered element.

Social Resources

Loyalty to Smallville is frequently cited as the reason for activities that undergird the village both socially and economically. People's patronage of local businesses sustains a vital main street with a variety of family-owned enterprises. "It is amazing that this town supports three garages. People come from all over. . . . That we still have a farm implement dealership is also amazing," said a farmer. "We try to support local businesses. My dad said 'Always buy everything in town,'" remarked a retired woman. A garage owner, proud of his son as the third generation in the family's fifty-year-old firm, reflects commitment to the community typical of local businesspeople: "I'm on the town board and have been for 25 years. . . . I've never run for mayor, but I've never needed to. I would run if no one else did. I wouldn't let the town go down."

Smallville sustains more businesses than does its closest neighbor, Bigville, a town twice its size, and Smallville's property has a higher assessed valuation (school report cards, 1990). One possible structural reason for the fewer businesses in larger Bigville is that it is closer to the county seat. Yet Bigville residents patronize the Smallville restaurant and have their cars repaired in Smallville. A professional woman whose husband farms near Smallville said, "We don't have that many businesses closing. The stores keep changing hands, but they don't close." Around the mid-1980s, Smallville was in danger of losing key main-street businesses. Prominent residents, organized by the mayor and the wealthy retired farmer who took over the failing café, also took over the food locker. "We all had the chance to buy shares. Nobody could buy more than $400 to $500 dollars," explained an elderly couple, who were investors. A recently received dividend from this community investment surprised the husband: "I got a check from the restaurant the other day for $250. I never expected to see that money again. It was a contribution to the welfare of the community."

The same investors financed a highly successful bowling-alley venture to provide families—but more importantly, youth—with a wholesome activity. To maintain a family atmosphere, the bowling alley serves no beer, and it stays open after high school football games so that youth have a place to gather. When the implement dealership threatened to move because no landowner would sell acreage to locate a larger store, a couple who were already shareholders in the cooperative restaurant and bowling-alley ventures reconsidered. "We didn't want [the dealership] to leave town. . . . It brought in a lot of sales tax," the retired businesswoman recalled. The cooperation that undergirds retention of Smallville's main-street businesses is indicative of a place attachment that generates human and financial resources as social capital available for other community endeavors.

Almost every active citizen alluded to a recently deceased wealthy farmer as a person pivotal to their community's integrity and connectedness. He is remembered as having "done a lot behind the scenes, helping out, trying to keep things going." Various people recall that he mobilized the community corporation that saved the restaurant, the bowling alley, and the food locker, just as he bought empty main-street storefronts, renovated them, and rented them to local businesspeople. It was he who purchased town lots, put trailers on them, and recruited family tenants to increase enrollment in Smallville schools. It was also he, as "one of the biggest landowners around," who gave land to the community college for its agriculture program. Commented a couple who invested in community endeavors with him, "He sure did care about Smallville. . . . He fought to keep this school and he was probably the one who paid the most money in taxes." In some towns the loss of such a dominant personality erodes further ventures (Flora, Sharp, and Flora 1997). In Smallville, however, others, such as the garage owner, voluntarily stepped into the breach. Furthermore, because the wealthy farmer never was eager to assume formal leadership but preferred working behind the scenes, others were accustomed to sharing authority in the town. Clearly, the deceased farmer provided Smallville with a committed community role model that they could emulate.

The way controversy is processed in Smallville produces social capital that is then available as a resource for dealing with other issues. People acknowledge community conflicts, but typically they report constructive resolutions. The town clerk noted: "Everyone is suspicious at first. It's only natural, but they eventually compromise." A homemaker expressed annoyance that "nobody minds their own business," but nonetheless she could describe how consensus emerges: "I don't think anybody makes decisions. I think it just happens. Some people are louder than others, that's all. But don't get me wrong, people stand behind our leaders." To an outsider, the slow pace at which decisions emerge is frustrating. The executive who retired to his family home is critical of what he considers inefficient problem solving: "People in Smallville aren't willing to rock the boat. . . . Everyone is . . . related. No one wants to cross anybody, to look foolish." A farmer's view of the characteristic consensus-making process is that "We're smaller than most towns so we get madder at each other. But we work together too." Trust in the basic goodwill of one's neighbor is evidenced in these descriptions of the community consensus-building process.

Smallville depends on trust and its customary ways for handling controversy to facilitate the generation of support even for unpopular issues such as taxation. For instance, Smallville successfully dealt with the controversial issue of high taxes to sustain its tiny school districts, while maintaining a cohesive community. Smallville has separate elementary and high school districts, but one supervisor and principal serve both. This arrangement, which allows both districts to assess taxes, is how the town taxes itself heavily enough to sustain the smallest school districts in the state (James G. Ward, personal communication, 1993). Property taxes in Smallville are almost double the rates paid in Bigville, where taxes are at the state average (Illinois State Board of Education 1992).

The strategy to preserve its schools by high taxes is not without local critics: "We've been fighting a long time. . . . landowners [farmers] outside the community make the decisions about Smallville's future, but they usually support the school," commented a parent. Smallville bears scars from the most recent struggle, when substantial property taxes were imposed in lieu of a school consolidation with Bigville, against the wishes of some farmers. People in Smallville say the vote "turned family members against one another." Two brothers, a farmer and a town resident, were on opposite sides and still do not speak to each other. A farm couple with children in the Smallville school, however, expressed a common view about the high property tax rate. Said the husband, "Local taxes are too high, but on the other hand we want to keep the school." His wife added, "If you're going to spend your money on something, it might as well be the school. It's money well spent." Despite voting to pay hefty property taxes, Smallville recently built a new gym and furnished it through community fund-raisers such as an annual smorgasbord.

The regular public forum that allows issues to be chewed over and negotiated to produce consensus is the informal, twice-daily gatherings at the Coffee House café. For example, the year Smallville was studied was the first time the school districts ran a deficit. The school superintendent recalled: "We had a meeting and over 100 people [one-quarter of the town] came; I was amazed. We had to cut $25,000 out of a $300,000 budget. People opted to cut sports rather than jeopardize the academic programs. The kids were surveyed about which sports to cut, and they chose softball, wrestling, and girls' basketball.

Then the booster club picked up softball and wrestling." From his point of view, the town sacrifices to keep its own schools because "when you lose your schools and churches from the community, you lose the heart." The Smallville mayor agrees: "When you take the school out of a community, you lose something. School functions bring people together." The fight to keep Smallville's tiny schools is also a fight to preserve Smallville as a community.

The state has exerted a great deal of pressure on Smallville to consolidate its small school system with Bigville, but Smallville has resisted. "Other towns think they're better than we are because we're small, but we're also closer-knit because of our size. Everybody's willing and everybody works to better our community. It depends on what you put into it," said a retired farmer. An insightful comparison was made by a businessman from a neighboring community about social processes in Smallville: "As I've gotten older, I've come to appreciate Smallville more; how the people there stick together and stick behind their community. People in Bigville are clannish diehards, even against local people. They don't stick together like Smallville people do." A succinct observation about the town made by a Smallville man commented on the place-specific nature of community social resources: "We all take care of ourselves, but if someone needs us we rally around. But we don't cooperate with other communities very well."

Cross-Age Relations

When Smallville people say "everybody's in everything," they mean school as well as community activities. Smallville children are highly valued as the town's future (Schwartz 1987). Because a sentiment prevails that children belong to the community, adults assume responsibility for all, not just their own children. A veteran school board member, who had served more than a decade (although having only recently become a parent), revealed an agrarian community commitment in her reflections on local youth and drugs: "I'd be lying if I said we didn't have problems. . . . we have some. You do what you can. . . . You worry though; those kids are like your own." A community farmer shared her perspective: "One thing's for sure, people around here will do anything for their kids."

Smallville considers its schools' intimate size critical to producing community-minded children. As "the heart of the community," the schools are the vehicles for nurturing citizenship and reproducing the place attachment that ensures the town's intergenerational continuity. "When you don't have many in the class, everybody has to take leadership," explained the retired teacher. A parent expressed a similar belief: "Everybody is either in sports, or a stats person or a manager. Everybody does something. They have to. When you got a school that keeps a kid that busy you don't have to worry about drugs." Each year the senior class takes a trip, to Hawaii, for example, with tickets earned beginning their freshman year through various fund-raisers. According to a low-income parent, community support is evident, because "everybody buys." Moreover, Smallville believes that a local school is better for children. The town has twice been "hardheaded" about resisting school consolidation with the nearest town. Smallville considers neighboring Bigville uncommitted to children, pointing to their unwillingness to make similar financial sacrifices. "They're selfish. They don't want to spend their money on the school, on something that really matters," according to the retired teacher.

Parental involvement in the schools is a community social resource known to positively affect children's academic performance (Coleman 1988; Coleman and Hoffer 1987). Do the social resources generated by parents' involvement in their community schools make a difference for Smallville children? Performances on nationally normed achievement tests were obtained to objectively assess whether Smallville's commitment to its schools has contributed to student performance, compared with neighboring Bigville. In Illinois, testing in reading comprehension and mathematics is carried out annually by state law for four grades. The number of students involved in each school, of course, is very small, so the average scores are merely suggestive. At the third-grade level, children in the two districts perform at approximately at the same level in reading. Among older children, however, Bigville's scores tend to go down in contrast to Smallville's, which improve. Smallville children score lower in third-grade mathematics, but by the time they reach the eleventh grade, the deficit is overcome. Approximately 50% of Smallville's eleventh-grade students ($N = 8$) ranked in the top quarter in all subjects, while around 30% of Bigville students ($N = 26$) scored in the bottom two quarters. Smallville's rankings in 1990 were consistent with its eleventh-grade ranking in the four previous years (school report cards, 1990; Salamon 1996).

Community involvement in Smallville schools is a factor in generating social resources available for other endeavors, such as the mobilization to save core businesses. It is interesting that despite having farms with comparably productive soils and a smaller population,

Smallville is wealthier than neighboring Bigville (twice its size), in terms of the property values on which taxes are assessed (Illinois State Board of Education 1992). The Bigville school district receives 60% of its revenues from the state; Smallville receives 41% from the state. It is difficult to determine the source of community wealth, but because the soil types of the two areas are similar, it is likely that town businesses, rather than farms generating differential returns, account for the difference in wealth between the two villages.

The social capital generated by community involvement in Smallville, particularly the deep engagement in the schools, has been productive. This small town has maintained a variety of businesses, whose higher assessed valuation attests to Smallville's vitality, when compared to the larger neighboring town. If state dollars for schools were, as the loyal retired teacher proposes, "based on how much the school is willing to help themselves . . . how much you're willing to sacrifice," Smallville would indeed be the recipient of more state aid.

REFLECTIONS

People in Smallville are realistic about their little community and its shortcomings. "This is not an exciting place to live. Brainwise, it's pretty dull. But you don't have to lock your house or your car, and it's a good place to raise kids," reflected a middle-aged woman who is active in civic affairs. The elderly retired teacher was more positive. "I love this town. I've lived here all my life, and I never wanted to live anywhere else." Social capital generated by actions to retain the local schools maintains this agrarian community in a postagrarian society. A cross section of citizens working together to preserve local sources of identity—the schools, core businesses, and public meeting spaces—has produced a community where a person is able to trust that all others are fundamentally committed to the community's welfare. Smallville's cooperation is of the ordinary taken-for-granted variety that suffuses highly personalized relation-ships, rather than a grand mobilization for out-of-the-ordinary events. Social resources are generated during the daily get-togethers at the village café and through activities based on the town's com-mitment to children. With its strong community identity and tight connectedness, Smallville shows cultural traits associated with an agrarian covenant: priority given to communitarian ideals for group welfare. How youth are treated and attitudes toward the schools, rather than economic development, indicate community social resources being produced by ordinary actions of citizens. Social capital generated through these actions is then available for other missions that sustain community (Coleman 1990; Schwartz 1987).

Rich social resources will not make Smallville grow, because the features associated with growth—location, ambience, size, and diversity of the economy—are absent. For community members, however, its size is about right. "I don't want it to get any bigger. On the other hand, if it gets too small there won't be anything left," reflected the retired schoolteacher. Smallville's community culture, with roots in an agrarian past, sustains a good life for its citizens (Kemmis 1995). Its agrarian culture shapes youth into citizens committed to their community; in contrast, the youth of many small midwestern towns are being socialized to leave permanently. A local minister explains, "Smallville kids are homebodies; they don't want to leave." Cooperative activities are a Smallville tradition motivated by a shared priority for preserving the town for future generations. Benefiting from the dedicated civic service of community members, each successive generation learns to be good citizens, to have respect for elders, and to develop a loyalty that cements a place attachment to Smallville.

Historically, the actions of Smallville residents are indicative of a concern for communitarian collective goals; this could be expected from a community sustaining an agrarian covenant (Bellah et al. 1985). The town of Smallville exhibits features such as acceptance of controversy as normal, depersonalization of politics, a long-term emphasis on school academics, investment of private capital locally, self-taxation to invest in the rural infrastructure, and a dispersed leadership—features that are linked to the persistence of rural communities today, a time when many are in decline (Flora and Flora 1990). These characteristics, although associated with communities that have successfully met current challenges with entrepreneurial endeavors, also represent historical ideals for agrarian communities (Smith 1966; Salamon 1992). Instead of inventing new strategies, then, entrepreneurial communities such as Smallville employ historical agrarian processes to cope with the changing social environment.

Although other small communities in the same county suffered fatal economic decline as a consequence of the 1980s farm crisis, Smallville maintained vitality. Ten years after the community study, I interviewed one of the last graduates of the Smallville school system, now working at the University of Illinois. Sadly for Smallville, in 1995 it was finally forced to consolidate its school system with Bigville's. No amount of community commitment could overcome the economic realities of Smallville's population decline and the continual state pressure to close its small schools. This student's graduating class numbered eight; two years before, there had been ten in the graduating class. Prior to the 1995 consolidation, the two school districts had already cooperated for team sports and the more costly classes such as agricultural education. Thus, the final closure did not come as a great shock, at least for the students.

Smallville stores, according to the native, "keep changing hands, but they don't close." Some have closed, but others remain. The café is still open, but under new and less skillful management. A new coffee shop is giving it some competition. As the study ended, the equipment used by the bowling alley was being recalled by the lessor. The bowling alley closed, but a gas station opened. Although the farm equipment store is no longer locally owned, this valuable service still is in operation. It was sold after the community-minded elderly owners died. One garage is open, as is the small grocery store. The latter has been under new management since the old owner died. The town food locker also closed just a few years ago, after the owner left town. A public library, funded with donations, is now open three days a week. It is run by a volunteer who is a retired school teacher. Pioneer Days was held in 2000, but the 2001 celebration was in doubt, because no new people volunteered to help. Someone always steps forward at the last moment, however, just as the garage owner finally accepted the duties of mayor when he was needed.

The young man working at my university, who provided the update on Smallville, thinks a newer mentality is replacing the community culture maintained by the oldtimers who lived in Smallville all their lives. The population is aging, and few young families are staying. Youth now schooled elsewhere may not be as locally committed. "It never is going to get bigger," he says. Would he go back if he could? His brother is farming with family, and if farmland were available, he would return. Smallville still creates homebodies.

4 UPSCALE SUBURBANIZATION: PRAIRIEVIEW

In collaboration with Patricia A. Howard, Consolata Kabonesa, Bret Kloos, and Stephanie Schaefer

Until the 1960s, Prairieview was a sleepy, modest farm town. Two events triggered explosive growth that irrevocably transformed the town. The first was the completion of an interstate highway in the early 1970s, which linked Prairieview to nearby small cities—Central City, less than a fifteen-minute drive, and others about a forty-minute drive. Several small subdivisions were developed next to the town before the highway's construction. The second event was the rapid expansion that occurred after the highway came through, as three landed families began to aggressively develop land tracts adjacent to the village (fig. 3). These local initiatives were soon dwarfed by upscale subdivisions built during the 1980s and 1990s by outside developers who quickly saw the potential of Prairieview as a bedroom community for Central City, in particular. This development sequence follows a nationwide pattern for exurban expansion (Rudel 1989). As a consequence, in just two decades the village transformed into an affluent residential community, suburban rather than rural small town in character, all white, and solidly Republican.

Prairieview was a prime candidate for suburban development. First, the interstate provided easy commutes to thriving urban centers. Second, Prairieview has rural ambience. The village nestles where a small river has cut a gentle valley, creating a hilly, forested setting unusual in the otherwise flat, open terrain of central Illinois. Stands of trees line the valley walls and the river banks, and woods cover the bottomland floodplain. Third, Prairieview, according to the "Village Comprehensive Plan" (formulated by the Prairieview Village Board in 1992), has an excellent school system, an adjacent

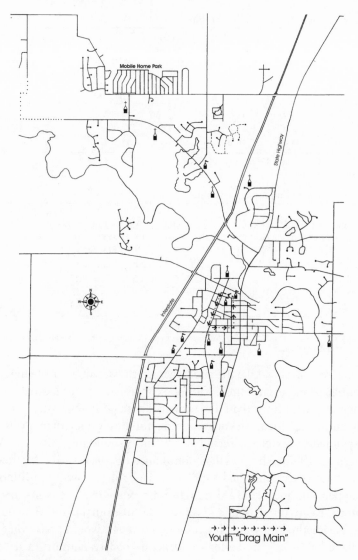

Figure 3 Prairieview town map

county park, and, according to developers, a "small town feel." These were key ingredients of the 150% growth in the town's population between 1980 and 2000. Prairieview newcomers are young, professional, and well educated (tables 8 and 9). An explosive growth in the number of Prairieview churches mirrors the growth of the town. As a farm town Prairieview was served by three traditional churches, but in the early 1990s the town of 4,800 had fourteen churches (about one for every 350 people), highly diverse in size, denomina-

Table 8 Prairieview Demographic Profile

YEAR	POPU-LATION	MEDIAN AGE	PERCENT RESIDING IN SAME HOUSE AS 5 YEARS BEFORE	MEDIAN VALUE OF OWNED HOMES ($)	MEDIAN HOUSEHOLD INCOME ($)	PERCENT BELOW POVERTY LEVEL	PERCENT FEMALE-HEADED HOUSE-HOLDS[a]
1980	1,986	29.9	46.6	52,900	20,723	5.2	6.8
1990	3,100	32.4	47.7	75,000	39,085	4.3	6.3
2000	4,870	34.0	46.1	113,600	54,574	5.1	7.3

Sources: Bureau of the Census 1980a, 1990a, 2001, 2002.
[a] With own children under 18.

Table 9 Prairieview Employment Profile

YEAR	PERCENT COMPLETING HIGH SCHOOL OR HIGHER	MEAN TRAVEL TIME TO WORK (MINUTES)	PERCENT OVER 16 IN LABOR FORCE	PERCENT EMPLOYED IN AGRI-CULTURE	PERCENT EMPLOYED IN PROFES-SIONAL SERVICES	PERCENT EMPLOYED IN MANU-FACTURING
1980	51.8	18.0	52.0	1.3	25.4	13.3
1990	89.5	18.9	77.6	1.9	32.8	12.9
2000	96.5	23.4	72.1	1.0[a]	44.5[a]	7.3[a]

Sources: Bureau of the Census 1980a, 1990a, 2002.
[a] Due to major revisions in the 2000 census classification of jobs by industry, these data are not exactly comparable with the 1980 and 1990 data.

tion, and doctrine. Like the subdivisions, the newer, more evangelical churches, and even a small Catholic congregation, are located on the edge of town rather than downtown. These peripheral sites symbolize an inward focus on congregation-building rather than a mission expanded by external, secular community-building activities (Ammerman 1997). The previous dominance of conservative Methodist and Baptist churches had kept the village "dry," owing to Illinois's emphasis on local rule. Although Prairieview itself remains dry, liquor is easily purchased in several stores just outside the village limits, beside the highway. Newcomers, however, would prefer that the village be "wet," the better to attract a good restaurant. Every few years a new ballot proposal to make the village wet is defeated, but the vote narrows as more upscale newcomers settle.

COMMUNITY CHANGE
Space and Place

The village downtown area retains marks of its farming past. A large grain elevator on a rail line anchors one end. Along the main street, businesses look prosperous, although smart boutiques, tea shops, and antique shops have replaced stores that originally supplied basic domestic and farm needs. Groceries, hardware, and other essential items are sold on the edge of town in a small strip mall next to the highway. Oldtimers report shopping locally, out of loyalty to town businesses. Newcomers, however, overwhelmingly say that they shop at the regional mall in nearby Central City, where they claim the selection is wider and prices are lower. Prairieview's transformation from farm town to upscale suburb is reflected in two new buildings on the main street. One contains the offices of the professional administrator who manages the village. He is assisted by a Central City engineering firm that has been planning the town's growth for about twenty years. The other houses a branch of a Central City bank heavily involved in home real estate loans.

The older parts of town, laid out on a square grid, have seen better days. The original tree-lined streets are now potholed. The brick sidewalks bordering several of these streets are also in disrepair. Complained an elderly widow, "The village doesn't take care of the streets and sidewalks in town." Prairieview's older housing stock resembles that of Smallville. The modest homes along the original streets tend to be covered with white clapboard or aluminum siding. Interspersed among well-kept homes are some in bad condition, rented to tenants. An elderly resident thinks such homes should be torn down. "They just make the neighborhood look awful. People have trash around their houses and they need fixin' up." It is clear from the modest nature of the homes that the forested areas so attractive to suburbanites never generated the handsome farm profits that arose from the flat prairie terrain, more typical of the Central City commuting zone.

Apparently, the town's leaders bought into the idea that residential development would bring public prosperity, and they permitted growth to control the village agenda. The first families to use Prairieview as a growth machine became wealthy by developing former wooded tracts or bottomland into subdivisions. These elite, major landowners were the principal local beneficiaries of Prairieview's growth (Logan and Molotch 1987). The subdivisions developed in the 1990s are decidedly more upscale than the original tracts and have a layout of culs-de-sac, sharply diverging from the original village grid plan (fig. 3). One of the newer developments has quarter- to half-million-dollar homes standing in what was formerly a cow pasture, much to the oldtimers' amusement. The growth was so rapid, more than 50% in each decade between 1970 and 2000 (57.2% in the 1990s, according to the 2000 census), that the village had difficulty supervising it or putting in place an appropriate infrastructure. For example, the earliest subdivisions were not connected to the city water system, and their old septic systems are a continuing problem. A local builder, also a subdivision resident, is frequently hired to repair the inferior construction allowed by the lax oversight of county inspectors. He said, "The building here is unlimited. It's growing too fast. . . . Bankers and suppliers are getting rich. . . . There are no building codes or inspection. . . . somebody must be getting their pockets lined."

Certain circumstances show that growth controls the town's agenda. In particular, newer residents are favored over old (Logan and Molotch 1987). Residents of downtown, for example, are saddened by losing a major chunk of a beloved park to a new sewer and water treatment plant. An elderly widow said, "They took our little city park. That hurt so much. It was the only park in town. . . . that's where they used to have the fall festival. There were people there all the time." Given the site's height relative to the river, the move was logical; but the newer parks, located on the town outskirts, are not easily accessible by the elderly. Likewise, elderly oldtimers conclude that the downtown area is neglected by village administrators when they see the potholed streets and broken brick sidewalks. A seventy-four-year-old resident remarked, "The subdivisions are well cared for and the town is neglected." Explosive growth also put pressure on the postal system. "They had to add one whole new postal zone in the last two years," explained a builder. Because of a post office policy of providing rural delivery service to the new subdivisions, town residents who live within a half mile of the post office no longer receive home delivery. A result of this policy is that that oldtimers, many over eighty years old, must walk to the post office to pick up their daily mail while youthful subdivision dwellers, who drive, have mail delivered to their doors. Such an unintended consequence of instituting rural delivery in a suburb illustrates how newcomers benefit and oldtimers lose from growth-machine processes.

Village personnel complain about the challenges facing the transformed Prairieview since "it's all boomed up." A local police officer points to the fluidity of the community: "People are constantly selling and buying houses. . . . There are 200 homes currently being built." Police like to know who lives where or who drives what car in a small town, the better to identify strangers. The professional village administrator feels caught between newcomers' and oldtimers' conflicting demands. He grumbles that "everyone feels free to criticize." Subdivision residents, however, tend to be the most disgruntled. "They have a consumer mentality" regarding the community. What he means is that people living in the subdivisions expect urban services as entitlements, because, as they constantly point out, they pay the highest property taxes in the county. Similarly, they feel that by buying an upscale home in a small town, they are entitled to a way of life that is safe, quiet, and family-focused. They fail to understand that volunteerism and shared values create these goods. Subdivision people are "too busy" to participate in the volunteer efforts that make a small town work as a connected whole.

Newcomers, preoccupied with property values and their invest-ment, put a positive spin on growth and other economic factors in their definition of community. Oldtimers do not voice an antigrowth sentiment, but they despair about the future of Prairieview as a real community. "People come from all over to do our strip of antique stores, but that doesn't pull our community together. It [just] helps our economy," explained an elderly widow. To her, a sense of com-munity differs qualitatively from simple economic growth. Elderly oldtimers say the subdivision residents "are money people." Subdi-vision people are so labeled because their homes or cars are chosen to display wealth and status. Oldtimers do not approve, and they sense the disdain of subdivision people for their own values. "The subdivisions are far enough away that I don't run into these people when I walk around. . . . no sidewalks go from here to there," said a retired farm woman who lives in the downtown area.

Thus, not only are the new subdivisions separated spatially from the original town on privacy-enhancing culs-de-sac, but also their residents operate in a world that differs according to generation and occupation from the world of oldtimers. The contrasts are evident in the income, educational, and occupational transformation of Prai-rieview between 1980 and 1990 (tables 8 and 9). Prairieview has be-come a midwestern version of a bifurcated community with few pub-lic spaces or activities that connect its entire population (Bradshaw 1993; Wuthnow 1998).

Interconnectedness

Newcomers and oldtimers uniformly like Prairieview, but each group evokes different social systems when describing their commu-nity. Essentially, as the subdivisions expanded adjacent to the origi-nal town, parallel communities evolved. A traditional agrarian com-munity, similar to Smallville, endures among oldtimers, who are connected by overlapping social networks through their civic par-ticipation, church membership, and downtown neighborhood resi-dence. Newcomers, in contrast, are focused on nearby Central City for work, shopping, services, and entertainment. They join local churches (often not downtown, mainline denominations) and in some instances participate in subdivision organizations. But they generally are absent from civic institutions, with the crucial exception of school activities and church. As a result, seldom are oldtimers and newcomers in situations that foster casual interactions. The segregation of these two parallel worlds erects barriers between them, and the connections that build community cannot form. Interconnectedness, when measured against the tight-knit agrarian community of the past, has declined with suburbanization. Prairieview lacks the crosscutting activities that produce the repetitive, densely overlapping, richly textured life that, in turn, creates community traditions constituting a shared history and culture (Williams 1988).

When oldtimers describe their Prairieview community, strong ties to the land and farming are evident. "Three-quarters of this town is related to each other," said a retired farm widow. These shared backgrounds and agrarian customs bind oldtimers by taken-for-granted understandings. An oldtimer widow commented, "As [Prairieview] grows, it becomes less desirable. It used to be small enough where everybody knew everybody. If you went to the hardware store and left your wallet, it was okay. You knew you could pay later." Oldtimers still live as they did before "[Prairieview] got too big." Neighbors say they look out for one another. "If she [a neighbor across the street] doesn't see my light on at night she'll call me the next day," related an elderly widow. According to an oldtimer, prior to the subdivision influx, "the moneyed people" in Prairieview were retired farmers, who moved into town late in life. Oldtimers live modestly, even if they were prosperous farmers or shop owners before retirement. Their generation shares a cultural belief that wealth should not be flaunted by conspicuous consumption. Oldtimers mourn the town's changing. A couple who ran the local newspaper until they retired reflected on the transformation: "We liked it the way it used to be. . . . Prairieview had a rural homeyness. . . . it's just not the same anymore."

Subdivision newcomers do not assume that they or their neighbors will live a lifetime in Prairieview, as do oldtimers. Subdivision residents represent a new form of sojourner, people who do not envision the place where they raise their children as their final destination (Siu 1952). A couple whose children are gone say that after twenty-seven years in an early Prairieview subdivision, they "want to move on." One young father thrives on the fluidity of his neighborhood: "Prairieview is a tremendous place to live. . . . All this town is is new people. . . . Everyone here is from somewhere else." Another newcomer, who had lived in his subdivision only two and a half years, said, "I've lived here the longest. My next-door neighbor doesn't expect to stay. He'll be out of here in three to four years. You see, he's still climbing the ladder. I think you'll find that a lot in this community, with young professionals." A fifteen-year-old was interviewed in a home with a For Sale sign on the front lawn. After living in this subdivision for four years, the family was relocating to a more upscale development in the Prairieview school district. He explained that they were moving "because my parents want a better home. . . . After we graduate from school, my parents will probably move somewhere in the Southwest. My mom likes the weather there." This sojourner family is there to consume the good school system for their children but do not have loyalty that extends past their need for that social resource. It is unlikely that community institutions other than the school or the church benefit from sojourner participation. Prairieview is viewed as a way station, a place to stay for a while before moving on. Sojourners remain relatively unconnected by choice.

The newcomers in the subdivisions like living in Prairieview, but their account of community pluses excludes the local oldtimers. A middle-aged newcomer arrived almost three years ago. What does he like about Prairieview? "The housing is cheaper. The school district has a good reputation. It's a growing area. I expect property values to increase." Like other newcomers, he thinks the property taxes are too high. Although oldtimers are typically elderly and putting few claims on local services, newcomers feel that their own property bears a greater tax burden than it should. "The new homes are carrying the [tax] burden. We pay more in taxes. Taxes are fixed in the old part of town." Oldtimers on the school board or the village boards are scorned as old-fashioned. A thirty-year-old newcomer father likes the small-town atmosphere but is critical of the oldtimers who ran Prairieview for years. "They have an archaic way of thinking. What they've done is not let any industry come to town and the tax base doesn't increase. They want to keep things the way they've been for years and years."

Rather than valuing Prairieview as a unique community, newcomers choose this town for instrumental means to specific ends. It has good schools and safe streets. Their children need not attend school with "undesirable" children, as they might in nearby Central City. They consider themselves too busy for much community engagement. When a specific life task, such as the children's schooling, is accomplished, the rationale for sojourner-residence ends. A typical sojourner life plan includes a move back to the city, to a warmer locale, or even to a more exurban place beyond Prairieview.

"The only time I see [newcomers] is in church," said a retired farm woman, but even her church is altered by the influx of newcomers. Prior to suburbanization, "You could look down the row of pews in church and you knew everybody in the whole row." Subdivision people have joined her church, but "it's difficult to get to know people. . . . Many come here for the good schools, but most kids leave when they graduate. . . . there are few job opportunities." Another retired couple also attend a local downtown church. "We don't see [socially] the new ones too much. . . . people just come and go." Oldtimers, now outnumbered, are resigned to life in a town and its institutions that are no longer familiar to them.

The Methodist minister confirmed the fluidity of Prairieview church membership. In his congregation of about three hundred families, at least one-third joined in the past decade, and one-half to two-thirds joined in the past fifteen to twenty years. "Some people are here for two or three years and then they move on." Oldtimers, the minister reports, had difficulty accepting the growth during the early stages, when they were younger and the newcomers fewer. "At some point resistance broke down and it's no longer a problem." As the oldtimers aged, and as newcomers outnumbered them, a tipping point was reached (Gladwell 2000). Oldtimers receded from centrality in their church congregations, as they have in the town.

Mainstream ministers report that newcomers consume not only town amenities but also religious activities. According to one minister, "people nowadays are not staying with the same denomination like they did years ago. Today people are looking for a church to meet their needs. It sounds crass, but there is an aspect of them being a consumer. So that when a church no longer meets their needs, they move on." It is the newer churches, the ones that have experienced explosive growth, that attract the newcomers. They are more likely than oldtimers to join the newer congregations on the outskirts of town, dedicated more to an inward focus on theology and to church as *the* community than to the greater community of Prairieview.

A sojourner, consumer mentality that focuses primarily on Prairieview schools and property values lacks appeal for a person who considers agrarian tenets to be the standard for community practices. A young mother, a subdivision newcomer, remarked about Prairieview: "I grew up in a small town. This doesn't feel like a small town. There's not a sense of community unless it's with the school.

. . . From a small-town person's perspective, the sense of community is not as strong as I'd like to see." But to a newcomer of similar age who is a product of a more urbanized place, the community is perfect: "Prairieview has kind of a small-town atmosphere, coming here from the Chicago suburbs." But Prairieview fundamentally has become suburban, with subdivisions segregated spatially and socially from the original town plan, so that it cannot function as a tightly inter-connected small community where neighborhoods and cultural beliefs are shared. Most important, the newcomers probably do not want to participate in an agrarian-like community; the social costs are too high.

Social Resources

Typically elderly, retired, and somewhat disengaged now, oldtimers were formerly highly involved in the community. Their commitment ran Prairieview and contributed to the good school system that attracted upscale newcomers. Their loyalty to local businesses sustained a viable main street. One elderly couple, who farmed and owned a main-street business, represent the traditional agrarian engagement pattern that generated social resources for agrarian Prairieview. He belongs to the Lions Club, the Kiwanis Club, the Rotary Club, the Masons, and the Farm Bureau (he is a board member), and he used to volunteer for the Agricultural Stabilization Conservation Service, the University of Illinois County Extension, and as a high school coach. From his perspective, people like himself still make Prairieview work. "I think community leaders are typically retired and business people, and elected officials. They're not necessarily wealthy, but they're well thought of." In the newcomer social hierarchy, however, such individuals would not rank so high; the newcomers' social system is more attuned to wealth and achievement outside of Prairieview.

Newcomers and oldtimers agree that Prairieview's good schools are its primary asset. Because newcomers choose school involvement if they are civically active at all, their engagement has maintained the quality of the district. In 2000 Prairieview third, fourth, fifth, and seventh graders ranked about ten points above the area average on the Illinois Standards Achievement Test (Central City newspaper, Feb. 5, 2001). Newcomers, focused on the school board, regard the village government as archaic. A subdivision man in his forties reflects the attitude of many newcomers: "The school board is the community. . . . People are less interested in village business because they consider it less important. . . . they just want growth to be managed well. Most people don't complain about services." He, like so many newcomers, ties his tenure in Prairieview to "after the youngest is out of high school." Because the real community for newcomers is the school district, and because so many choose Prairieview for the sake of their children, school board meetings are well attended. In contrast, the town administrator complains about the difficulty of getting anyone but members to attend village board meetings.

Whether or not to continue a latchkey school-aged child care program, which occupied school space needed by the burgeoning student population, was a major Prairieview community issue in 1994. The actions taken by newcomers using the program contrast with those of the more elderly oldtimers and reveal how each group approaches community welfare. Serving 170 children from kindergarten through grade five, the full-day latchkey program had about 40% low-income children. A mother from a dual-earner, middle-income subdivision household that used the program single-handedly led the fight to retain the latchkey program. Being a newcomer, however, she did not understand how to tap wider community social resources for support. To her, Prairieview is simply a bedroom community, not a special place whose welfare should be of general concern.

Newcomers, seeking monetary or professionalized solutions rather than those that require commitment of self, tend to claim that an abstract "they" should provide this or that in Prairieview (Kemmis 1995). The newcomer-activist believed that oldtimers on the school board whose wives never worked outside the home would be unsympathetic to the need for local child care among dual-earner families. She complained, "On the school board, we have some men near retirement who just don't understand." It never occurred to her to seek allies among the retired women or in the community churches. She just assumed that oldtimers would naturally be opposed. As a newcomer, she is not aware that small towns can be rallied to support institutions that benefit the general community. Thus, the newcomer's campaign was based on statistics about program use and its value to individual working families rather than trust that the oldtimers as a group would care. An elderly woman, a retired farmer, was sympathetic when she learned about the latchkey issue. "I feel sorry for the parents," she said. Although never approached by the newcomer spearheading the campaign, she had constructive suggestions for sustaining the program that utilized churches or service groups. But to a newcomer, an oldtimer by definition was not a useful social resource that inspired trust.

During 1994 a natural disaster occasioned the rapid mobilization of Prairieview. Heavy spring rains on ground still partially frozen caused the river to flood at the highest level on record. About a thousand volunteers (one-quarter of the town) responded to radio and television appeals for help. The Central City newspaper reported that they sandbagged all night to save the water treatment plant and the supermarket in the shopping plaza near the river. Although a major disaster was averted by the effort, it was a chaotic endeavor. People were not accustomed to cooperation. The town lacked an organized plan; materials were not stockpiled, nor was an efficient system developed for bagging and carrying bags. A subdivision built beside the river was partially flooded despite the heroic sandbagging.

Although local pastors considered the substantial response to reflect a caring community, the city administrator recounted the hostility he experienced, particularly from residents of the flooded, upscale subdivision. "They're out there trying to hang the village and the developer for the fact that [the river] flooded. . . . They are saying they were lied to [about a flood threat]. . . . It was a 100-year flood and they took the risk of buying a house near a river. Of course, you can't tell them that. It's always somebody else's fault." To the administrator, who deals with the entire community, the emergency crystallized the differing group cultures in the town. Oldtimers, although they complain about receiving unequal treatment relative to the subdivisions, nevertheless serve the community. Subdivision people, however, demand services as their due as taxpayers. They accept as entitlements the well-run village and good schools produced by the long-term, unselfish commitment to Prairieview by oldtimers.

Social resources generated during the recent agrarian past are available to the Prairieview community today because oldtimers remain civically involved, but these resources are eroding as this engaged group ages. Oldtimers do not voice an antigrowth sentiment, but they worry about the future of Prairieview as a "real" community. Newcomers are engaged in the community, though typically more narrowly than oldtimers and only where a direct personal benefit is obvious (Bellah et al. 1985). Furthermore, the two groups may not see themselves as social peers. That is, the higher-income, lavishly housed newcomers may feel that the local social clubs and other community organizations are beneath them. Newcomers gauge themselves by nearby urban Central City rather than by the agrarian community social system in which the oldtimers prefer to be embedded.

Cross-Age Relations

As a school social worker pointed out, "a sense of community is based in the schools, not based on the community. . . . It's not [Prairieview]; it's 'We're the [mascot].'" High school sports, in particular, are keenly followed by newcomers and oldtimers alike. The Prairieview high school band has won national contests and frequently is invited to march in parades all over the nation. Photos of the basketball and football teams past and present line the walls of the newspaper office. It is evident in the local newspaper that academics also are important. Scholarships available and awarded, the dean's list, honors awarded, and college acceptances receive notice in every issue along with the school sport events. Implicit in these lists is the priority of academic achievement in Prairieview. The school system emphasizes its academic record proudly. "They are excellent schools. . . . Some schools only emphasize athletics. They do that pretty good here, too, but the academics is really the first thing. I like that," said a newcomer approvingly.

Prairieview's commitment to its schools does not extend to sympathy for all youth outside the school. Adolescents in Prairieview, for example, lack public spaces where they can see and be seen, and they are not generally well tolerated by other generations (Childress 2000; Schwartz 1987). By not nurturing its youth so that they become strongly attached, Prairieview resembles the suburbs, where youth are expected to leave rather than to stay or return as they are in agrarian communities. The lack of public gathering spots indicates not that adolescents are ignored but that they are segregated. Youth are a great local concern, particularly in regard to alcohol and drug abuse. Because the village is dry, alcohol use is taken as evidence that outsiders are seducing town youth. Outsider status tends to be associated with housing enclaves on the outskirts of town for lower-income families, whose children attend the cherished Prairieview school system. Differential treatment of youth from a low-income versus a high-income family is related to the emerging postagrarian culture in Prairieview.

In an unincorporated area about a mile from Prairieview stands a mobile home park with a densely platted grid of six hundred lots, where fifteen hundred people live (fig. 3). Several apartment complexes adjacent to the mobile home park and some near downtown have additional low-income housing, and these two areas tend to merge in the minds of Prairieview residents. The park was built on family land by one of the local families that used the village as a growth machine. Residents and others agree that as mobile home parks go, "Riverview Terrace" is a quality one, because residents own their homes and rent only the land (MacTavish and Salamon 2001). An elderly woman expresses the widespread community bitterness nonetheless felt toward the park developer: "He'll use any excuse to make a buck. . . . it hurts the value of our houses." Although Prairieview has an aggressive annexation policy for the area within three miles of the town corporate limits, outlined in the progrowth town plan, the Riverview Terrace trailer park is unlikely ever to be incorporated into the village (village board, 1992).

The rapid rise in community home values (table 8), and therefore taxes, has indirectly displaced area lower-income families. Both lower-income and higher-income residents agree that the only affordable housing available is in the mobile home park or the apartments. "Families move to [peripheral places that resemble Splitville or Arborville] because the cost of living is cheaper. . . . The cost of living is going up in Prairieview," explained a school social worker. The trailer park attracts working-poor families who are fairly transient, as indeed are the subdivision families. In a 15% randomly selected household survey of the 560 park units, over half of the 85 households interviewed had lived in the park four years or less (MacTavish 2001; MacTavish and Salamon 2001). School administrators remark on the mobility of trailer-park families but not on the mobility of the subdivision families. One social worker gave an example of a trailer-park child who was in school only a week before the family moved on. It is likely that trailer-park families move randomly throughout the school year owing to the unpredictability of their poorly paid hourly jobs. In contrast, subdivision families, as salaried professionals, can schedule moves when school is not in session and thereby minimize disruptions for their children and the school.

The trailer park and the apartments, however, account for any diversity within the Prairieview student body. Among subdivision people, trailer-park families in particular are stigmatized as high-risk families (Fitchen 1981). Mobile-home-park families, as owners of their homes (if not the land), feel that they, like other residents, are entitled to good schools for their children. "Junior high and high school living in [the trailer park], it's the worst. It's torture. You're not treated fairly by any means," said a woman who grew up in the park and now is raising a family there. Indeed, the reason for moving to Prairieview given most often by trailer-park families is the quality of the Prairieview schools—the same reason that the higher-income residents give (MacTavish and Salamon 2001).

Some agreement exists among education professionals that trailer-park children often bring problems to school. According to a school social worker, "Prairieview is definitely the haves versus the have-nots. . . . People think Prairieview is all white, upper-middle-class, but it's not the case. . . . There's a transient population in the trailer parks and the apartments. . . . a huge percentage of the kids I work with come from that population." Furthermore, to the upscale subdivision people, trailer-park and apartment-dweller families represent all that they sought to avoid by moving to Prairieview. One subdivision father resentfully explained, "The problems at school come from [the mobile home park]. They don't pay as much for the education of their kids, but they get the same education." Yet school administrators admit to having similar problems with children whom one labeled as the "trophy kids"—those neglected by dual-career couples in the subdivisions.

School staff members say that class differences are most apparent in children's motivation toward educational goals. Subdivision people, as professionals or management types, see good schools as the first rung on the ladder that leads to acceptance by a good college. "There's a very high academic expectation. . . . We push and we push and we push," commented a community youth worker about the schools. Explained a thirty-four-year-old father, "Everything [in Prairieview] thrives around the school unit. . . . The advantage is the high standard of education. You'll be college-ready by growing up in Prairieview. It's middle-upper class mostly." Working-poor trailer-park and apartment-dweller families in most cases also want the best for their children, but they do not understand as well as subdivision parents do what is involved in school or college achievement. Among some trailer-park families, however, explained one teacher, "there's a blue-collar attitude . . . in which parents say that school wasn't important for me, so they don't support their kids' academic work." Attracted to Prairieview by the schools, subdivision parents place high demands on their children and on the teachers. Thus, if a youth is not motivated academically in a school where the majority of students are motivated, this contrast fosters stigmatization or causes placement in a lower academic track. Trailer-park and apartment youth therefore are often labeled as problem students, academic underachievers for whom little family support can be depended on by teachers. Realistically, these children reflect class differences in parents' educational expectations and goals (MacTavish 2001).

Economic segregation, arising from the spatial segregation of lower-income Prairieview families in distinct enclaves, is reinforced by academic segregation in the schools. High school youth from the trailer park, despite attending schools designed to foster academic achievement, find themselves treated as a distinct minority and categorized as "trailer trash." An elderly oldtimer who has offered her home to many troubled adolescents from the trailer park and the apartments was alarmed by their treatment in the high school. "Prairieview schools are good, but . . . they persecute the kids who come from bad homes. They label them." A subdivision mother of relatively modest circumstances shows awareness of the implicit tracking in the Prairieview schools: "We have lots of kids who don't fit into the molds, like Jock or Student. A lot of it has to do with social status. If you live in the trailer parks or the apartments, you're really stereotyped." One school social worker believes the community is too quick to assign at-risk behavior only to lower-income youth. "The problem is perceived as a [trailer-park] problem and nonexistent in the Prairieview community, but I can tell [alcohol and substance abuse] is right here too. . . . The problem is seen as a [trailer-park] problem because kids from [there] are more likely to talk about their problems than the more affluent kids from the Prairieview community. It is a cultural difference that kids here protect their parents and their families." Apparently "the trophy children" are more sophisticated about handling themselves.

Prairieview as a community shows some collective responsibility toward the trailer-park youth. Public meetings were held in 1994 to discuss establishing a Boys and Girls Club, aimed at "keeping kids out of trouble." To a certain extent, the Boys and Girls Club gained widespread community support (in contrast to the latchkey program) because unsupervised adolescents after school posed a potential threat to town property from involvement in drugs, alcohol, or sex. Although most funding eventually came from the town, a dilemma arose about where to locate the facility, according to the village administrator who led the initiative. The solution was to have trailer-park children stay downtown for the after-school program.

Community concerns about the Boys and Girls Club suggest a contagion theory of risk attached to the trailer park, according to the Prairieview administrator who was active in organizing the club: "If the program moves to the trailer courts, there is some fear that village kids hanging out there may get into trouble. . . . Also the police are in the village, and it would be easier to control the kids at school." Defining trailer-park and apartment children as a group at risk ensures that they will be treated as such. Trailer-park adolescents feel that they are assumed guilty when community transgressions occur, as a result of their being stigmatized. One youth went so far as to term the park a "galvanized ghetto." Marginalization of the trailer-park children by the schools and the community of Prairieview makes it more likely that these students will reject the model of middle-class academic achievement that the school can provide (Mac-Tavish 2001).

In contrast to the stigmatizing of trailer-park youth by subdivision people, the oldtimers show an inclusive tolerance toward all town children. Although retired, and bearing a relatively large share of the tax burden from the growth machine, a farm couple voted for the school referendum (at the time of the study) that would raise their taxes (Daniels and Bowers 1997). "Prairieview is a good place to raise children. It must be because of the way people move in from outside. They're coming here for the school," said the old farmer. This oldtimer was shocked to learn that his neighbor, a relative newcomer, voted against the referendum for building a new school. "His wife sells homes around here too. He [the neighbor] figured since his kids were grown he didn't have to vote for it anymore." From an involved oldtimer's perspective, good schools benefit everyone and should be supported because local children belong to everyone in the community. Newcomers, perhaps because they are sojourners, are less altruistic with their time or money.

REFLECTIONS

Prairieview represents a suburbanized town, one in which growth-machine processes in a previously agrarian community have created stark spatial and social segregation by income and age. In the town's agrarian past, the social resources from committed citizenry produced a school system (through civic engagement and capital investment) that appeals to upscale families with a high priority for education in a context of gentrified rural ambience. The newcomers, however, neither understand nor respect the social resources that generated the attributes that attract them to Prairieview. That is, they are not looking for a true agrarian community. Although the school system benefits from newcomers' involvement, other community issues are of less priority to those who distance themselves as sojourners. Prairieview is becoming a suburban nontown. The small-town sense of community that urban newcomers believed they wanted is eroding with time and as a result of their taking it for granted.

Churches, another community institution that draws newcomers, are also being transformed. A twenty-five-year-old church, described by the minister as "nondenominational, mission-driven, and not based on nostalgia," lies on the outskirts of town. The church shares the same growth agenda that altered Prairieview. Becoming an area church with a thousand families was the minister's goal. He has met that goal with great success, and the church is involved in its third building program. The church is not driven by community-minded goals. Instead, the minister believes his church's mission is "to lead unchurched people to be full devoted followers of Christ" (Central City newspaper, Aug. 4, 2000). Although the church will grow by attracting newcomers, the entrepreneurial minister also views local churches as a source for growth, a strategy arising more from suburban than from agrarian-community attitudes. Thus, even an institution that has been central to community-building in the agrarian community is motivated by narrow, individualistic growth and moral goals rather than engagement agendas that serve the general good. His church helps the poor of Haiti instead of those in the trailer park or in nearby Central City.

It seems unlikely that Prairieview will long retain many cultural markers from its agrarian past. A recent election crystallizes the suburbanization of the town. The longtime mayor, a retired tradesman, was voted out of office—a revolution referred to by an oldtimer board member's letter in chapter 1. A newcomer who runs a Web page design business out of his home is the new mayor. (His spouse, however, is from an oldtimer family.) Newcomers can now freely shape the town in their image. Rapid growth powered by upscale families and low-income, trailer-park residents mirrors the divergence in income that the nation as a whole is experiencing. Oldtimers truly are wedged in the middle, by income and by community practices. So many oldtimers are elderly, however, that their bridging ability and energies are unlikely to span the widening gap. It may be that with time newcomers who choose to remain in Prairieview will feel a responsibility to invest in the community beyond the schools or their church. Financing the Boys and Girls Club is a step in this direction.

In the emergent hierarchy of places in the region, Prairieview represents the top, economically and socially. Its population is wealthier, younger, and better educated, and its homes are of higher value than other towns in the commuting zone (table 4). Its purposeful exclusion of the trailer park portrays the emerging rewoven social fabric of the region. Highlighted are the homogeneity within each of the adjacent places—subdivisions and trailer park—and the heterogeneity of economic and social discrepancy between them.

The suburbanization process in the midst of a productive landscape (photo by David Riecks)

Trees define an agrarian community's boundaries, seen
from the air (photo by David Riecks)

A historic main street typical of midwestern small towns (photo by David Riecks)

An old tree-lined street that encourages visiting from porches (photo by David Riecks)

A town that tolerates youth hanging out on the main street
(photo by Gary Beaumont)

A town that provides public spaces where cross-age interactions occur (photo by Brian Stauffer)

A town farmer's market, a site of community-building and celebration (photo by David Riecks)

A school is the heart of a small town (photo by David Riecks)

5 BOOSTERISM BREEDS SUBURBANIZATION: BUNKERTON

In collaboration with Cynthia Loula

Bunkerton serves as the county seat. The handsome early-twentieth-century courthouse in the town square reflects actions by a past prosperous and committed business community. Main-street business vitality and residential growth to support local commerce consistently rank as high priorities for Bunkerton leaders. An early-spring all-day community sale run by volunteers brings people from all over the Midwest to buy and sell farm implements, household goods, cars, and antiques (Gengenbacher 1980). It is fitting that for four decades Bunkerton has hosted this annual festival dedicated to commerce. Bunkerton exemplifies a town whose existing housing stock was used as a growth machine to preserve local businesses. After decades of decline, merchant-led initiatives during the 1990s achieved a population gain of 5.5%, which represented a small newcomer influx (table 10). Before boosters began marketing its housing stock and its Swedish ethnic heritage, Bunkerton was mainly a working-class town. The newcomers are blue-collar and lower-middle-class families attracted by the small-town ambience, the fine old homes, the good schools, and the adjacent interstate that takes a person from Bunkerton to Central City in about thirty minutes. Tensions now exist between tendencies to suburbanize and resistance to these trends by both old-timers and the newcomers who long for an agrarian community.

From the mid-nineteenth century through much of the twentieth century, Bunkerton was an agrarian community dominated by Swedish farmers (the pseudonym Svedberg was used almost twenty years ago in Gengenbacher 1980; Salamon 1984; and Salamon, Gengenbacher, and Penas 1986 to reflect the Swedish ethnicity of its farmers). From the 1850s through the 1870s, the recruiting efforts and the

Table 10 Bunkerton Demographic Profile

YEAR	POPU-LATION	MEDIAN AGE	PERCENT RESIDING IN SAME HOUSE AS 5 YEARS BEFORE	MEDIAN VALUE OF OWNED HOMES ($)	MEDIAN HOUSEHOLD INCOME ($)	PERCENT BELOW POVERTY LEVEL	PERCENT FEMALE-HEADED HOUSE-HOLDS[a]
1980	4,250	32.8	62.0	35,900	15,935	7.0	6.2
1990	4,290	33.4	57.0	45,600	23,770	10.5	6.7
2000	4,500	37.8	61.4	69,000	37,804	4.8	5.6

Sources: Bureau of the Census 1980c, 1990a, 2001, 2002.
[a] With own children under 18.

charisma of a Lutheran minister attracted immigrants from Sweden, as well as Swedish farmers who had earlier settled elsewhere in Illinois and Indiana. His dream of a rural Swedish enclave surrounding a theological seminary collapsed, even though revenue was earned toward seminary support from sales of a railroad company land grant. In the mid-1880s, he moved the seminary to northern Illinois, where more Swedes had settled (Hasselmo 1976). The farmers remained. Today the Evangelical Covenant Church is still controlled by descendants of the original Swedish settlers, but neither it nor the original Lutheran church is now led by Swedish-origin ministers. Swedish ethnicity is often cited to explain the community personality of Bunkerton (Perry-Jenkins and Salomon 2002). The Methodist minister commented, "Bunkerton is a great place to live, [but] I don't think I've been welcomed as completely as in other communities where I've worked. I'm not sure why that is, but there is some sense of exclusiveness and isolationism among the old-time, particularly Swedish, residents." Other than these traits, many Swedish names in the phone book, and a Swedish gift shop on the main street, however, Bunkerton's identification as a Swedish ethnic enclave has faded.

Bunkerton's population started declining in the 1970s and continued to do so through the 1980s (Bureau of the Census 1960, 1990a). In the 1980s the county for which it is the county seat experienced a 32% decline in number of farms (table 1), which changed its major economic activity from agriculture to service (table 2). A consequence of the dwindling countryside population was the 1990 consolidation of the Bunkerton school system with smaller school districts in the area. In addition, when the nearby military base closed in the early 1990s, Bunkerton rapidly lost critical businesses and services. Fifty years ago, Bunkerton had eleven grocery stores. Now only a single supermarket operates, and there is widespread complaint about its high prices. A café, clothing stores, and other main-street businesses closed in the 1980s, as did the local hospital. Near the highway on the outskirts of town, a new pizza restaurant and a franchised fast-food restaurant are doing well. The fast-food restaurant fills the gap left by the main-street café's closing as the spot for twice-daily coffee-time meetings of retired men. Other businesses that have survived include a variety store, several new-car dealerships, and a television sales and service shop. Some amenities endure, reminders of a vibrant past. Bunkerton, for example, is the smallest town in Illinois to support a daily newspaper. As the location of the district high school and as the county seat, Bunkerton continues to be the center of activity for the county.

On a quiet side street stands a substantial, historic Carnegie library. The library's location, where it is visible from the Illinois Central rail line that simultaneously divides the town and parallels the main street, is a testimony to the business elite's past influence. Like the grand old county courthouse, the landmark library symbolizes the ability of early-twentieth-century Bunkerton community boosters to mobilize for large projects. Much commitment was needed to obtain a Carnegie Foundation building grant (Van Slyck 1995). As a condition for receiving Carnegie money, politicians and business leaders had to demonstrate financial support for the institution. The town had to be willing to tax itself 10% of the value of Carnegie's donation each year to operate the library. Bunkerton's is one of only two Carnegie libraries among the six communities that we studied.

On another side street is an old city park complete with a well-kept pavilion and clean restrooms. During the early twentieth century, Chautauquas were held in the park. Residents heard lectures and music, and they could even camp out there. The annual Fourth of July community activities are now held in that park, as are several other festivals. Another park gives residents access to other public spaces: a civic center, a swimming pool, and several ball fields and basketball courts.

Oldtimers and newcomers agree that the town is safe and slow-paced. A middle-aged woman commented, "Bunkerton is a quiet and peaceful little town, with virtually no crime." Another woman, an oldtimer, said, "I like small towns, the friendliness of the people here. There's a lack of crime and we have no fear of our neighbors. It's a safe feeling." A middle-aged oldtimer remarked, "We rarely ever lock our front door and have never had anything stolen or vandalized. It's safe." The sense of security that residents find in Bunkerton is something they regard as absent in Central City, where most of them work. Safety is highly valued. A newcomer said, "It's a safe community, a nice place to raise children. The kids can walk to and from school, and you don't have to worry about them."

Bunkerton is relatively homogeneous in terms of class and race (Bureau of the Census 1980c, 1990a, 2001). Based on census occupational categories and accepted definitions of working-class jobs, approximately 70% of Bunkerton's employed adults held blue-collar jobs in 1990 (Perry-Jenkins and Salamon 2002; Gilbert and Kahl 1993). In 1990 the median family income was $23,770, and about three-quarters of the population had at least a high school education (tables 10 and 11). Bunkerton is clearly a community mirroring major national demographic trends, except for its lack of diversity. Specifically with regard to women's employment, in 1980 40% of women with children under six years of age were working outside the home, but by 1990 that proportion had risen dramatically to almost three-quarters of such women (table 12). An advantage of living in this small town, when compared with nearby Central City, is the relatively low cost of living. For example, the estimated value of a Bunkerton house in 1990 was $45,600 (table 10). Thus, a blue-collar family can live comfortably in Bunkerton on a relatively modest income, although generating the income means that households with

Table 11 Bunkerton Employment Profile

YEAR	PERCENT COMPLETING HIGH SCHOOL OR HIGHER	MEAN TRAVEL TIME TO WORK (MINUTES)	PERCENT OVER 16 IN LABOR FORCE	PERCENT EMPLOYED IN AGRI-CULTURE	PERCENT EMPLOYED IN PROFES-SIONAL SERVICES	PERCENT EMPLOYED IN MANU-FACTURING
1980	69.2	14.0	62.4	2.6	18.7	26.5
1990	74.1	15.8	64.9	1.2	24.0	19.3
2000	88.0	21.5	65.1	0.3[a]	31.7[a]	22.7[a]

Sources: Bureau of the Census 1980c, 1990a, 2002.

[a] Due to major revisions in the 2000 census classification of jobs by industry, these data are not exactly comparable with the 1980 and 1990 data.

Table 12 Bunkerton Household Profile

YEAR	PERCENT OF FEMALES 16 YRS. AND OLDER WITH CHILDREN UNDER 6 YRS. IN LABOR FORCE	PERCENT BORN IN ILLINOIS	PERCENT HOUSING OWNER OCCUPIED	PERCENT OF POPULATION AGE 65 OR OLDER	PERCENT OF POPULATION UNEMPLOYED
1980	39.8	76	75	15.7	7.6
1990	72.4	75	77	17.9	6.2
2000	71.8[a]	77.6	78.3	18.7	2.2

Sources: Bureau of the Census 1980c, 1990a, 2002.

[a] Data represents "all parents in family in labor force." Data for females only was not available at publication time.

young children also are dual-earner commuters (Perry-Jenkins and Salamon 2002). But the newer upscale subdivisions on the edge of town and some fine old homes reflect the presence of an elite—professionals, lawyers, county officials, and businesspeople, including the management of local industrial plants—associated with Bunkerton's status as the county seat and with the prosperous 1990s.

COMMUNITY CHANGE

Space and Place

Starting about 1920, nonfarmers in Bunkerton depended on several small local industries or on the nearby military base for well-paid, stable jobs. In 1993 the base closed permanently, but because it began downsizing a decade before, the impact was felt earlier on the local economy. About the same time, several town factories closed, and warehouses along the rail line stood empty. Real estate entrepreneurs divided the abandoned commercial buildings into apartments that attracted low-income families (Fitchen 1991). These newcomers probably account for the 3% increase in persons below the poverty rate that occurred between 1980 and 1990 (table 10). Along with more low-rent housing, Bunkerton developed a market glut of single-family homes after the base closed. Faced with a saturated and deteriorating housing market, the business community was finally motivated to act. Their plan linked the turnover of the large pool of available good-quality homes to ultimately revitalizing local businesses. In essence, the town housing stock was to be employed as a merchant growth machine.

Advertisements placed by the Chamber of Commerce in the newspapers of central Illinois small cities (fig. 1) touted Bunkerton for its low home costs and small-town lifestyle. After the initiative, 1992 home sales were double those of the previous year, according to the president of the Chamber of Commerce. Eventually, the demand created by more than one hundred buyers from Central City alone caused home values to rise by 10% (Central City newspaper, 1993). Because of the housing turnover, neighborhoods in Bunkerton now mix older, long-term residents and military and professional retirees with newcomers attracted by the affordable housing.

At the same time, the main street was beautified by a dedicated Downtown Revitalization Committee working jointly with the Chamber of Commerce to fill empty storefronts and remodel landmark buildings such as a theater. As it was hoped, the housing initiative indirectly helped improve main-street business. By 1994 the

mayor could remark, "We're very pleased with the way the downtown has developed in the past few years. . . . We've had new,
younger [business]people willing to invest time and money, trying
to make it work. . . . A lot of small communities are going by the
wayside. We're on a roll and we want to continue that." Retail sales
in Bunkerton had grown by about 35% during the 1990s (Central
City newspaper, Nov. 11, 1994; Aug. 30, 2001).

Bunkerton's older neighborhoods are on the grid, radiating east
and west from the main business street (fig. 4). Following a Swedish
custom, farmers of the late nineteenth and early twentieth centuries
moved into town when they retired and erected fine homes. This
practice left Bunkerton with an amenity that attracts home buyers
willing to invest time and money in restoration. On several older
brick-paved streets stand rows of large, stately, two-storied mansions
of a square shape with dormers in a clipped gable roof, a style related to the town's Swedish ethnic heritage (Gengenbacher 1980).
"Swedes built them sturdy," commented an ethnic Swedish farmer
proudly (17). These large, well-crafted homes are snapped up as soon
as they are put on the market.

Elsewhere in the established neighborhoods, older two- and three-
story frame homes alternate with newer ranch-style, brick homes
built after houses were torn down or where empty lots existed. Some
older homes are run down, but others are maintained impeccably.
In one block alone, a large two-story home, well kept and landscaped,
stands near a shabby, one-story home with peeling paint and a clutter of objects covering the yard. At the edge of town in the newer
Heights subdivision and along Swedish Road, the grid is broken by
curved streets and culs-de-sac. This, "the richest part of town," by
spatial separation and by its grander home size, marks Bunkerton's
social divisions, which are emerging more pronounced with the progress of suburbanization.

During the 1990s the housing turnover transformed a Bunkerton
neighborhood that was targeted for study (see appendix B). De-
pending on who moved onto a particular block, oldtimers viewed
the transformation positively or with despair. For an oldtimer, home
upkeep is crucial to preserving a neighborhood and housing values.
Indirectly, well-kept homes and higher property values benefit the
entire community. Care of property therefore is the measure used
by oldtimers to judge newcomers, since they cannot base such ap-
praisal on long-term family reputation (Salamon and Tornatore
1994). Established residents are most favorably inclined toward new
neighbors who maintain their homes according to oldtimer custom-

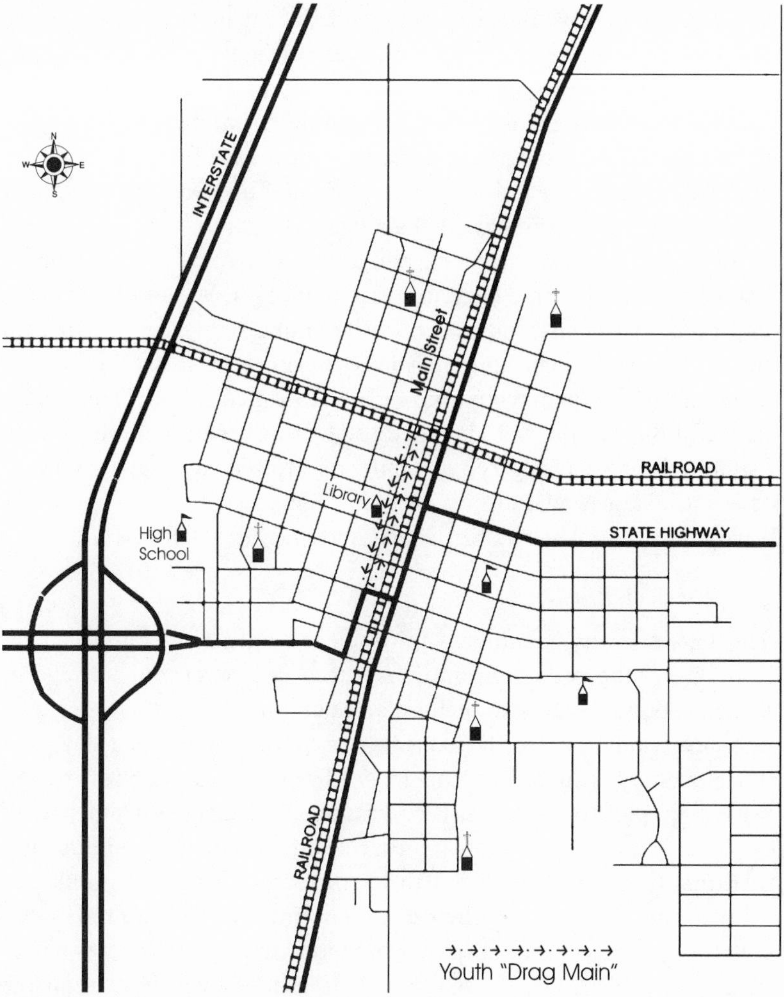

Figure 4 Bunkerton town map

ary expectations. One middle-aged oldtimer approves of her new neighbors. "I actually think our neighborhood is improving over the last few years. . . . Some houses have recently been sold, and the new owners are really putting a lot of work into restoring them and fixing them up." A newcomer who is engaged in an ambitious remodeling project reveals, however, that his focus is on his house more than on the community: "There's a lot of flavor in these older homes. They're well made and are interesting. People here take a lot of pride in their homes and restoring them to their original specifications. [Houses are] also very reasonable. . . . Only $250 a month and that includes taxes and escrow. The price of the house outweighed the disadvantages of living here. . . . it's a very conservative town. . . . the people really are not very friendly."

Having lower incomes and property norms diverging from what is customary keep some newcomer families from ever obtaining acceptance. The newcomers most alienated from the Bunkerton neighborhood studied live either in rented houses or in apartments, or if home owners, they maintain their property carelessly ($n = 6$). An oldtimer on a block with such neighbors despairs: "Our neighborhood has gotten worse over the past ten years. We used to have a lot of older residents, but now that the younger ones are moving in, they just haven't kept up their yards or property as well." Likewise, a woman with a poorly kept home, even though her husband was a native of Bunkerton, was alienated and cynical about the community. Thus, upkeep of property, an easily monitored indicator of family status, constructs an oldtimer-neighborhood response that reinforces a particular social status for newcomers in this small town.

Interconnectedness

The Chamber of Commerce initiative brought new families to a tight-knit, blue-collar community with a unique ethnic heritage in German-dominated central Illinois (Salamon 1984, 1987, 1992). To one newcomer couple, "Bunkerton is a Swedish town and if you're not born here, you don't fit in. They have their own cliques and are not very open to having any newcomers." A businesswoman who is a relative newcomer feels rebuffed by the exclusive business elite of Bunkerton. "The town is run by the same faction of people for time immemorial. . . . When it comes time to choose officers for clubs . . . , they want to keep that old blood in there as long as possible." The difficulty in breaking in was echoed even by a minister who is new in town: "There is a good park district recreation program here in town for varied ages. Now, I'm an avid basketball player. . . . But they have the same teams from year to year. You can't get on one unless someone moves away or dies. . . . That's been really frustrating for me." Bunkerton is a dynamic community, but by not being very inclusive, the social system forfeits some trust.

Middle-class newcomer home buyers find a certain narrow-mindedness in homogeneous Bunkerton. To a young, middle-class couple attracted by the inexpensive housing stock, the town is provincial: "There is absolutely no cultural diversity in Bunkerton. It's a very conservative town, and we're not terribly conservative. It's also very bigoted. There are no blacks, Asians, or Hispanics. . . . The people really are not very friendly at all. It's the type of place that's

really hard to fit in." To oldtimers and blue-collar newcomers, however, homogeneity is desirable. An elderly widow says, "[Bunkerton]
is a particularly nice place for older persons to live. . . . I feel very
safe. There aren't any colored people in Bunkerton either, in case
you're interested." A newcomer who shares her priorities says,
"There's not a whole lot of riffraff here. . . . there aren't any blacks
here, not a single one. I don't have nothin' against blacks, but it
seems like wherever they are, there's a lot of trouble going on." For
blue-collar oldtimers, a retired mail carrier, for example, the local
economy rather than diversity is of greatest concern. "The only
downfall [about Bunkerton] is the cost of living is getting real expensive. . . . We keep getting our taxes raised to build the jail, to better
the schools. . . . We're kind of afraid if we don't get more stores or
industry in here, Bunkerton could become a ghost town before too
long." It is such sentiment that provides the business elite widespread community support for its growth initiatives that have altered
Bunkerton as a place.

A profile of fifty households drawn from the five-block neighborhood studied, which has a high residential turnover (table 13), reveals the social changes generated by the Chamber of Commerce
housing initiative. Two ideal types, as identified by residents, divide
the neighborhood: oldtimers ($n = 33$), insiders socially well inte-

Table 13 Residential Profile of a Five-Square-Block Bunkerton Neighborhood

HOUSEHOLD CHARACTERISTICS	OLDTIMERS ($n = 33$)	NEWCOMERS ($n = 17$)
Age***	30% over 55	100% under 55
Income (mean)	$15,000–$20,000	$20,000–$40,000
Retirement status	30% retired	0% retired
Education	33% high school 52% college or higher	35% below high school 65% much college
Percent with Swedish ethnicity	21	0
Percent home ownership**	97	69
Family mobility**	6% moved more than 5 times since marriage	37% moved more than 5 times since marriage
Birthplace*	60% born in community	0 born in community
Social network*	64% over half in community	77% up to half elsewhere
Church membership*	85% local	59% elsewhere

Source: 1991–92 neighborhood survey (see appendix B for details).

Note: Oldtimer versus newcomer households discriminated according to criteria developed inductively: length of
residence, place of birth, local church membership, and location of major proportion of the support network. A 98%
reliability was achieved by coders.

* $p = <.01$
** $p = .01$
*** $p = .03$

grated in Bunkerton; and newcomers ($n = 17$), less well integrated, by virtue of their outsider status. Particular family circumstances are associated with a well-integrated household (table 13). Home ownership, to a certain extent class-determined, distinguishes the two groups: the oldtimers are overwhelmingly home owners; only two-thirds of the newcomers are. Household mobility divides the groups: more than one-third of the newcomers have moved more than five times since marriage, but less than one-tenth of the oldtimers are that mobile. Newcomers account for the 5% decrease since 1980 in the number of people residing in the same home they lived in five years before (table 10). Income is, of course, linked to age, and almost one-third of the oldtimers ($n = 10$) are retired or widowed. Reflecting the original ethnic population, about one-fifth ($n = 7$) of the oldtimers are of Swedish origin, but no newcomers reported Swedish ancestry. Thus, as a consequence of housing turnover, the Bunkerton neighborhood studied has newcomers who, compared with oldtimers, are more likely to be younger, at a higher income level, better educated, and more mobile and who are not native to the community.

An elderly widow on a block where newcomers now occupy most of the homes comments: "When we moved here, 31 years ago, it was mostly old people . . . but most of them are gone now. . . . My neighbors are very considerate and really do look after me. . . . I'm the old one on the block, you see." About one-quarter of the newcomers in the study neighborhood are involved in renovating old homes, are small-town boosters, and have joined a local church. Such newcomers are candidates for eventual incorporation into the community by oldtimers and, moreover, are those potentially desiring incorporation.

In the transformed neighborhood live two full-time homemakers in their early thirties with preschool children; their well-tended homes are directly across the street from each other. One, a newcomer, has rented a home for a year. She has this to say about her neighborhood: "It's a very friendly community; there are nice people here. It's quiet, and our neighbors are very nice." Across the street, the other home owner, an oldtimer, measures the neighborhood against when she was a child: "There ain't no close ties in this neighborhood. I grew up in this house and we used to have great neighbors, but . . . it's really kind of gone downhill. . . . I used to know all of the neighbors and was on good terms with them, but now I couldn't even tell you their names." She feels surrounded by "pot-smokers," rude neighbors whose garbage is always burning. She now locks her doors since a robbery occurred next door. Life on the same street is experienced differently for two seemingly similar women. The oldtimer expectations for community include frequent interaction and reciprocity from neighbors. The urbanite newcomer apparently wants her privacy to be respected and thus is satisfied that Bunkerton neighbors leave her alone except to greet her.

Table 13 shows that neighborhood oldtimers were born in Bunkerton or have lived in town more than twenty years (mean 25.9 years). A young mother, an oldtimer businesswoman who bought a home in the targeted neighborhood, sees the town differently from the way it is seen by newcomers who seek small-town hospitality and find Bunkerton standoffish: "Once you're in Bunkerton, born here and under its wing, everyone is friendly. The neighbors all watch your house for you when you're on vacation. We have mostly elderly neighbors here and [my son] thinks of them all as his grandparents." Longer residence means that one's kin and friends are more likely to be nearby. For about two-thirds of the oldtimers, over half of the people in their social networks live in Bunkerton. Newcomers' residence ranged from less than one year to at most about a decade in the community. In contrast to oldtimers, three-quarters of the newcomers have up to half of the members of their social network living elsewhere. If newcomers have kin living in Bunkerton, these relatives represent more than half the family's network, a characteristic of blue-collar families generally (Perry-Jenkins and Salamon 2002; Komarovsky 1967; Rubin 1994).

Some oldtimers emphasize that church, rather than the neighborhood, provides their real community. (These churches are mainstream dominations, however, unlike the rapidly growing suburban church in Prairieview.) An elderly widow explains the centrality of church in her life: "Most of my support is from the church, and that's where all your friends are." A young single mother, also an oldtimer, a member of the same church, comments, "In a way I think the church forms its own little community within a community to offer activities and support to its members."

According to four Bunkerton ministers of mainstream churches, they do not actively recruit newcomers for their aging congregations. It is not surprising that the oldtimer-dominated mainstream churches do not invest great social resources in recruitment efforts, given the meaning of a church to oldtimers. The minister of the Evangelical Covenant Church leads a congregation of about two hundred members, predominantly of Swedish background. "The Methodist, Covenant, Lutheran, and Catholic churches provide a foundation for the community to rally around. . . . We send letters to all of the newcomers in town. We try to emphasize a person-to-person outreach from the congregation to the community. I've found door-to-door visitation and welcoming just doesn't work in this community." Church affiliation is a gauge of local attachment and a crucial indicator of community contrasts: 85% of the oldtimers belong to a Bunkerton church, whereas 59% of the newcomers belong to a church elsewhere (table 13). Newcomers from the targeted neighborhood who are beginning to assimilate, owing to their middle-class status, home ownership, and preference for a small town ($n = 4$), are also those newcomers who have joined a mainstream Bunkerton church.

The response to newcomers brought to the community by the growth-machine housing initiative in Bunkerton has not been wholly inclusive. The vast majority of the 63 households (both newcomer and oldtimer) interviewed for a study (linked with the neighborhood study) of dual-earner Bunkerton working-class families (see appendix B for details) liked Bunkerton as a town. But about 35% ($n = 22$) made typical comments about the downside of a small community, citing in their criticisms the gossip and nosiness, along with racism and a cultural narrowness (Perry-Jenkins and Salamon 2002). A blue-collar woman whose husband's kin live in town summarized her concerns: "Everybody knows everybody's business. They don't give anybody a break. If someone does something wrong, they don't forget." Of those who dislike Bunkerton ($n = 6$), the majority fit the profile of the single-mother or the lower-income family. One single mother said, "The town is prejudiced. People are stuck up. . . . If you don't have a lot of money, you ain't nobody." A middle-aged welfare recipient feels real rejection: "The people in Bunkerton, they snub you, the neighbors just ain't helpful." Snobbery and being made to feel like an outsider were some major criticisms of Bunkerton voiced by these lower-income newcomers. Similarly, newcomers from the neighborhood study who think of themselves as urbanites are critical of the very small-town qualities that oldtimers prefer (Hummon 1990).

Bunkerton thus includes oldtimers socially embedded in local networks and newcomers who simply live there as disengaged consumers of the town's affordable housing. The expectations for community held by each group shape diverse experiences. The strength of contrasting perceptions of family and community is so strong that neighbors on the same street can live in "different social worlds . . . that are separate and socially distant" (Lamphere 1992, viii). The neighborhood transformation of Bunkerton by the housing initiative decreased community interconnectedness, despite improving the local economy.

Social Resources

Bunkerton has the reputation of a business-friendly community. After the successful housing initiative, the business district revived. The long-term mayor remarked: "You look downtown and you see a thriving business district. We have a unique combination of history, business and industry, recreation, and safety. . . . I think Bunkerton's the best kept secret in east central Illinois as far as the quality of life and services we provide" (Central City newspaper, June 11, 1995). In a newspaper profile of a central Illinois family-owned pizza chain, the owner referred to his new Bunkerton restaurant as doing well because the town favors economic development. "I took over an abandoned [snack store] in Bunkerton because I really wanted a restaurant there. In Bunkerton, if someone has a good idea, everyone gets together to make it work." He contrasted Bunkerton with another central Illinois community (also in the Central City commuting zone) of similar size, where "when someone comes up with a good idea, everyone fights about it" (Central City newspaper, Apr. 24, 1994). Because his pizza restaurant flourished beside the interstate exit, it attracted another fast-food restaurant and a car wash. Bunkerton business leaders point to such growth as a validation of the community priorities they endorse (Logan and Molotch 1987).

Bunkerton was selected as a participant in a pilot state program, the Rural Downtown Revitalization Initiative. A citizens' committee formed for the pilot program also operates in conjunction with the Illinois Historic Preservation Agency. Its aim is restoration of the main-street row of architecturally distinctive buildings, with the expectation that the structures' historical uniqueness will foster tourism. Another community project is Swedish Heritage Days, a festival created in the 1990s to attract tourists by mining the ethnic origins of its settlers. Committee members together with the Chamber of Commerce recently celebrated their progress in a newly restored building that dates from the 1860s, part of the rehabilitated downtown block that includes an old movie house and the remodeled city hall.

Good schools are regarded by local businesspeople as a prerequisite for attracting more middle-class families to Bunkerton. Broad community support for the schools is evident from their success in garnering funding for extracurricular activities. About every four years, for example, the high school band has marched in national celebrations such as the Washington, D.C., Cherry Blossom Parade. For such a trip the band must obtain fifty thousand dollars through fund-raising activities. To march in a recent parade, band members conducted a raffle, washed cars, sponsored a dinner dance, and received a substantial donation from Bunkerton's service clubs (Central City newspaper, Apr. 1995).

Seeking to grow by attracting more upscale home owners has social costs as well as economic benefits for Bunkerton. For example, the good schools help attract families who want to raise children in a small town, but these families lack community commitment to anything but the schools. Explained one woman: "It's a good place to bring up kids. It gives them time to grow up. . . . There's a drug problem and alcohol abuse you see in larger towns, but not the total criminal element you'd see. When [the children are] older and moved out, we'll probably move closer to our jobs." A blue-collar man explained why he lives in the town: "So my kids can finish school here. Other than that, I have no special ties to Bunkerton." These sojourners, like those in Prairieview, are motivated by a single purpose—to consume specific quality-of-life community goods. Rather than identifying with Bunkerton as a unique place, sojourners focus on a narrow set of advantages—good schools for their children and a family-friendly town (Hummon 1990; Siu 1952, 1987; Wuthnow 1998).

Rich community social resources are apparent in the Bunkerton business elite's mobilization to revitalize the downtown. However, the initiative was built on defining community growth as a good thing; therefore local policy has required business priorities to be favored even over the priorities of some oldtimers. In 1994, for example, the Bunkerton Women's Club Community Improvement Committee gathered signatures on petitions against permitting semitrailer trucks and trailers to park on residential streets, as had been the custom. The confrontation pitted middle-class property values against property practices of oldtimer blue-collar residents. Remarked the wife of a trucker, "We've had this discussion in this town for 12 years. . . . As home owners who pay our taxes and maintain our property, we feel we should be allowed to park a truck, a camper, a boat, or a wrecker. . . . We [truckers and families] aren't deadbeats. We're making an honest, hard living." Community property norms, this conflict illustrates, are being transformed by the middle-class newcomers settling in Bunkerton. The Bunkerton Women's Club, firmly on the side of the middle class, got local real estate agents to attest that parked trucks lowered property values in other towns

(Central City newspaper, Nov. 1994). Thus, the growth-machine, business-led housing initiative has had the unintended consequence of making Bunkerton public spaces contested territories. Newcomers and the business community both want to attract higher-income residents to increase the tax base. They unite to struggle against long-time residents with blue-collar attitudes and blue-collar utilitarian land-use norms.

Cross-Age Relations

Having a single consolidated high school assures that all Bunkerton youth—oldtimers, newcomers, country, and town—are thrown together. The high school principal proudly describes the early 1990s environment, from his perspective: "Our mobility rate is 13.1%, which is considerably less than the state average of 20.6%. . . . Nearly 96% of our students graduate, and about half (51%) go on for higher education of some sort." The high school student body (480) is about half the size of Prairieview's high school (800), despite the similarity of the towns' size in the 2000 census (tables 8 and 10). Bunkerton students scored above the area average but not as high as the ten points above average achieved by Prairieview students in the 2000 Illinois Standards Achievement Test (Central City newspaper, Feb. 5, 2001). These scores probably reflect the differences between the more upscale population in Prairieview and the lower-middle-class and working-class population of Bunkerton.

High school looms large in a Bunkerton adolescent's experience and social status, according to the principal: "I really think the school becomes the social center of the community for teens. We have school activities almost every night of the week. There's not much else in the community for them. . . . Even in the summer, we have camps going for band and volleyball and football, etc. So we're always busy here." Because school activities revolve around sports, academics, and the arts, there are few outlets for youth not athletically, academically, or artistically inclined. The lack of activities or a community gathering spot, such as a club or a café, was repeatedly cited as the most serious problem for Bunkerton youth. Such a complaint is similar to suburban complaints and is symptomatic of Bunkerton's transformation into a bedroom community with increased age segregation (Childress 2000; Gans 1967; Hollingshead 1975).

School social relations show Bunkerton to be a small town and friendly, says the high school principal. "The school is just a reflection of the community operating. Our kids here are especially open to strangers. The kids will welcome you if you want to be accepted."

However, a fifteen-year-old newcomer who has lived in Bunkerton for a year said, "[The students] are real cliquey and it made it a little hard to adjust at first, but now it's okay." She has made two good friends, but she does not want to live in Bunkerton when she grows up; this testifies to an absence of community processes that create attachment, which are evident in Smallville.

According to a variety of residents, being poor or a newcomer negatively shapes school and community experiences for Bunkerton adolescents (Hollingshead 1975). A pastor commented, "A person coming into town has a strike going against them from not being born here." A young mother and business owner reflects on the implications of her oldtimer status: "I was born and raised here and so was [her husband]. If you're one of Bunkerton's children, you've got it made." A blue-collar parent is critical of the differential treatment that stigmatizes some children: "I wouldn't live here if it wasn't for the kids. There are cliques, favoritism in the school system too. Certain kids get more [sports] playing time based on who's their parent. They don't take the kids' feeling into consideration and it rips out the kid's heart." A cynical oldtimer commented, "If you aren't born and raised in Bunkerton, you are just considered a live-in. It's very hard to integrate." But for lower-income children, the cross-age barriers are highest.

Bunkerton's downtown revival made business leaders more vigilant about the image that is presented by town public spaces. Congregating adolescents apparently undermine the desired ambience of spiffed-up rurality that potentially attracts tourists or home buyers. A 1994 City Council meeting was attended by youth ages 15 to 18 and by Bunkerton businesspeople. It crystallized the tolerance quandary created by the presence of adolescents in a village being used as a merchant growth machine. A heated exchange took place during the council hearing concerning the removal of two main-street benches to discourage youth from loitering. A Bunkerton mother and businesswoman addressed the council and asked the youth in attendance, "Do you kids have homes?" Replied a youth defending his group's right to congregate, "Were you ever a kid?" (Central City newspaper, Aug. 25, 27, 1994). Of course, in this small town the businesswoman knew who the youth were, but her question emphasized that these youth were not "anybody," just the children of poor newcomer families who had arrived in the 1980s when Bunkerton was down on its luck.

Who has rights to Bunkerton's public spaces? Why does youth behavior previously tolerated by a small town become redefined as deviant? The council action is evidence that in a suburbanizing town not all youth are considered to be "our children." Community treatment of these youth, carried out by the council, provides clues to the social fabric emerging as Bunkerton is transformed by newcomers into a sleeper town, a modest suburb of Central City.

Outside of school, Bunkerton adolescents—all agree—"drag main street" (fig. 4). As in many other small towns, Bunkerton youth jam themselves into cars and drive around and around the town square, past the county courthouse, displaying themselves and their cars, greeting friends, and filling time, especially in the evenings. Alternatively, some hang out on benches along the main shopping street talking, fooling around, and sometimes being rowdy. In Bunkerton the social class and community status of the youth determine which activity is engaged in. Youth from oldtimer or middle-class newcomer families typically have access to cars. After dragging main, they favor "road parties" out in the countryside, where they sit on their car hoods and socialize.

Youth from lower-income families are those whose main-street "loitering" is objectionable to businesspeople. Lacking a car, a youth can only hang out on the main street to be seen. Bunkerton police can more easily ignore adolescents driving cars to road parties than tolerate others congregating in this public space. A blue-collar mother explained the rift developing in Bunkerton as a consequence: "There's not too much to offer for the high school kids or kids in general. . . . There's no movie theater or what else they'd do. There's no place to shop. Because there's not a lot to do there's a lot of drinking and they cruise. You can't get around downtown on Saturday night. Now the businessmen and cops are trying to stop it and they're causing a lot of negative attitudes from the kids."

Unlike the police and the main-street businesspeople, elderly oldtimers still consider Bunkerton an agrarian town, and they regard local adolescents as a homogeneous group—newcomers indistinguishable from oldtimers—as "basically good kids." An elderly widow, for example, said: "I really think the teenagers around here are all good. I don't think there are any problems with drinking and such. The kids are very considerate of me. . . . I'm not saying there isn't some problem with vandalism and problems in some areas of town, or on Main Street, but I haven't had any trouble here." Another frail widow in her eighties sees only a basic goodness in Bunkerton youth: "Have you heard about how the kids drag main? Well, they are very polite about it. If you're coming out of a store, they let you cross the street, back your car up, or whatever."

Newer businesspeople and village officials, without such agrarian-community tolerance, complain that youth hanging out on the main street use profanity, litter, and in other ways "intimidate" downtown visitors. During the conflict over the sidewalk benches where youth gathered, an owner of a recently opened bar argued before the city council, "I've got $70,000 in that building and I want that sucker [bench] gone. Put it in front of a business that isn't open in the evening." The pizza-parlor owner described previously, who numbers adolescents among his clients, argued to keep the benches (Central City newspaper, Sept. 4, 1994). But the bar owner is not the only one who stigmatizes the youth (Goffman 1963). Revealing the community business priority for a revived main street over tolerance for adolescents, the city council voted to remove the benches (Central City newspaper, 1994).

Adults raised in Bunkerton remember a place where adults watched out for all children (Benson 1997; Freudenberg 1986). Recalled a blue-collar father, "My sister used to say Dad would find out about things before she got home from school." Newcomers choose the community believing it to be a good place for families. Another blue-collar father said, "I like the small community because of security, friendliness, lack of big city problems, and good schools. Bunkerton is big enough to have things for the kids to do yet small enough to feel safe." But the belief that children belong to the community, indicated by tolerance of their use of public space, seems to be a cost of the community transformation triggered by the housing initiative.

The main-street public space, contested by lower-income youth and business interests, was eventually lost to adolescents with the approval of Bunkerton authorities. Growth is defined as the primary good, and other community priorities have become subordinated to that goal (Logan and Molotch 1987). Loitering on main street rather than dragging it marks a group of undesirable youth in the community and probably in school. As a consequence of the actions of the authorities, some youth are essentially stigmatized, increasing the likelihood that they will reproduce the marginal position of their parents. Little chance exists for such youth to achieve upward mobility either in the town of Bunkerton or in school. It is their town because they grew up there. But as the town transformed and gentrified, poorer youths' claims on public spaces were sacrificed. In other towns, the authorities may be more sympathetic to teens' congregating; that would be in accord with sympathy for adolescent restlessness and the optimistic belief that teens represent the future town and belong to everyone (Schwartz 1987). In Bunkerton, an emerging bedroom community, youth are being segregated as in suburbia rather than given the tolerance of an agrarian community, as in Smallville.

REFLECTIONS

In contrast to the lack of tolerance shown toward some Bunkerton youth, another county seat in the Central City commuting zone of similar size (one where the pizza-parlor owner found little business support) is more open-minded toward all town youth. Said the police chief of Bunkerton's counterpart: "Yes, you do have problems up there [in the downtown square] from time to time, but kids also have a right to be up there. . . . You have to kind of balance it out. . . . Are you better off leaving kids the uptown where at least you know where the kids are and what they are doing, or do you run them off and have no idea what's going on. . . . They have to go somewhere" (Central City newspaper, Sept. 4, 1994). Perhaps, however, this latter county seat has fewer lower-income families, like those who aroused the ire of Bunkerton. Bunkerton youth, forced to congregate on main street for want of financial resources to drag main street or attend road parties, are constant symbols of the recent, depressing bad times to the businesspeople responsible for the town revitalization. Emphasizing tolerance toward youth flies in the face of the business-first policy taken by Bunkerton's Chamber of Commerce to achieve the town turnaround.

In 1999, five years after the city council removed the main-street benches, a coalition representing Bunkerton area churches, schools, and businesses commissioned a survey of their high school youth (Central City newspaper, Aug. 20, 1999). The coalition was alarmed by the survey findings that less than one-fifth of the students felt that their community valued youth or that they had useful roles in Bunkerton. Although the coalition commissioning the survey was motivated by a concern for keeping youth from using drugs, their concern seems to be inclusive. In response to the survey findings, a couple relatively new to Bunkerton who are parents of two teenagers offered to fund a youth hangout downtown. Their vision was for a place where kids could get off the streets, out of the countryside, and be monitored from 3:30 to 10:00 P.M. weekdays and until curfew on weekend nights. An adult who was raised in Bunkerton commented on the need for such a space in the changing town: "We always dragged Main Street and hung out, but they [town officials and the police] don't want them to do that anymore."

It seems that although Bunkerton is now home to many newcomers, it still has a rich store of social resources to draw on when concerns about the community welfare are raised. An oldtimer with adult children reflects this tolerance and sympathy: "There are mostly good kids in Bunkerton, not to say there aren't any bad ones. Teenager years are a world in itself, but it seems that all the problems of a city are in a small town, too. They're more controllable here. There's more opportunity for the kids to have support and recognition here, and more kids can achieve things." The main-street growth-machine dynamics have elicited an opposing social response that draws on aspects of the town's agrarian-community past. As least some residents of Bunkerton are resisting the social by-products of suburbanization.

Bunkerton represents a dilemma facing small towns that are intent on growth: how can they balance economic development with the small-town norms that shape cross-age respect and a shared sense of community ownership? Bunkerton shows how with suburbanization, even oldtimer rights can be overshadowed by business and growth priorities. Social capital created by this business community is not a resource equally accessed by all town residents. Small-town public spaces, in particular the downtown main street, become contested spaces where hanging out can be defined as deviant and youth as outsiders. Yet, as sojourners, the middle-class families that the business boosters desire to recruit contribute only sporadically over the long term to the store of social resources. By catering to sojourners, Bunkerton is in danger of alienating its original blue-collar residents, such as the enraged truck-driver families, who are committed to lifelong residence and the community.

6 BLUE-COLLAR ETHNIC ACCOMMODATION: CORNTOWN

In collaboration with Stacey Williams

A two-lane state road leads into Corntown, which lies at the county's edge. The town is visually defined by agriculture. On one side is a cattle feedlot, on another side a grain elevator; and the town is surrounded by farms. Beside the rail line dividing the town at one end, the skyline is dominated by the true lifeblood of Corntown, several food-processing and manufacturing plants. Key to Corntown's economy, the factories capture value-added profits from agriculture. Widely cited as the worst feature of the town is a pervasive rank stench from these food plants and their waste-water treatment lagoons. Such smells are an unwelcome food processing by-product, which constantly reminds the blue-collar residents of the bitter that accompanies the sweet in agribusiness manufacturing jobs.

Corntown's economy, because of its stable, well-paid, blue-collar manufacturing and food-processing jobs (the county as a whole also has a manufacturing-dependent economy; see table 2), supports a vibrant main street near the factories. A supermarket, a variety store, and a hardware store are among more than two hundred local businesses that serve Corntown residents. Although youth all agree that there is "nothing to do," Corntown has a pool hall, a bowling alley, a video store, and a cinema. A Masonic Temple, a country club with a golf course, and American Legion and Veterans of Foreign Wars posts supply additional meeting spaces. What distinguishes Corntown from nearby towns are the institutions and shops catering to Mexicanos (people of Mexican origin), both settled-out families (former migrants who have left that way of life) and annual seasonal migrants. Main Street has a small Mexican market, and the cinema occasionally shows Spanish-language films. Across from the city hall are the Migrant Health Clinic and Council offices. Mexicanos are visible shopping on the main street or visiting in neighborhoods all over town. In summer, Corntown Anglo youth cruise the main street on weekends or gather to party in the countryside, where "every kid in town will be there." Mexicano youth, however, are more prone to home-visiting than dragging main street. "We all hang out together, walk around, and go to each other's houses and stuff, but mostly just walk around. There isn't anything else to do," said a fourteen-year-old Mexicano boy.

Because the town lay at the intersection of two railways, it was originally expected to boom. In 1875 the first canning factory was built, situated to take advantage of the vegetables raised by local farms and the good rail transportation. Another cannery soon followed. By 1877 the town was incorporated. By 1940 the town had a can manufacturing plant and two canneries packing 30 million cans of corn, lima beans, and red beans annually (Federal Writer's Project 1983). Asparagus also was raised and packed locally in the 1960s and 1970s. The can plant and two canneries remain in the 1990s, although one cannery, after being bought by a national conglomerate, scaled back production. Sweet corn, pumpkins, and navy beans are the vegetables packed today. About 65% of the sweet corn packed is grown near Corntown; the remainder is shipped in from elsewhere in Illinois or from Wisconsin (farm journal, Nov. 15, 1996).

Corntown's agribusinesses served early as a magnet for rural workers. Immigrants from Kentucky and Tennessee doubled the village population between 1890 and 1900. Despite the influx from the upland South (Mexicanos refer to the town as "Little Kentucky"), local farmers and the canneries required additional seasonal labor for harvest and canning. Economic downturns, such as the Great Depression, generated sufficient seasonal workers from the countryside. During World War II, barracks were erected on the cannery sites to house German prisoners of war, who kept the vital food industry going. After World War II, the canneries, seeking a dependable seasonal labor supply, tried Haitians for several years but soon settled on recruiting American workers, Mexicanos from the Texas Rio Grande Valley, starting in 1947. The migrants from Texas were housed in the former prisoner barracks, still ringed by barbed-wire fence, a setting that provided little privacy and did not enhance family life (Williams 1975).

At the height of migrant employment, the population swelled by 50% when more than two thousand migrant workers arrived in spring and stayed until fall to work the fields, detasseling corn and harvesting asparagus, and to pack vegetables in the Corntown plants and factories. Such a large influx of a distinctive minority produced sharp community tensions (Lieberson 1980). Townspeople were hostile toward what they considered an annual alien invasion of their cohesive and homogeneous community. Migrants, crammed together in inhospitable and strange prison surroundings, felt equally threatened by the town (Williams 1975, 1979, 1984).

Housing its migrants as prisoners gained Corntown unwanted national notoriety through a widely watched television special in the late 1960s that documented the abuse of U.S. migrant workers. Eventually the media exposure embarrassed the canneries into making some changes in their migrant housing (Williams 1975). Nonprofit agencies also intervened with support programs. The Community Health Partnership of Illinois, based in Chicago, established a health clinic, subsidized by government programs. A Head Start program was set up for preschoolers whose parents both worked all day. Summer programs for school-aged children were established and administered by the Illinois Migrant Council. Despite these improvements in health and educational opportunities, former migrants say that camp life today is only somewhat improved. The current number of migrants, however, is only a fraction of the 1960s and 1970s migrant population. Several Mexicanos, community activists with long residence in Corntown, claim that the canneries continue to exploit migrants. They cite a practice of garnishing extended family members' paychecks to pay for medical problems incurred by kin on the job. Locals, in the meantime, have come to recognize that migrants boost the town coffers. "Migrant workers bring in revenue to the community because they buy food, a lot of them buy cars, a lot of clothes," according to the mayor (farm journal, Nov. 15, 1996).

Despite their troublesome welcome, some Mexicano families chose to leave the migrant stream and settle-out in Corntown starting in the 1960s. Seeking a better life, they remained behind after the main group returned to Texas in late October to the Texas Rio Grande Valley (Williams 1975). Their numbers grew modestly to total 5% of the town by 1990, or fewer than 300 people when the study was conducted (table 14). These former migrant permanent residents all speak fluent English. With the number of Mexicanos reduced to about 500 (a seasonal trickle of 200 migrant workers plus the settled-out Mexicanos), the Mexicanos no longer are so threatening to Corntown Anglos (Lieberson 1980). Although the settled-out families agree that racism and discrimination occur, they do not report experiencing the virulence of the past. By 2000 the census reports that 500 Hispanic residents account for 8.4% of the town population. Thus, without the Mexicano migrants who settled-out, Corntown would not have achieved the 1.4% increase in size that occurred between 1990 and 2000 (table 14). Clearly, their presence also helps the local economy.

Corntown is struggling to preserve its manufacturing base in the face of a national restructuring of the food-processing sector. One Corntown food-processing plant was downsized during the 1980s, and a major employer, a heavy industry in the county seat, gradually phased out its operation. By 2000 the sweet corn–packing operation had ended. Sweet corn was too expensive for Illinois, where producers had to be paid high premiums (farm journal, Nov. 15, 1996). The loss was 450 jobs employing workers in all capacities, from haulers to pickers. As the county manufacturing base weakened, people left. Corntown's population peaked in 1960 at around 6,500. The decline thereafter is thus related to a countywide manufacturing decline rather than to the rural-manufacturing national trend—nationally, there was a moderate increase during that period (Cook and Mizer 1994). The unemployment rate hovers around 8%, higher than the county rate of about 7%. Yet a large proportion of Corntown's blue-collar workers remain employed in manufacturing jobs (table 15). As

Table 14 Corntown Demographic Profile

YEAR	POPU-LATION	MEDIAN AGE	PERCENT RESIDING IN SAME HOUSE AS 5 YEARS BEFORE	MEDIAN VALUE OF OWNED HOMES ($)	MEDIAN HOUSE-HOLD INCOME ($)	PERCENT BELOW POVERTY LEVEL	PERCENT FEMALE-HEADED HOUSE-HOLDS[a]	PERCENT HISPANIC
1980	6,411	31.0	54.2	30,500	14,992	10.8	7.3	4.7
1990	5,880	35.7	62.5	33,000	22,266	14.2	6.8	5.0
2000	5,965	39.8	65.5	48,700	31,940	13.8	7.3	8.4

Sources: Bureau of the Census 1980c, 1990a, 2001, 2002.
[a] With own children under 18.

Table 15 Corntown Employment Profile

YEAR	PERCENT COMPLETING HIGH SCHOOL OR HIGHER	MEAN TRAVEL TIME TO WORK (MINUTES)	PERCENT OVER 16 IN LABOR FORCE	PERCENT EMPLOYED IN AGRI-CULTURE	PERCENT EMPLOYED IN PROFES-SIONAL SERVICES	PERCENT EMPLOYED IN MANU-FACTURING
1980	54.4	11.8	62.7	1.9	13.5	43.7
1990	68.7	15.5	63.3	1.1	12.9	37.7
2000	76.4	24.1	58.7	1.6[a]	31.3[a]	29.1[a]

Sources: Bureau of the Census 1980c, 1990a, 2002.
[a] Due to major revisions in the 2000 census classification of jobs by industry, these data are not exactly comparable with the 1980 and 1990 data.

the town entered the twenty-first century, however, the historically plentiful supply of good, stable jobs was slowly dwindling. "It's a depressed area right now," said the president of the Corntown Chamber of Commerce, referring to the closing of some companies and the downsizing of others (Central City newspaper, Aug. 5, 2001). A new state prison that many had hoped would create local jobs went to another town. An alderman speculates that for the first time Corntown may be evolving into a sleeper town, albeit a blue-collar one.

The plants process agricultural products and provide jobs, but they are owned by large national corporations, and most of the profits flow out of town. An interesting effect of the absentee ownership of Corntown's major plants is that no small wealthy elite has ever controlled the political structure. The plants have been managed by workers who rose through the ranks, and this has muted social distinctions between management and the plant rank and file. How this relatively shallow stratification shapes Corntown's social structure is strongly related to the town's treatment of Mexicano newcomers.

COMMUNITY CHANGE

Mexicano Newcomers

Before the 1980s, Anglo oldtimers recall, the settled-out Mexicano migrants were simply ignored. "Many [residents] probably felt like I did . . . that it was okay that [settled-out migrants] were there, but that they had nothing to do with me," recalled an Anglo nurse at the Migrant Health Clinic. She explained that her attitude changed after working with migrants and getting to know them as individuals. For the most part, the nurse characterizes Corntown Anglo-Mexicano relationships this way: "[Anglos] aren't real prejudiced, they just don't mix with [Mexicanos]." She now sees herself as a community advocate for the seasonal migrants.

Most Anglo community members treat them well enough, say Mexicanos. "The ones who don't are never going to accept us anyway," remarked a newly settled-out woman. She thinks that "some of the Spanish people who've settled-out are the worst [toward migrants]." Settled-out families, having improved their life chances through extraordinary efforts, emphasize differences between themselves and those who are still migrants (Hondagneu-Sotelo 1994). Longer-established Mexicanos in Corntown are proud of their achievements and criticize recent settlers for, among other things, accepting any government supports. One family, recent permanent residents, brags about never receiving food stamps or other welfare entitlements. "There were times when we could have used them, but we got by," said the woman. Mexicanos who use entitlements are considered by those who are well established to deserve poor treatment.

The process by which Corntown becomes home to Mexicanos is reflected in the history of an original Mexicano settled-out family. They first came to Corntown as migrants in 1951. Not until 1963, when the man obtained a cannery job, did they stay year-round. Soon after that, he was hired by the can company, which has what are considered the best local factory jobs. An Anglo coworker sold them their home. In the late 1970s, the settled-out man opened a store that caters to the Mexicano population and began to work as crew leader, recruiting seasonal migrants to detassel corn. His wife never got beyond the sixth grade, but he eventually obtained a GED. In contrast, their six children all graduated from the Corntown high school. One is a college graduate, and the others either have attended college or have received vocational training. The father is justly proud of the distance the former seasonal-migrant Mexicano family has traveled in a single generation.

Once a few families settled-out in Corntown, their relatives followed in chain-migration fashion from Texas. Settling-out is begun by extending the migrant season with cannery work. Essential to the process is for one adult to find a full-time job in a local factory. Stability is erratic until that happens. Some families have a circular migration history, living in Corntown, returning to Texas, and then moving back. The experience of a Head Start aide in the program run for migrant children typifies the uneven migration process that often occurs before a family establishes permanent residence. She and her husband and children return to Corntown annually and stay from March through November. "If things were different, we would stay. Every year we say that maybe we'll stay this time, but there is never any money here after the season is over." They tried staying one year after the season ended but could not make enough money. Her sister and several cousins already live year-round in Corntown, and her family's goal is to eventually join them.

Push and pull factors provoke the supreme effort migrants make to settle-out in Corntown, far from extended family. The strongest push comes from the dramatic urbanization and population growth of the place where most of the migrants originate, the Texas metropolitan statistical area (MSA) McAllen-Pharr-Edinburg in Hidalgo County's Lower Rio Grande Valley. In the largest area, McAllen, the population increased by 65.8% during the 1950s. Between 1970 and 1980 the McAllen-Pharr-Edinburg MSA grew by an astonishing 75.8%, with another 65% added in the 1980s as a result of substantial Mexican immigration and the high Hispanic fertility rate (Bureau of the Census 1960, 1991a, 1991b). Such rapid growth severely overtaxed the predominantly (85.2%) Hispanic county, which was already beset by a number of socioeconomic problems. By 1990 Hidalgo County Hispanics were young (36.6% under eighteen years of age), poor (47% below the poverty level), and often unemployed (16% of the workforce over the age of sixteen lacked employment). It is also an undereducated population. In 1990 in Hidalgo County, about 54% of persons twenty-five years of age and older had dropped out of high school; the high school dropout rate was 31% for the same age group in Corntown (Bureau of the Census 1990a, 1991a). Such conditions push migrants outward, just as conditions in Mexico had pushed out their parents or grandparents (Williams 1996). "It's dangerous. There are gangs," explained a recently settled-out migrant mother.

The pull factor that attracts the settled-out migrants to central Illinois, in addition to good jobs, is that Corntown represents small-town life for families who identify themselves as small-town people (Hummon 1990; Williams 1996). Such families value Corntown's good schools and the security of living where everyone knows you and watches your children as if they were their own. Commented the same mother, "I'm at peace here. . . . We leave our door unlocked sometimes here, and we could never do that in Texas." Her daughter agreed: "There are gangs in Texas, lots of violence. Here you don't hear nothing about that. You feel more secure here, because you know everybody. And the education is definitely better. It wasn't very good in Texas." Despite being over 90% white, Corntown as a blue-collar agrarian community represents a way of life familiar to settled-out-migrant, small-town Mexicanos (table 14).

Space and Place

Corntown's street plan deviates little from the original grid platted in the early 1870s (fig. 5). On the outskirts of town, farthest from the processing plants, stand several small subdivisions with newer homes, some on culs-de-sac that break the uniform grid. Older homes are well kept but modest, standing along curbed brick streets with sidewalks. No single neighborhood departs from the overall homogeneity of modest homes not beautified by suburban landscaping or gentrification touches. Most important, Corntown has no barrio in which permanently settled Mexicanos live in a segregated enclave.

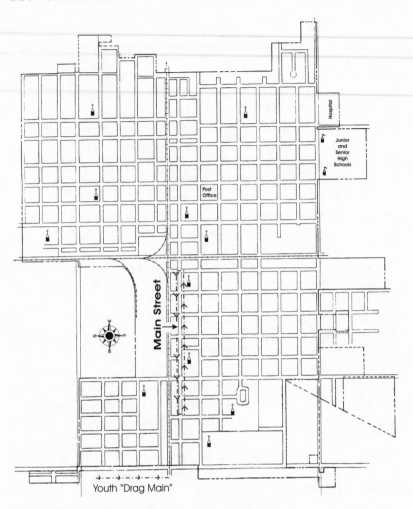

Figure 5 Corntown town map

Some older homes in poor condition are grouped near the largest cannery, where a few recently settled-out families live. New arrivals use such homes to gain a foothold in the town. Once established, Mexicanos move farther away from the plants, in an ethnic pattern similar to the one followed in Chicago (Kornblum 1974). That their homes are scattered throughout town indicates a lack of bias in the local housing market. According to our survey, Corntown Mexicano incomes cluster above $35,000, with three-quarters of them higher than $50,000 (typically derived from dual-earner households). Hispanic-owned homes in Corntown, however, have a lower median value ($27,013) than the median home value for the town of Corntown as a whole (table 14) (Bureau of the Census 1990a).

After settling-out, Corntown Mexicanos aim to quickly achieve home ownership. At first, such families had difficulty buying homes, but once the early Mexicano families proved trustworthy, other migrant families experienced few problems. Although a "Little Mexico" label is attached to the poorer-quality housing in the undesirable location near the manufacturing plants, proportionately few minority families live there. According to the high school principal, housing is not segregated except for a recently built subdivision where Mexicano families congregate because the houses and some apartments there are reasonably priced. "We have no 'across the tracks' here in Corntown," he commented. Mexicano newcomers have bought homes all over town rather than settling as a group. They live next door to Anglos in every Corntown neighborhood. Mexicanos and their blue-collar Anglo neighbors both place a high value on owning a home and on the upkeep of their property.

Interconnectedness

Corntown stands out from Prairieview, Bunkerton, Arbordale, and Splitville in absorbing newcomers because it incorporated them without being wholly transformed. The newcomers, despite being a distinctive minority, have specific assets that promoted their integration. One crucial factor is that the Corntown newcomers chose a town that was losing population. The Mexicanos, although only 5% of Corntown (at the time of the study), stabilized a population that otherwise would have declined more. The Mexicano families also are young. Their children helped ensure that Corntown's high school, rather than one in another town, would serve a school district that consolidated with four nearby districts in the early 1990s. According to the high school principal, it is "the only school system in the county that is operating in the black, and we have the cheapest tax rate around." Because the school district is efficiently managed, no oldtimer criticism has surfaced regarding the few special summer programs that have been introduced for the minority newcomer students.

According to the median income and types of jobs held (tables 14 and 15), Corntown is a blue-collar community. In addition to living as neighbors, Mexicanos and Anglos work side by side for similar wages. For both groups, the best local jobs are in the Corntown can manufacturing plant, but some from each ethnic group commute to plants in the county seat or in Central City. (Corntown is at the periphery of the Central City commuting zone.) Both Mexicanos and Anglos work in production lines or serve as line foremen in Corntown's several plants. Mexicanos, especially those who have settled-out, say they are accused by some Corntown Anglos of "taking our jobs." One cannery sets aside a certain number of jobs to offer Anglo townspeople but must always recruit local Mexicanos to fill some of the jobs, because Anglos reject jobs that Mexicanos willingly take. The high school principal believes that the blue-collar status shared by Anglos and Mexicanos and, until the late 1990s, a high employment rate have dampened the potential for racism. He commented: "Corntown is basically a working-class town. Most people here are employed in the factories or in retail and sales-type positions. Fewer people are in the professional occupations that you would find in more urban areas. That's one of the reasons that the Hispanic families have found acceptance here. In other communities where you see sharper class divisions, an ethnically diverse group would have a more difficult time being accepted. But in this town, most people are about on the same level, economically."

Mexicanos do not just live in Corntown. The small core of Mexicanos who settled permanently more than thirty years ago became integrated into Anglo Corntown while simultaneously providing leadership to the highly cohesive ethnic community. Both women and men (one-third of the parents interviewed) report being civically engaged (table B2, in appendix B). Almost all of the Mexicanos participate actively in the Catholic Church. One family provides the music for Spanish-language masses. Mexicano women volunteer for the United Way, belong to the Jaycees and the Rotary Club, work at the Planned Parenthood and Migrant clinics, and serve as voter registrars and election judges. The men volunteer as Little League coaches and for the PTA and also belong to the Jaycees. A son from an original Mexicano family is a police officer. Another son was elected as alderman to the village board. One Mexicano volunteers as a disk jockey for a local "Mexican Hour" radio program and is a member of the Lions Club and the Moose Lodge. A Mexicano woman formed a partnership with an oldtimer Anglo couple and opened a Mexican café. Length of residence is significantly correlated with both involvement in community activities ($r = .43$, $p < .05$) and voter registration ($r = .47$, $p = .05$) (Williams 1996).

Children from the longest-settled families are also actively engaged in school. Four have been elected high school homecoming queen, some have been band members, and some have made the football and wrestling teams. An adolescent from a recently settled-out family attributes such achievements to longer Corntown residence: "That family [with a homecoming queen and athletes] has lived here a long time. That's how they can be so popular."

Settled-out Mexicanos like living in Corntown. "Some here don't like Mexicans," commented a longtime resident, who says he never lets latent Anglo racism bother him. "I may not be educated but I think that prejudice is just ignorance. Some insult me, but I just ignore them." That almost half of the first settled-out cohort who grew up in Corntown married Anglos shows extensive accommodation. An Anglo woman who married a man from one of these early settled-out families said, "My sister and I used to work at the corn-pack with Mexican kids. We always thought they were a lot of fun." When she told her father they wanted to marry, he protested. She recalled: "He said that Mexicans were lazy and shiftless and have no ambition. But I told him that [her husband] had already enrolled in college and wanted to make something of himself. That's why his parents came here from Texas. They wanted that for their children. So finally, he agreed." In contrast, almost three-quarters of the members of the later settled-out cohorts, who had a larger ethnic-minority mate pool, chose Mexicano spouses. Intermarriage is seen by later arrivals as a threat to maintaining a strong ethnic identity. A man in his forties, whose sibling married an Anglo, explained, "My wife and I don't believe in mixed marriages. When that happens, the person who is Spanish ignores their culture" (Williams 1996).

Community acceptance for Mexicano newcomers was pioneered by the original families who settled-out, bought homes, and initiated civic engagement in Corntown. These early families became upright citizens respected by their blue-collar neighbors. The children of original families who intermarried with Anglos have, as town residents, integrated the two parallel and cohesive groups. Their small-town ideology, which motivated their transplantation to Corntown, inspires citizenship among these families (Hummon 1990). Commitment is evident in their civic engagement and loyalty to the town. For example, a woman who was a child when her family settled-out almost thirty years ago is now a Mexicano oldtimer and has apprehensions about the future for Corntown. "So many businesses in town are closing. But I think we have only hurt ourselves. We go out of town to buy in the stores, too. So we are just as bad as everybody else."

Social Resources

Mexicano families agree that decisions about Corntown are made by those with the longest residence rather than by a wealthy elite. Mexicano families do not point to any Corntown Anglo family as the most powerful or wealthy. A prominent Mexicano woman from a family that has been settled-out for more than twenty years commented, "The mayor used to work at the same place my husband does." To her the mayor, a retired thirty-five-year veteran of the can company, is a regular guy rather than a powerful community leader. A typical blue-collar example of who governs Corntown is provided by one Anglo man. A longtime alderman on the village council, he is also the fire chief. After retiring from a local construction firm, he served as a grade school custodian and ran a tool-sharpening shop out of his home. A daughter married a Mexicano from a long-settled family. He and his family also exemplify a civically engaged citizen and a family in the vanguard, accommodating and connecting with Mexicanos. His life course shows how the two ethnic groups live and work together. In Corntown, mutual respect and familiarity developed as the pioneering, settled-out Mexicanos gradually integrated themselves into the community and contributed to the stock of social resources.

When in 1992 a boiler explosion rocked the 125-year-old town cannery, both Anglos and Mexicanos were concerned about losing jobs. At the time four hundred people, both townsfolk and seasonal migrants, were canning corn. An Anglo quality control worker in the plant said: "This is going to hurt. This is the place people look to earn extra dollars to buy things like school clothes for their kids. It's a sad situation" (Central City newspaper, Sept. 12, 1992). Local citizens agreed that the community had pulled together in crisis. "It was amazing," said the plant manager. "If you think about it, you'll cry about it." An area not-for-profit agency was quickly mobilized to open its community center as a free cafeteria for firefighters, workers, and residents. Town restaurants, stores, individuals, and other companies donated food, cups, and drinks. "Nobody asked them to bring it. It just started coming," commented the agency's director. The center also served as a gathering place for migrant families temporarily evacuated from company housing behind the burning building (Central City newspaper, Sept. 13, 1992). A Mexicano from an original family was also impressed by how Corntown rallied after the explosion. "It was incredible. I was very proud," he said.

For more than fifty years the village has relied on volunteer help to produce a fall community festival. In 1992 this annual festival drew fifty thousand for a parade with more than one hundred entries, including bands, floats, a queen, and, as the grand marshal, an area Olympic athlete. In conjunction with the festival, the town organizes a flea market, three days of entertainment, and an antique auto show on one day. "It's the most exciting things that happen here all year," said a local resident (Central City newspaper, Aug. 3, 2001). The explosion happened a week after the town put on what was thought their best festival ever. Townspeople had invested months of planning, hard work, and cooperation to bring off the event. Keeping a large festival going for more than five decades using volunteers contributes to the high levels of social resources available in Corntown for other purposes (Putnam 2000).

Among Mexicanos, strong networks of kin and friend quickly mobilize for crises. During the study, a well-connected couple was killed in a crash while driving to work early one morning. They left seven children, the youngest a four-year-old. Although in shock, the entire Corntown minority community mustered to help, many reported. "Everyone was involved, and the children were never alone," explained a middle-aged mother. The event shook the small, highly connected community. "Every Mexican in town was at the church for the funeral. Even the ones that you never see. I think we're all concerned about each other's welfare," said a young woman. She believes the wider Corntown community would react similarly, although Mexicanos think that Anglos "mind their own business . . . ; [however], I think when you know them, they aren't like that. My friends aren't, and my Dad's best friend is white. He's helped us out a lot. But if you don't know them, that's how they seem."

An organizing engine for Corntown Mexicanos is their link to the local Catholic Church. Although only forty families out of the approximately eighty in town attend regularly, every family interviewed reported having religious identification. For more than ten years, a particularly sympathetic and well-loved priest ran the parish, holding regular Spanish masses. Around 1990, he moved to the larger, county-seat parish. "They're a good people. . . . They're very trusting of the church, and that's a cultural trait," said this relocated former priest about the Corntown group. A newly appointed Spanish-speaking priest now ministers to the parish. He characterizes the settled-out families as "very Americanized. . . . They greet me in English even after I give a Spanish mass." In winter he conducts a monthly Spanish mass, but when summer migrants swell the ethnic population, the Spanish mass is weekly. "I think if we had it weekly throughout the year that would be encouraging a separation. We want the community to be interrelated. It's harder to feel prejudice, I think, when you are always sitting next to that person in church." Unlike the previous priest, he seems to have an assimilation agenda, and the Mexicanos are less enamored of him.

Through the 1980s, when the migrant stream was high, Corntown had a Mexicano association organized by several original settled-out families. Financed by regional organizations and an area philanthropist, it was originally started to fund a migrant day-care center. Land was purchased in town and an office established. The group's mandate was expanded (after the Head Start was established) to encourage the maintenance of ethnic identity through college scholarships and help for needy families. Dances were also sponsored so that adolescents could socialize under supervision. Unfortunately, the organization fell apart after its assets were depleted by helping families who were laid off during an economic downturn. The families never repaid the funds, and the main leader of the association quit in disgust. Yet enough social capital had existed to maintain an active organization for many years. Because the association owns the land, renewal is potentially an option. Among the postagrarian communities, Corntown alone sustains a civic organization to further a newcomer agenda.

Cross-Age Relations

Nationally, Hispanic children are more likely than non-Hispanic children to drop out of high school before graduation (National Center for Educational Statistics 1992). Although Hispanic high school completion rates are improving, they remain much lower than those of non-Hispanics (Chapa and Valencia 1993). In contrast to the high dropout rate (8%) for Hispanic youth nationally, during each of four senior-high years, the Corntown adolescent dropout rate ranged from 0% to 3.13% ($t = p < .005$) (Williams 1996). These impressive local statistics result from the combined efforts of Mexicano families and from accessible community social resources, which reinforce positive developmental outcomes in these minority children (Elder and Conger 2000).

Mexicano families settling-out in Corntown are a self-selected group with the energy, commitment, and independence typically associated with immigrant success. In addition, although former migrants, the families provide their children with important family social resources. Home ownership among Corntown Mexicano parents is at a higher rate than that found nationally among Hispanics (57% versus 38%). Almost all of the Mexicano children of Corntown live in a two-parent home (Bureau of the Census 1990a). (One female-headed family was interviewed, but that family moved in 1991 after the census was taken.) None of the originally settled-out Mexicano parents graduated from high school. Nearly three-quarters (72.7%) failed to even finish elementary school (Williams 1996). More than half (53%) of the first-generation parents interviewed, however, say they moved to Corntown specifically so that their children could attend good schools (they were able to evaluate the schools during their annual residence before they settled-out). They purposefully chose the small-town environment that they consider fosters school success. Mexicano parents thus endow their children with substantial human capital despite having little education themselves.

Undereducated parents are unable to help their children with homework, yet they appear successful in transmitting educational priorities to them. Almost all of the youth who were interviewed reported a desire to fulfill the high expectations their parents had for them. A sense of responsibility to her parents was expressed by one high school girl: "I've never considered dropping out of school. My parents would be very upset if I didn't graduate. They want what's best for me—the things they didn't have." Mexicano adolescents in Corntown recognize the difficult choices their parents made to better their offspring's lives. Older siblings willingly help younger ones. Almost every adolescent interviewed indicated an intention to graduate from high school. A typical remark was made by a sixteen-year-old girl: "I never considered quitting because my parents would get mad. They didn't graduate from high school, and they want to see us [the children] graduate." A high school junior with college as his goal commented, "My father always says that if you don't want to work in a factory all your life, you have to go to school."

Corntown Mexicano mothers have altered how they treat their daughters, by transforming ethnic gender roles (Hondagneu-Sotelo 1994). A mother of two daughters, who was taken out of school at age twelve by her own sickly mother, recalls, "My father always said that women only need to learn how to write their own name because when they get married their husbands will take care of them." She is now a teacher's aide, and she values education and regrets not finishing school. "I tell my daughters to go to school so that they don't have to depend on anybody else." Another message Mexicano parents preach to both daughters and sons is the importance of education to economic security (Williams 1996). Explained a high school senior, repeating her family's incessantly asserted beliefs: "You need to graduate from high school to get a job; you probably need to go to college now, too."

Numerous indicators show that Mexicano youth brought up in Corntown are improving their life chances with education. In one family both parents had quit school before the age of fifteen to do migrant labor; all seven of their children graduated from Corntown high school. Two of them have bachelor's degrees, and two more have completed some college. Of the thirty-three children of sample families who have passed through Corntown's school system, most (88%) have graduated from the high school. It is impressive that almost 40% of these graduates have attended or are presently attending college. The families in the first cohort to settle-out produced children with the highest social mobility. These educational achievements could be attributed entirely to the local schools. But the scholastic successes would not have occurred without the Corntown parents' commitment to education, their trust in the schools, and the respectful school environment that the town provides (Williams 1996).

"What we have here is what was intended for the *Brown vs. Board of Education* decision. Corntown is living this," according to the principal. When compared with schools elsewhere in Illinois, the Corntown high school has fewer low-income students (15% versus 32% in the state), a lower truancy rate, and a lower student mobility rate, as well as a lower dropout rate and a higher graduation rate (86% versus 78% for the state) (Illinois State Board of Education 1992). Children of settled-out migrants make up approximately 7% to 8% of the high school student body. In spite of their small numbers in a school of about five hundred, the minority students have a large impact on the school; in turn, the school shapes their lives in profound ways (Williams 1996).

The high school principal contributes vitally to the impressive educational achievements of the Mexicano adolescents, normally a high-risk population (Williams 1996). He is committed to helping his minority students achieve success so that they do not reproduce the low educational status of their parents. His school does not track Mexicano students into lower levels. "Their academic performance is indistinguishable from that of white students. Where there is a problem, their parents are just as involved. . . . They come for open houses, athletic events, plays, etc. Their children are just as involved as the Anglos—they play sports, are involved in the yearbook, drama, and the honor societies." He can recall only one case of a severe behavior problem among Mexicano students in his fifteen years as high school principal. "[A problem child] is very unusual for Hispanic families. They have even more respect for authority than Anglo families do, because it's an important part of their culture. Their family units are strong, so the parents naturally want to be involved in the school. [Youth] have no lack of role models, because they have this solid parental backing. They have a good Catholic base as well. That adds to the stability of their families. When kids have such strong support from family, community, church, and school, they have a greater reason to succeed in school." The school policy, explains the principal, is to encourage all Corntown students to pursue higher education. Through the Illinois Migrant Council (for which he served as a consultant for many years) and other organizations, about thirty college scholarships are available to Mexicano high school students. "The money is out there. We try to prepare our students to compete for the scholarships because we want them to go to college," he said. The local community college works closely with the Corntown high school to guarantee placement for students desiring a vocational education program.

Although the principal believes his teachers are more liberal than Corntown itself, some local conservatism permeates the school. For example, a young woman who was a member of the Honor Society and went on to a university felt that the guidance counselor automatically steered Mexicano students toward the community college, when higher education was their goal. "I didn't want to go to [the community college], although he tried hard to talk me into it. He was always questioning my judgment, but I knew exactly what I wanted to do." In contrast, one teacher "pushed me harder than she did the other kids, because she expected that I would do better. . . . she would say, 'I know you can do better.'" Although Mexicano students can point to some negative events in school, on the whole their Corntown education has been a positive experience that has motivated them to stay in school or go on to a community college or a state university.

Corntown's police are somewhat less tolerant than the high school in their treatment of minority youth. A Mexicano serves on the force, yet several other police officers, according to particular male adolescents, are downright racist. Young adolescent males, especially those who are relatively recent arrivals, feel labeled as troublemakers. Of course they are not as familiar to the police officers as are children from families with a longer history in town, and they bring something of an urban street attitude. One of these youth said:

"Sometimes we like to hang out at the benches across from Subway. But at night the cops come and say we have to leave. They don't tell the white kids outside Subway to leave. They say it's okay to sit there, but that anybody who sits at the benches is a troublemaker. ... They won't let us ride our bikes on the sidewalk. . . . They won't let us stay in the parking lot at the [elementary] school even for a minute. I think it's hard for Hispanics to live in Corntown."

However, a Mexicano father whose son ran into trouble with the local police recalled how an officer explained Corntown's interethnic relations: "We don't have to like each other. We just have to respect each other." Mutual respect despite recognized differences seems on the whole (except for certain young men) to describe Corntown's tolerance of ethnic youth. Although Corntown police are not as tolerant as high school authorities, law enforcement seems to be tempered by some trust; Mexicano adolescents as a group have not experienced consistent, outright racism or punitive treatment. Mexicano girls and boys experience freedom and security in the town because of a trusting, tolerant social environment. Moreover, migrant parents could not achieve their familial goals without the aid of key cultural brokers among Corntown Anglos. Minority youth have the option of fulfilling their potential because authority figures—the high school principal, the parish priest, some police officers, and a guidance counselor—provide tacit support and tolerance (Schwartz 1987).

A threat to the persistence of vitality in this small ethnic-minority community is the diminished employment opportunities for youth coming of age in the early twenty-first century. As early as the mid-1990s, a Mexicano mother of six children commented, "The only thing is, when the kids grow up, Corntown has no jobs for them. They have to go somewhere else." The canneries that originally recruited migrants closed in the late 1990s. Corntown has mobilized to seek another base industry but with little success. In addition, Mexicanos' success in encouraging their children to attend college—usually elsewhere—makes their return to blue-collar Corntown less likely.

REFLECTIONS

Corntown, at the county line and on secondary roads, attracts only committed newcomers. Of the transformed agrarian communities, Corntown has succeeded best in incorporating its newcomers, formerly seasonal-migrant Mexicanos. It is particularly remarkable that settled-out migrants are being integrated into a cohesive rural white Illinois community when only twenty or twenty-five years ago, these ethnic groups were actively hostile to each other. Certain characteristics of the newcomers and the oldtimers gradually fostered mutual respect. Corntown oldtimers are blue-collar people who work in the local or county manufacturing plants. Mexicanos, once they had settled-out from the migrant stream, eventually rose to share the occupations and blue-collar status income of the oldtimers. These newcomers, moreover, chose Corntown and have plunged into civic engagement, demonstrating a commitment to the town itself, not just to the jobs it provides. They arrived at a time when the town population and the school system were declining, and their presence helped somewhat to stabilize the downward drift. Mexicano children raised in Corntown have embraced the town, some by intermarrying with Anglos. To them, Corntown is a special place, as it is for old-timers. One reason for the accommodation of the town to the newcomers, however, is that the Mexicano influx remains small and is unlikely to increase to a level that would intimidate Anglo oldtimers (Lieberson 1980).

Minority youths' success in Corntown is linked to their parents' adopting a town whose collective norms and values matched their own: working-class, a strong work ethic, a preference for small-town life, a high priority for home ownership, and commitment to community involvement (Williams 1996). This congruence of values allowed Mexicano parents to place their trust in the town and the schools and to expect that the community would reciprocate. Social resources accessible to youth, in the form of sympathetic, well-placed community authority figures, structured their world with caring adults; they were not left to their peer group (Elder and Conger 2000; Schwartz 1987). Because of family resilience in the form of tenacity and determination to settle-out in an environment that was initially hostile and to overcome prejudice in order to gain access to community social resources, a group of minority youth, normally at risk, are beating the national odds by achieving family educational and social-mobility goals. An agrarian community with rich social resources and a self-selected group of minority parents combined in such a way that minority children develop successfully in a supportive environment. Their small numbers and their strong character aided the incorporation of the settled-out migrants. The Mexicanos also mobilized in ways that sustained their ethnic identity and their strongly interconnected ethnic group, even while they took on aspects of a new identity as midwestern small-town citizens.

7 ETHNIC SUCCESSION IN PROCESS: ARBORDALE

In collaboration with Patricia A. Howard

Arbordale is situated amid three major highways that serve as primary routes for heavy commercial and passenger traffic flowing north to Chicago and south to the five central Illinois small cities (fig. 1). South and west of the village stand fields with rows of nursery-stock trees and bushes, evidence of the main local agribusiness. On its eastern side, bounding the village, are a subdivision of somewhat more upscale homes, compared with the modest homes of the old town, and fields of soybeans and corn. Downtown streets follow the grid, leading away from a central town square lined on one side by a state highway that runs alongside the railroad tracks and several grain elevators that serve the local family-run grain farms (fig. 6). Arbordale peaked at a population of approximately 1,450 in 1930, declining by 1980 to approximately 1,270 (table 16). During the 1990s a steady influx of Mexicanos (all of Mexican origin) stabilized the population decline, and by 2000 they constituted 35% of the town. The presence of the Mexicanos reflects Arbordale's location on a midwestern migrant workers' pathway from Texas to Illinois; from Illinois it divides, heading north to agricultural areas in Michigan and east to others in Indiana. Their presence also reflects the century of labor demands for the nursery and other nearby agribusinesses in the Central City commuting zone.

Arbordale was settled by German farmers in the mid-nineteenth century. Farmers still move into town when they retire. Because Arbordale was religiously diverse from the outset (German Baptist Brethren Dunkers were one of the religious groups), it lacked the unity of other central Illinois German towns where church and community overlapped (Godina 1998; Salamon 1992). Arbordale has

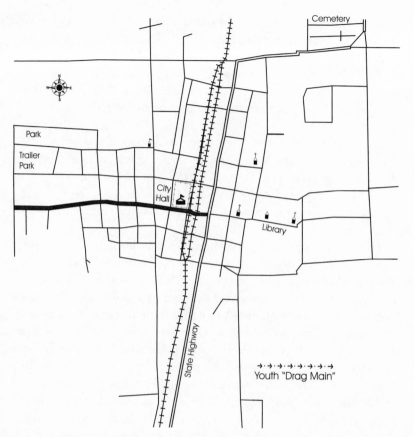

Figure 6 Arbordale town map

Table 16 Arbordale Demographic Profile

YEAR	POPU-LATION	MEDIAN AGE	PERCENT RESIDING IN SAME HOUSE AS 5 YEARS BEFORE	MEDIAN VALUE OF OWNED HOMES ($)	MEDIAN HOUSE-HOLD INCOME ($)	PERCENT BELOW POVERTY LEVEL	PERCENT FEMALE-HEADED HOUSE-HOLDS[a]	PERCENT HISPANIC
1980	1,269	33.3	57.2	25,500	13,393	12.8	4.9	18.5
1990	1,280	33.4	64.9	27,500	22,365	14.6	7.3	24.7
								32.0[b]
2000	1,430	29.9	62.0	69,000	35,850	10.9	6.8	35.3

Sources: Bureau of the Census 1980a, 1990a, 2001, 2002.

[a] With own children under 18.

[b] 1995 result of a windshield survey of every house, conducted jointly with a Hispanic resident.

always been deeply committed to education. Its business leaders, like those in Bunkerton, won a grant in 1906 from Andrew Carnegie to build a library, which is still in existence (Godina 1998).

Arbordale supports a variety of businesses, particularly those that meet the needs of seasonal Mexican-national nursery workers who tend not to have transportation. Lining the main square are a small grocery store that carries Mexican items, a barber shop, a tavern, a coffee shop, a sports equipment shop, a cinema, and a substantial, imposing bank where Mexicanos are seen cashing paychecks on Fridays. The grocery store is busiest after work hours, from four to six in the afternoon. Anglos and the Mexicanos who are permanent residents do their main shopping in the county seat, which has a chain supermarket and a Wal-Mart.

Three elite families, who own major local businesses, have long controlled Arbordale. The long-term mayor is from one ruling family, and other members of the principal families serve or have served on the village board. Although they are civic-minded, the elite families, to a certain extent, run Arbordale to maintain the status quo. The economic importance of agriculture to Arbordale perhaps explains why certain policies have been unchallenged in the past. From the perspective of Mexicanos, the mayor and his allies "don't want to allow too many businesses to come in." For example, a prominent businessman who has been a village board member for more than a decade argues that a past decision to remain on a septic system, rather than to invest in a city sewage facility, dooms any growth initiatives. "That's one of the first things that businesses ask about, whether or not our sewage can handle a big business or factory moving here. To change over means more taxes, so I don't think it's going to happen any time soon." Despite his criticism, he is an ardent Arbordale booster who sees the town as a "dynamic community" because it has young people. Furthermore, he says, "it's a peaceful community. It's a loving community. The relationship between the Mexicans and Anglos is excellent."

A county history chronicles the growth and decline of the various agribusinesses that have dominated the Arbordale economy (county historical society, 1985). In the early 1900s, a canning factory was built to process sweet corn, but it burned in the late 1940s and was never rebuilt. One family has raised garden nursery stock for more than a hundred years. Recently the family opened a retail outlet in Central City to tap the nearby urban market. Around 1950, when a large tract of land became available, a second family, involved with the oldest nursery firm, spun off to establish a new business, which gradually eclipsed the original nursery. The second firm now controls more than one thousand acres and employs more than fifty year-round workers in its commercial nursery production, according to the owner. Arbordale also has a small factory, and there was a private school that closed in the early 1970s. About five years ago, the empty school facility was converted to a center that houses primarily African American school-aged boys who have been removed from abusive homes in Illinois cities. The center brought in its own professional staff but employs a few locals in maintenance. After these well-paid professionals arrived, village housing became somewhat more scarce and expensive for other newcomers.

During the busy nursery seasons of spring and fall, seasonal workers are the source of a continuing trickle of Mexicano newcomers, who constitute a growing proportion of Arbordale (table 16). After initially working in the nurseries, they tend to move into other industrial jobs within a twenty-five-mile radius of the village that, unlike the seasonal nurseries, provide full-time employment and fringe benefits. Mexicanos seek jobs in small plants or manufacturing firms, including a meat-processing plant that employs more Mexicanos than does the major nursery, a rubber-stamp manufacturing plant, a plant that makes harvesting machines and wagon boxes, and a plant that manufactures grain bins. Arbordale Mexicanos are also employed by a large confinement hog operation and by several factories in nearby Bunkerton. These jobs account for the higher-than-average town employment in agriculture (table 17 and tables 3 and 5 in chapter 2, above): the surrounding countryside provides more employment opportunities than settled-out Mexicanos find in Arbordale, although Arbordale is where they choose to live.

Despite more than four decades of a Mexicano presence in Arbordale, there is no mention of Mexicanos in the local "official" histories. This appears to be a purposeful omission when one considers

Table 17 Arbordale Employment Profile

YEAR	PERCENT COMPLETING HIGH SCHOOL OR HIGHER	MEAN TRAVEL TIME TO WORK (MINUTES)	PERCENT OVER 16 IN LABOR FORCE	PERCENT EMPLOYED IN AGRI- CULTURE	PERCENT EMPLOYED IN PROFES- SIONAL SERVICES	PERCENT EMPLOYED IN MANU- FACTURING
1980	41.5	15.1	76.2	12.0	18.7	29.2
1990	63.5	15.1	64.2	17.5	14.9	24.9
2000	64.4	20.8	62.7	7.5[a]	27.4[a]	25.9[a]

Sources: Bureau of the Census 1980a, 1990a, 2002.

[a] Due to major revisions in the 2000 census classification of jobs by industry, these data are not exactly comparable with the 1980 and 1990 data.

that a revised 1985 county history, published after the 1980 census, reported almost one-fifth of the population to be Hispanic. Similarly, Mexicanos rarely appear in the local newspaper (Godina 1998).

COMMUNITY CHANGE

Mexicano Newcomers

Mexican nationals fueled a rapid Mexicano growth in Arbordale during the 1990s (table 16). Their numbers account for an 11% increase in the town population. From one-quarter of the town population in 1990, the proportion of Mexicanos increased to 35% by 2000 as a result of immigration. There were 58 Hispanic (the census term) households in 1990 (Bureau of the Census 1990a). A long-term-resident Mexicano male assisted with a windshield survey in 1995, which counted 92 Mexicano households. Extrapolating from the 1990 census rate of 4.8 persons per household, the 92 households would yield about 440 Mexicanos. Thus, steady growth occurred throughout the decade. Arbordale's increase in Mexicanos during 1980–2000 seems to follow a rural midwestern diversity trend, except that elsewhere meatpacking plants typically are the labor magnets (Aponte and Siles 1997). During the 1980s, Mexicanos accounted for half of the midwestern population growth. The bulk of the decade's growth was centered in Illinois (especially Chicago), a state without major meatpacking plants. Arbordale—and Corntown—provides clues to explain the non-Chicago, downstate growth.

A local businessman speculates that Mexicano migrant workers from Texas first came to Arbordale in the 1940s to work in the corn-packing factory that was later destroyed by fire. According to several original families who settled-out, starting in the 1960s they left the farm-labor migrant stream that flowed through Arbordale on the way to the fruit orchards of Michigan. This handful of Mexicano families, originally from Texas, have lived in town for more than thirty years. Mexicanos have not really experienced the town's brotherly love described by the elite Arbordale businessman. Yet Mexicanos say they have bettered their lives by uprooting their families and moving, either as part of the early pre-1970s wave of migrants, primarily from around Laredo and south-central Texas, or as part of the later wave in the 1980s and 1990s from around Guanajuato and other parts of central Mexico. Their migration pattern resembles that of Mexicanos throughout the nation (Hondagneu-Sotelo 1994; Wilson 1994). Arbordale Mexicanos make distinctions among themselves based on the number of generations that have passed since their settlement and on whether they have gained U.S. citizenship. Those who migrated more recently, directly from Mexico, and who have less facility with English, for example, are accorded lower status than those who migrated thirty years ago from Texas and have good facility with English. The Arbordale measures of social inequality between "Texans" and "Mexicans" are documented elsewhere in the United States also as dividing the ethnic-minority population (Zavella 1994).

Because within a twenty-five-mile radius the diverse manufacturing plants and factories offer good jobs, the village remains a magnet for Mexicanos. According to the nursery owner, the nurseries technically have not employed migrants (whom he defines as workers who leave after doing a particular job and then return each year) since the late 1970s. Nonetheless, his nursery business continues to bring in legal Mexican nationals, typically single men who are housed in a dormitory facility. Somehow, some of these Mexicans eventually bring their families to Arbordale and stay.

Families describe settlement via a chain-migration process with kin mediation. "We were migrants . . . and my mother was getting a divorce. We went to Michigan and . . . the following year we went to Indiana. . . . My mother came here to visit my uncle and she really fell in love with the town, so we stayed," explained a twenty-year resident, a mother of three. Settled immigrants from Mexico function as a sort of halfway house to accommodate relatives or friends from their native village who are new "first comers." Long-term families typically speak Spanish at home and English elsewhere, although those who were raised in Arbordale speak English at home. Neither long residence nor Mexicano origins necessarily translate into English fluency and easy assimilation. Several elderly Mexicanos from Texas, despite living many years in Arbordale, speak very little English; a few Mexicanos are unable to read or write.

All but one Mexicano couple interviewed were dual earners. In the past, women worked in the nurseries. Now they are more likely to work in one of several small factories (making coils and thin wire) located in the county seat. One woman, one of three who work as bilingual aides in the school district, explained, "You don't find a lot of men working in factories. Men tend to work outside or at industrial jobs. I've never seen where the husband and wife work in the same place." The only exception, the only place where couples work together, is the packing plant for summer vegetables and corn.

Mexicanos, regardless of when they arrived, report experiencing racism in Arbordale. They all say that Anglo racism moderated with time but that it seems to be exacerbated by the recent Mexican immigrant wave. Commented a woman from a Texas Mexicano family that settled-out in the 1960s: "They accept us now, compared to when we first got here . . . but I think they're also getting to the point now where they're saying 'there's too many of you coming to Arbordale.' . . . A lot of people are putting their houses up for sale . . . because the community's become really big in Spanish people." Mexicanos, however, carefully distinguish between tolerant Arbordale Anglos and intolerant ones. A lifetime resident and bilingual teacher's aide who has wide contact with both ethnic groups explained: "You have your 'yes' and you have your 'no.' There are some that are still not quite used to the Hispanic community, and there are some that have accepted. Like the grocery store. It's run by Anglos. . . . So they would lose a lot of business if [Hispanics] weren't there. . . . So I wouldn't say there's a problem. It's a quiet town and everybody seems to get along. There have been marriages between Anglos and Hispanics. We've learned and they've learned."

Space and Place

In 1990, 75% of Arbordale Hispanics were home owners (Bureau of the Census 1990a). The home owners interviewed had bought homes from Anglos using loans from the previous owner, contract mortgages, or standard bank mortgages. Several have contract mortgages with family members. Mexicano-owned homes are scattered in Arbordale's older, more run-down neighborhoods, which extend out from the main square but are separated from better Anglo homes by the railroad track. Some large, older homes house multigenerational extended families. In their backyards the Mexicanos tend extensive vegetable gardens.

The area on the "wrong side" of the track (from the Anglo perspective) is *Little Mexico*, a term used by both ethnic groups. Little Mexico includes a distinct neighborhood of neatly kept older homes and a nearby densely populated mobile home park. Mobile homes serve as first homes for the newest migrants and as permanent dwellings for the persistently lowest-income, longer-term Mexicano families. Mexicano home owners in the neighborhood are critical of how some trailer-park families maintain their homes. Their fear is that Anglos will think all Mexicanos are negligent.

Through the 1970s, the early Mexicano families made an hour's trip to Corntown to attend a Catholic church with Spanish masses. Children took their first communion and young couples were married in Corntown. But the long trip was hard to sustain on a weekly basis. About fifteen years ago, unhappy without a local church, Arbordale Mexicanos mobilized, collected three thousand dollars, bought a vacant town building, and established Our Lady of Guadalupe Church. Today the only link between the two Mexicano communities is that Corntown musicians occasionally play at Arbordale fiestas or weddings.

Twenty years ago, reports an elderly Mexicano couple, numerous stores on the main square made Arbordale feel more like a community: "People used to walk around uptown and talk and visit with one another. There was a shoe store, a men's clothing store, two grocery stores, and other businesses. . . . It used to be that we would never go to a tavern. But now that's the other place [besides church] where we can go and be together." La Curba, a rural roadhouse tavern with drink and music on the outskirts of town, was bought a few years ago by a Mexicano couple and has become a de facto social center for the ethnic community (Godina 1998). Families rent the bar to celebrate weddings, first communions, Quinceañeras (a girl's fifteenth-birthday fest), or other fiestas (the alternative facility is the Lions Hall, considered too expensive). On those nights entire families come to dance and socialize. On other nights the bar is open to everyone. Several Arbordale families have formed bands that play regularly at La Curba. The tavern is patronized by nursery field hands, meatpacking-plant butchers, and factory workers and their families. Youth are attracted on weekends by the music and dancing, although legally they cannot purchase alcohol. Few Anglos patronize the tavern, and Mexicanos do not go to the bar on the village square.

In exclusive, inward-facing worlds, Mexicanos and Anglos live near one another and cross paths in the public spaces of school and the town square, but they attend church, socialize, and work segregated by space and networks among their own kind.

Interconnectedness

No one describes Arbordale as a tight-knit community. The town functions as a mosaic of small worlds, each homogeneous and internally interconnected; there is little or no social network overlap. According to a middle-aged Anglo woman, who has the perspective of a relative newcomer: "I see the town as a three-department community. One is the Chamber of Commerce, the business people. The next are the family groups, and then the Mexican population. They're all separate. The first group . . . does things for the community. It's always the same people. They don't have outside support from the rest of the community. We have strong churches, too." Even after a decade of residence in Arbordale and civic engagement in the Women's Club, schools, and her church council, she considers herself an "implant" among the Anglos: "I've made every effort to be active and a part of this community, and [Anglos] still see me as an outsider."

Segregation is reinforced among Arbordale's small worlds by class and ethnic differences (Elder and Conger 2000). Anglo elite business families understandably employ only their own. Mexicanos also are highly cohesive and exclusive, according to a Mexicano woman who has lived in the town for twenty-five years: "As far as Hispanics and other people, they don't mix." From her perspective, Mexicanos share the fact "that everybody comes from Mexico. . . . They know how hard it is to live down there, and it's . . . kind of like a bind. . . . Maybe it's the language barrier too, that has a lot to do with it." The Anglo woman "outsider" agrees with her depiction: "In general, I found that if you don't mess with them [Mexicanos], they won't mess with you." Indicative of the Mexicano community's cohesiveness is the uniform complaint about gossip—that nothing is private in Arbordale. "Everybody knows everybody here in town; kind of like a family," said a mother whose Texas Mexicano family settled-out in 1965.

High school adolescent friendships span the ethnic divide, but the community norm is that extended interaction between the groups seldom continues after graduation. An example of how the segregation of social worlds emerges was described by a young Mexicano. He recalls hanging out with Anglos in high school because they were on the football team together. After graduation all contact ended, but the division was evident earlier. "When I was in school, I wanted to work. . . . I applied a couple of places. I'd tell my football buddies [Anglo], hoping we could get hired together and have somebody to talk to. . . . Well, it would usually end up that they'd get hired and I applied first." Over time he associated more with Chicanos (his term) and dropped his old Anglo buddies. "I needed some backup in a fight or . . . two bucks, and [Chicanos] had it. It was mine. They wouldn't even say pay me back. . . . It was more like family. . . . With the Anglos, it was more like 'Well, when are you gonna pay me back?'" He sees cultural differences other than generosity between the ethnic groups: "Another thing I didn't like about [Anglos] is they're always talking stuff about their parents. . . . The guys I hang out with, we respect our parents. We got a lot of respect for them—parents and elders . . . and sisters. They look out for my little

sister, and I look out for theirs. It's like a family. We're real close."
Mexicano youth report getting along best with Anglo farm boys.
One Mexicano commented: "The country boys, the farmers; they're
really nice. They feel like they have to be nice to you. They're more
like scared of you. . . . Usually they hang out by themselves. Once
in a while we'll get invited to road parties and stuff like that. . . .
We just go out there and we party. Usually, country music is all
they listen to." Although they meet Anglo girls at road parties, Mexicano boys do not encourage Mexicano girls to come along to meet
Anglo boys. Ethnicity is thus subtly reinforced, as are gender roles.

An exception to the rigid social boundaries that divide Arbordale
can be seen in the annual Fourth of July festival, the town's biggest
local celebration. Mexicanos operate food stands and enliven the parade with young dancers coached by the Catholic Church paraprofessional. Thus, one day a year Arbordale celebrates its multicul-
turalism and the importance of Mexicanos to its economy and
community vitality.

Social Resources

Longtime Mexicano residents of Arbordale serve as a community
resource to facilitate the adaptation of later arrivals, a familiar immigrant community pattern (Portes and Sensenbrenner 1993). Women
from the longest-settled-out Mexicano families, fluent in both Spanish and English, are school district bilingual aides (at least one with
some community college training). They frequently are asked, by
newly arrived Mexicans with little English, for assistance with interpretation or with filling out forms or for guidance in dealing with
Anglo institutions. "A lot of the kids' parents . . . come to one of us
three. . . . We're like the go-between. . . . They try to offer you
money and you tell them, 'I won't take it. This is a favor. . . . Then
one day you'll be doing me a favor.' We're there if they need anything," commented one school aide. Arbordale Mexicanos, however,
are realistic about the diversity in their ethnic "family." According
to a thirty-year Mexicano resident, a mother of four: "Some of them
will help you out. Some are out for what they can get. Really, you
have a mixture of both."

Elite Anglos have reached out to Mexicanos in key ways, contrib-
uting to the feeling of trust Mexicanos have toward Arbordale. The
major elite employers, for example, are never criticized by Mexicanos. Bridging the ethnic gap has thus generated social capital between Anglos and Mexicanos. One businessman, although defensive
about recruiting Mexicanos to Arbordale, reflects respect in his char-

acterization of them as a group: "They have a work ethic. The Mexicans come to work every day and they're on time. They're not taking jobs away from anybody. It's not because they're getting paid less than anybody else. . . . It's because they want to work. In this town, unemployment is low, but among the Mexicans it's very low because they want to work." He has promoted Mexicanos to foreman positions when they have proved competent. Clearly he knows his long-term workers personally: "You've got to realize that the Hispanics are family-oriented people. They don't like to have cousin away from cousin and mother away from children. So, they came for work here, but then they brought their families. . . . You won't find many on welfare. Maybe they have some tough times and they might take food stamps or something, but they're a working-class people. The sooner they get off the food stamps or welfare, the better they feel about it."

A young married Mexicano woman who had moved many times received Anglo help with buying a home. An elite businessman helped to stabilize her life by referring her to someone who had an Arbordale home for sale. "The guy who owned it . . . loaned us the down payment. It was $5,000 and let us move in. If it hadn't been for the owner loaning us the money, we wouldn't have gotten the house." Perhaps it was difficult for the Anglo to sell his home after he retired, but his Mexicano buyer has never forgotten this crucial assistance.

Our Lady of Guadalupe Church, which resulted from Mexicano mobilization, is in a yoked parish that includes a church in a nearby, mainly Anglo, town. The relatively new priest prefers working with the sister Anglo church. The diocese, however, has placed a Mexicano woman in the Arbordale church as a full-time community organizer. Working actively to establish more educational and cultural activities for parish members, she has organized premarriage and communion classes and fiestas such as Dia de la Independencia (Independence Day on September 16), La Virgen Guadalupe (December 12), and Los Posadas at Christmas. Mexicano families applaud her efforts to preserve their cultural identity by working with youth, in particular. Consistently, Catholic Church membership was cited as the single community engagement of Arbordale Mexicanos. Church membership is a way that community identification can be redefined for Arbordale Mexicanos. Catholicism allows them to live peacefully among Anglos while simultaneously celebrating their ethnic heritage and sense of community and place (Hondagneu-Sotelo 1994).

It appears that some Mexicanos were community activists in the

1970s and attended village board meetings. But those activists have either left town or lost interest. Mexicanos' trust in the community leaders explains the lack of Mexicano involvement, according to a woman from an original Mexicano family: "They're all trying to make Arbordale stay a peaceful community. I think they're all working at it, not just one family. . . . Everybody's trying to pitch in to keep it as it is." She feels that Mexicanos are not aroused by political concerns but that, furthermore, they may be wary of attracting attention: "Maybe getting involved might create some kind of problem. I guess we feel comfortable the way it is. . . . If anything needs to be decided, we leave it to the town. . . . Like for instance, whenever they have a referendum, there's not many Hispanics who vote. So it would be the decision of the . . . Anglos what's gonna be done. I don't think there are a lot of Hispanics that can vote." None of the Mexicano families interviewed, for example, are engaged enough to subscribe to the local weekly newspaper, although most of them say they frequently purchase it. A middle-aged Mexicano father of three who is happy with the status quo explained: "Oh, we'll be here forever. It's a good place to raise kids. There's no fighting or nothing. No gang members or nothing. . . . It's not the best to get a job, but it's good to raise kids."

Thus, Arbordale Mexicanos are more passive as community members than Corntown Mexicanos are. Arbordale Mexicanos tend to concentrate on internal ethnic-community issues, such as the church or the festivals, rather than on obligations to the wider community. Of course, Corntown is a town run by a blue-collar electorate, whereas Arbordale is run by a small group of people who control the economic structure. The size of the Mexicano population in relation to the Anglo population may also be a factor. The actual numbers of Mexicanos in the two towns are similar; but because Arbordale is smaller, the Mexicanos are proportionately a larger group, and they may sense that their presence is threatening to Anglos (Lieberson 1980).

Arbordale and three neighboring towns had consolidated their school districts several years before the study. Mexicano experiences in the combined schools contrast with their acceptance in Arbordale. The entire school district staff is Anglo, with the exception of the three bilingual aides. Arbordale Mexicanos thus for the first time encountered staff and students who were unfamiliar with them. An eighteen-year-old Mexicano high school graduate and Arbordale native remembers that just after the consolidation it was common to hear students from the other schools say: "'Watch out for the Mexicans 'cause they all carry knives, and they'll stab you.' I thought it was kind of funny." Enhancing this negative image, to the dismay of the Mexicano community, five adolescent Mexicano girls became pregnant in 1993. A fifteen-year-old girl explained: "Everybody was like wow. They were shocked. . . . They all would say 'yeah, you're gonna get pregnant,' but they never got pregnant until all of a sudden they did." None of these girls cared about school, she felt: "They did good in school, but they didn't like it. Another reason that I stopped hanging out with them was because I was scared that I was going to get pregnant. I don't want to have kids yet. I see what my mom went through." The boyfriends of the pregnant girls, it was rumored, were not from Arbordale.

The Mexicanos share the small-town ideology of Arbordale Anglos: they see danger as coming from outside rather than being locally generated (Hummon 1990). According to a Mexicano woman, this ideology accounts for Arbordale Anglos' suspicions: "They're warm and friendly with [local] Hispanics. . . . The ones they're leery about are the ones who come from Chicago . . . because they're afraid they'll bring the gangs down here." Outsiders from Chicago and Kankakee, as well as recent, and therefore outsider, Mexican migrants, were associated with a couple of vicious fights that broke out at La Curba in 1995. Relatives of the victims initiated a petition signed by thirty Mexicano and Anglo Arbordale residents to demand that the village board regulate the tavern. Arbordale's village attorney drafted two amendments to the liquor license that suspended or revoked the license if too many fights occurred in a given period of time and prohibited persons under twenty-one from being in the bar after 10 P.M. (Godina 1998). When motivated, the Mexicano community could mobilize and act in its best interests and gain Anglo cooperation.

Arbordale Mexicanos recognize the Catholic Church as the lone institution connecting them as an ethnic community. "The church in Arbordale has to do a lot of activities to raise money just to keep the church going here. The priest doesn't do much," explained a woman from an original Texas Mexicano family. The possibility that they might lose their church, compounded by their priest's lack of sympathy for them, keeps Mexicanos galvanized for action—both Texans and Mexicans. Their food booths at the Fourth of July celebration and other ethnic festivals such as the Cinqo de Mayo celebration are used to generate funds to support the church; indirectly, they also generate a sense of community in a diverse group of Mexicanos. Having the church paraprofessional initiate activities that encourage ethnic pride, support of needy families, and church participation creates community social capital that is available as a resource for these families.

The nurseries have recently adopted newly developed mechanized techniques to replace much of the seasonal field labor that they formerly needed. As a consequence, young Mexicanos, such as one dropout from the community college, have difficulty finding jobs locally. Times have changed, he argues, since his parents arrived with little education but were still able to better themselves. "It was simpler back then. Back then, if you were a hard worker, a good worker, you could make it. Now, it don't matter if you work hard or not, unless you got that piece of paper saying you got so many college hours and all that crap. That's the only way you're gonna make it." His experience is typical for second- and third-generation Mexicanos, whose limited access to what seem to be declining community economic resources may alter the tolerance shown by Anglos and the cooperation among Mexicanos.

Cross-Age Relations

Arbordale authority figures—and indeed, those in the neighboring town—show a great deal of tolerance for their adolescents (Schwartz 1987). To village authorities, Arbordale Mexicano youth are "our kids," just as Anglo youth are. Familiarity is the key. Every Mexicano adolescent interviewed described freely cruising Arbordale's main street or the square of the sister town. A Mexicano mother recalled that as a youth she, like her own adolescents, drove around, parked at the school or the church, turned on the radio, and talked. An 8 P.M. town curfew is imposed, and after that time the cruisers are no longer permitted to honk horns or play loud music. "You know the old people go to bed early and they don't want to be bothered," said the mother. It is evident that the curfew is a community compromise that allows youth ample latitude without violating the rights of older citizens.

During autumn, one of the Arbordale homecoming-week traditions is for high school students to "egg" each another. "They're throwin' out eggs and tomatoes. They've been cruising every night this week," said the Mexicano mother of a daughter who was participating in the activities. Arbordale and the sister town apparently have tried to crack down on the egging of cars and people by instituting a seventy-five-dollar fine for each egg found in a car. One fifteen-year-old girl described her experience with a local policeman the first year she went egging: "We got stopped . . . but he didn't search the

car. He just asked [whether they had eggs]. We said no, and he believed us." Clearly, the policeman knew they had eggs and used the
stop to scare them into civility. But by not enforcing the town ordinance, which is too punitive for a minor crime, the policeman showed
his tolerance of youth (Schwartz 1987). The mayor of the sister town
even gave a Mexicano friend six or seven dozen eggs. His daughter
explained: "They [the police] didn't cause a problem because they
know it's homecoming week. But some of the kids were getting carried away and egging old peoples' homes, which isn't necessary. Instead of . . . hauling them off to jail, they just took the eggs away.
. . . So [the mayor] was giving away the eggs they had confiscated."
Tolerance permeates ethnic interactions in this situation.

The police chief, who lives in Arbordale and knows Mexicano
youth and their families, has the reputation of being the most tolerant officer. "We never lied to [the police]. If they ask if we'd been
drinking, we'd say yeah. Like the police chief, he would just tell us
to empty out the rest. Then he would follow us home and that would
be it." The local police do not all show tolerance, however. According
to an eighteen-year-old Mexicano boy, "It seems that the new
cops that come into town—they pull you over just because you're
Mexican." But the youth know that Arbordale is relatively tolerant because of their bad experiences in neighboring towns
where the police are unfamiliar with Mexicanos. A sixteen-year-old
girl said, "Bunkerton, like, if you go over there and you walk around
town . . . it's like 'whoa, what are these people doing here?'" The
social capital generated by tolerance makes most Mexicano youth
say that although they want to leave, returning when they have a
family is an option, for Arbordale is a good place to raise children.
They have developed a place attachment to the community (Chawla
1992).

Adolescents in particular evoke a Mexicano (and at times Anglo)
community watchfulness that applies to all children (Freudenberg
1986). One young man recalled: "I used to drink a lot and I used to
get kinda rowdy. Pick fights and stuff like that. It's a small town.
Word gets around too quick. By the time I'd get home in the morning, my parents would already know what I was up to the night
before." Similarly, a middle school girl explained why she liked her
small town: "If you just went into the grocery store and stole a candy
bar . . . you're just so horrible and everything. . . . In Chicago, you
can do it and it's just you and the cop, or whoever finds you . . . but
now the reason I like living in Arbordale, I'm not into too much

trouble." Thus, there are Anglo police officers in Arbordale who are as watchful toward youth as are Mexicanos.

Another tolerant authority figure is the librarian at the Carnegie library. Mexicano youth frequent the library to work on school assignments but also to socialize with friends and relax. Youth feel particularly comfortable in the library because the librarian makes a special effort to buy books in Spanish and on culturally relevant topics, such as the pop singer Selena. An Anglo school-bus driver organized male Mexicano and Anglo high school students (almost equal numbers of each) into a city-league soccer team. Two older Anglo males were coaches. The Mexicano community turned out when the team played in Arbordale. In 1996 they won the Midwest Conference trophy, an event that resulted in one of only two photographs of Mexicano youth featured in the local newspaper during the year (Godina 1998). Unfortunately, Mexican surnames tended to be misspelled in the articles about the games. Most unfortunate was that the team was not officially recognized by the high school. The principal claimed that if he formalized soccer, some Mexicanos would be ineligible to play under a rule that student athletes must have passing grades in all classes.

Two members of original Mexicano families who were interviewed are graduates of the University of Illinois. A handful have completed some coursework at the nearest community college. Their success reflects parental goals. A twenty-year-old Mexicano man recalled his mother's saying about him and his siblings: "For her, we are like a piece of gold. . . . Because we are getting an education . . . and that it's going to be better for us, getting a better education." One university graduate, from a long-settled Arbordale Mexicano family, says her mother stressed education. She remembers, however, being discouraged by the guidance counselor from applying to a university. Most of the successful high school experiences of Mexicanos took place before the school district consolidated. These days, owing to attrition, the number of Mexicano high school students becomes progressively smaller as they move from the freshman to the senior year (Godina 1998).

Middle school experiences seem to be better than high school ones, in a reversal of the Corntown situation. A fourteen-year-old who is active in sports considers that at her middle school "they pretty well treat me equally." Like many youth, she finds that some teachers are more sympathetic than others, but, like most of the students at that school, she described the female middle school principal as "pretty nice." In contrast, almost without exception, Mexicano youth and parents voiced criticism of the high school principal. Said a young woman, now a university student, "He wasn't very good. I mean [he makes] you feel like a smart aleck. . . . As you come in, they have this picture of what you're gonna be like, and automatically you're like that to them. . . . [Mexicanos] get in trouble a lot more than the Anglo kids do." The tolerance shown Mexicano youth by village authorities such as the police chief, the mayor, and the librarian is not duplicated by the consolidated school district, according to almost every Mexicano family interviewed.

School authorities make a great deal of difference in how minority students perform, whether they drop out or whether the learning attitude is developed, as seen in Corntown (Schwartz 1987). The current high school principal explained his philosophy regarding Mexicano youth: "Kids are kids. I don't notice if they're Hispanic or whatever." His assessment of his minority students was that "most of the Hispanic kids don't go to college, but most of them graduate [from high school]. Those who don't graduate get their GEDs." He saw a pattern for those dropping out at age sixteen: "A lot of them go to work. . . . That's why they were brought here. . . . that's the family tradition. . . . that's a real tough nut to crack . . . as a school" (Godina 1998, 59). By implication, according to the principal, Mexicanos differ from Anglo students with regard to their educational goals.

Adolescents, even from completely bilingual families, feel that the high school resists tracking them into the programs that foster social mobility through higher education. Mexicano students are considered low achievers and are enrolled in low-track, general education classes more often than Anglo students are (Godina 1998). A graduate of the high school recalls another rule, which devalued their language: "One thing that caused a lot of problems was that people would get in trouble for speaking Spanish in school. Everybody thought that was unfair. If you were in a classroom and speaking Spanish . . . they'd send you to the office." An unsympathetic high school principal and policies that ignore cultural differences while emphasizing language differences cause some Mexicano youth to drop out—first mentally and then physically (Godina 1998).

Mexicano students' perseverance in the Arbordale consolidated high school can be related to pressure applied by parents who regard school as a priority or to resilience in the face of racism (Elder and Conger 2000). Adolescent males, in particular, feel that differential treatment is accorded Mexicanos by high school staff. A young male graduate recalls:

I thought they were more favored, the whites, I should say the
Anglo Saxons. . . . They'd believe them before they'd believe
me, you know . . . Cause you got certain last names that are
very popular [those of the elite families]. The parents own businesses and all that kind of stuff.

I got a lot of cousins . . . messing around in grade school. By
the time you got to middle school, the teacher's already saying,
"Ah, these kids, they're troublemakers," categorize 'em. Same
way through high school. They categorize.

According to another recent Mexicano high school graduate, the
authorities hold grudges: "Here if you say something smart to the
principal, he'd hold it against you until the next time you got in
trouble." He recalled how the principal kept a book to record every
time he was sent to the office. "Kind of like a school criminal record."
As this young man described it, the sports coaches were aligned with
the principal. "I was in football in my freshman and sophomore
years, but that was it. The coaches are the same way. They would
pick their favorites and after that, nobody else gets a chance. . . .
They wouldn't cut anybody from the team, but if you were picked
not to play, you wouldn't play." Not surprisingly, the high school
principal remarked that according to their percentage in the student
body (12% to 15% of 280 students), Mexicanos were proportionately uninvolved in school activities. In 1996 no Mexicano students,
male or female, played on any team (Godina 1998). Although several
girls are on the pom pom squad, for example, none are members of
the student council. By and large, Mexicano students do not participate in school activities that are the source of high status (Godina
1998). Mexicano youth say it is difficult to get their parents to attend
school activities. Dual-earner parents say their limited time (and
sometimes language) precludes their involvement in the schools.

Different characteristics of Mexicano families shape the educational aspirations of their youth. The bilingual school aides, voicing
class as well as ethnic biases, attribute lack of school success to contrasting socialization about the importance of education for success
by the established Texan versus the newer Mexican families. A university student thinks Mexicano parents stress education but not
higher education. "They emphasize graduation [from high school],
a lot of them do, but get a job after that. If [students] are not being
encouraged by educators, or their families, it makes it kind of hard."
There are committed students, however, among both the Texans and
the Mexicans, although pressure is exerted by their peers (especially

recent Mexican immigrants) not to work hard in school, youth say. A college student recalled: "In high school, a lot of my Hispanic friends, they'd be, like, 'wannabe white girl' because I would study. I'd try to be better in school and to them it was, like, 'oh whatever.'" That is, a focus on education was equated by some with being a "coconut"—brown on the outside but white at the core. As a consequence, explained a mother of three from a well-established family, "The girls are more into school than the boys. . . . I liked school, but then this is a different generation and they just don't like school." Gender differences also are reinforced by church programs aimed at gaining the participation of girls more than that of boys. Thus, girls have access to more community resources.

Although more education is needed to improve one's life chances, key Arbordale authority figures are not promoting educational achievement among Mexicano youth to the extent that similar figures in Corntown are doing so. School experiences influence whether Mexicano youth gain the resilience and persistence required to attain even the level of success achieved by their parents. The children of Arbordale's elite Anglo business families, however, are perceived as reproducing their privileged position with little effort. Mexicanos apparently feel stereotyped by the high school as poor prospects for higher education (Godina 1998). Thus, the school system subtly fosters reproduction of the community hierarchical social system, which can be overcome only by heroic strategies on the part of Mexicanos.

REFLECTIONS

Despite being located an hour's drive away from Central City, Arbordale has maintained population stability and high employment by being a magnet for Mexicano migrants (Gruidl and Walzer 1990). Agricultural work ceaselessly attracts Mexicanos, who have come first from Texas and later from Mexico, especially those whose small-town place identity makes them leery of city life. However, only a small number of Mexicano families from those who settled-out twenty-five to thirty years ago have moved into managerial or professional positions equivalent to those of Arbordale Anglos. Class differences, now drawn along ethnic lines, reinforce a division instituted in the past between the business elite families and the rest of Arbordale.

Long-established Mexicano families paved the way for later settlers in Arbordale. The first wave of settled-out Mexicano migrants came as families, bought homes, emphasized education to their children, and worked hard to better their lives. Village business leaders and authority figures, observing their drive and commitment, gradually awarded them tolerance and respect. A recent wave of Mexican families accounts for an almost 50% increase in the minority population (table 16). As the Mexicano proportion of the town population rose rapidly to about one-third, community dynamics were altered. Increased community resentment, even among established Mexicanos, focuses on the Mexican newcomers who neither are citizens nor speak English well. Mexicanos are now more visible on town streets, adolescent pregnancies among Mexicano females have increased, and a local minority-owned bar attracts troublesome behaviors and outsiders. These visible changes are negatively reinforced by clear class differences associated with the newcomer minorities— Mexicans and the African-Americans who have been sent to the school for troubled youth. Together, these conditions arouse local emotions against Mexicanos. As one Anglo woman commented, there is concern about teen gangs "coming into our community."

Rural Illinois is nervous about teenage gangs. Small towns, although racially homogeneous, seem to fear that gangs can spontaneously generate as do the corn and soybeans every spring. In 1993 Harvard, Illinois, a town of 6,500, sixty miles north of Chicago, passed ordinances that allowed the police to arrest teenagers wearing clothing assumed symbolic of gangs, such as a Chicago Bulls jacket, a University of Michigan baseball cap, or a rolled-up left pant leg (Terry 1995). Youthful gangs give a focus to latent community racism. In Arbordale the school district invited outside police officers with the DARE program to come and combat an imagined gang problem. The problem was evidenced by a single gang graffito on a high school wall. "According to the police . . . the first sign of gang activity is graffiti. And we do have it in town. Nobody knows what the graffiti means; it just looks like art or people's initials, but the signs are there for the gangs," was a comment by a middle-aged Anglo woman at the 1994 special meeting where DARE representatives spoke.

The meeting was attended by one hundred Anglos, who complained about the "outsiders" (a code word for Mexicanos) invading their community. Only two Mexicanos attended, and they remained silent. Arbordale Mexicanos see their youth, gathering in the park near Little Mexico, as exhibiting dress and style that make them "wannabe" gang members, rather than actual ones (Monti 1994). But even wannabes seem like the real thing to Anglos feeling threatened by a growing minority in their midst. In contrast to this alarmist response by the school district, Arbordale police still treat Mexicano youth with tolerance. Arbordale confirms the theory that the greater the size of a minority population relative to the majority (32% at the time of our study), the greater the threat that the majority feels (Lieberson 1980). One casualty of the Arbordale overreaction to one gang graffito is community trust on the part of upstanding minority citizens.

Corntown, where Mexicanos constituted only 5% of the town when studied, has absorbed the minority group more readily. Corntown minority youth, moreover, have benefited from having sympathetic Anglos in key positions who are allies with the Mexicano parents in structuring an empowering environment for youth (Elder and Conger 2000). When the Corntown principal dealt with a scuffle at his high school, he downplayed the event as a sign of gang presence and thereby de-emotionalized the issue. He commented: "It wasn't really a gang. . . . I really don't think that a gang could gain a foothold in a town like Corntown. There is nothing here for them. The whole incident was blown out of proportion. . . . The parents were as upset about it as we were." The Corntown principal, a key cultural broker sympathetic to Mexicano families, also worked behind the scenes to allay suspicions among his staff (Williams 1996).

If Arbordale's Mexicano youth are disillusioned by finding that the pathway to a better life than that achieved by their parents is blocked, it is possible that gangs might become established in this small town. Disillusionment has occurred elsewhere in rural America among similarly discouraged Mexicano youth (Finnegan 1996). Essentially, Mexicanos born in Arbordale are small-town youth who cherish being known by all and who care about their parents' feelings. Several key figures in authority, especially the police chief, the librarian, and the business families, have been tolerant and accepting of them. Local jobs, it seems, are a critical intervening variable between actual gang behavior and producing Mexicanos who value work, marry, settle down with a family, and lead productive lives. The historical U.S. patterns of steady immigrant progress economically and socially may not apply to these recent rural arrivals, or indeed even second- and third-generation small-town Mexicanos. It is possible that these groups may be trapped into living lives of class status even lower than that of their parents, because they are a rural minority. The rigid actions of the Arbordale high school in tracking minority students and assuming that they will drop out seem destined to maintain the Arbordale class structure of elite Anglo families supported by Mexicano menial labor.

8 A SHABBY, DYING TOWN: SPLITVILLE

In collaboration with Jane B. Tornatore

Splitville is bisected by a state highway running from north to south. Each side of the village, west and east of the road, has a mixture of rundown and well-tended homes (fig. 7). A home in Splitville is typically a small clapboard box, white-sided or painted white, with little design distinctiveness. Although some homes are kept neat and repaired, no single building looks as if its owner is affluent. Most residents park their cars in the street in front of their homes or in their driveways, because few homes have garages. Behind the houses run alleyways—evidence of village planning by the founders to hide trash and other unattractive objects. The lawns are mowed, but decoration in the form of trees, bushes, or flowers is absent. About one in five homes is badly in need of repair and paint. Porches are falling down, walls are sagging, and roofs are missing shingles. The yards around the shabby homes are littered with a clutter of toys, bicycles, cars, or car parts. The largest cluster of such homes lines the highway, termed "Welfare Road" by some residents.

Nestled among the homes along the village streets are a shuttered school and a church with a For Sale sign on the front lawn. The other church in town shows signs of activity. East of the state road stands a block of connected buildings that constitutes the Splitville business district. The buildings are modest, plain, one-story structures. One holds a café that is open six hours each day (started by the Lions Club in the 1960s), another the post office, and another a bank. Some buildings stand empty. At one end of the main street rises a grain elevator, and at the other end there is a small park with a slide and some swings. Built and maintained by the local Lions Club, the park often stands vacant, even during the summer when children are out of school (Tornatore 1993). Oldtimers still mourn the closing twenty

Figure 7 Splitville town map

years ago of the local tavern, which served as a village meeting place where farmers could visit and play cards. A village hall where community dances were held was demolished years ago and never replaced (a Splitville history, 1988).

Originally a railroad town, Splitville was founded as an agricultural trade center by a wealthy family with extensive land holdings who until recently still controlled the local bank. Oldtimers and newcomers alike claim that the bank's lending policy irreparably damaged the village. Credit other than for farm loans, according to a farmer, was always difficult to obtain: "The bank wasn't thinking of the future. They wouldn't lend the money; they were tight fisted." A newcomer who has his own business blames the bank's commercial lending policies for strangling village growth: "There'd be five or six businesses here if the bank would've helped. . . . They just sat on all that money." The same family also owns the city water system, decried by all for its poor quality. In addition the family owns many village businesses, using its holdings mainly for wealth extraction. For example, one land tract on the main street is leased to a man

Table 18 Splitville Demographic Profile

YEAR	POPU-LATION	MEDIAN AGE	PERCENT RESIDING IN SAME HOUSE AS 5 YEARS BEFORE	MEDIAN VALUE OF OWNED HOMES ($)	MEDIAN HOUSEHOLD INCOME ($)	PERCENT BELOW POVERTY LEVEL	PERCENT FEMALE-HEADED HOUSE-HOLDS[a]
1980	207	32.2	71.8	19,500	15,625	21.6	3.8
1990	180	35.9	69.1	27,500	22,083	10.5	7.1
2000	150	32.8	75.3	37,500	31,875	15.2	9.8

Sources: Bureau of the Census 1980a, 1990a, 2001, 2002.
[a] With own children under 18.

who operates an auto repair shop. The lot is an eyesore, but the tenant rather than the landlord is blamed by residents for the situation.

Splitville's population declined after 1930, when the village peaked at about 300. By 2000 only 150 people called the village home (table 18) (Bureau of the Census 1950). Between 1960 and 2000, about half the population left. A janitor enumerated forty-one former farmsteads, existing when he arrived in 1954, that now are cultivated as open fields because of farm concentration. The decline of the farm population meant that fewer people came to Splitville for shopping. From an apex of several grocery stores, a meat market, a garage, a pool hall, a restaurant, a hardware store, an elevator, and a bank, main-street businesses began to dwindle after 1930. Local business was drawn off by Central City, only a twenty-minute drive away by good roads. One farmer thinks the shift in shopping patterns shows a lack of loyalty: "They lost the stores because people didn't support the businesses." Both newcomers and oldtimers bemoan the recent closing of the gas station owing to lack of customers and repeated vandalism. The Splitville school district was merged with two nearby school districts in the 1950s. The remaining elementary school, still used by the consolidated district, finally closed in 1990, causing a mother of school-aged children to complain, "It's gonna contribute a lot to the death of Splitville."

Splitville at one time benefited economically from a nearby coal mine. About twenty years ago, the coal mine shut down because the high-sulfur coal it contained was no longer marketable. With the closing a local source of well-paid blue-collar jobs disappeared. A well-educated male newcomer commented on the impact: "The closing of the coal mine was a disaster to the whole area." What few agricultural jobs are available locally are seasonal ones such as corn detassling or canning, which provide workers no benefits. Lamenting the lack of local work opportunities, an unemployed newcomer said,

"If you're goin' to do anything, even detassel [corn], you have to leave town." The loss of most of the businesses, the mine, and much of the population destroyed Splitville's economic base. Without an economic base, a village is subject to forces that cause growth or decline different from those in effect when productive or distributive capacities exist (McKenzie 1967).

Its physical attributes shaped the town's transformation process. Splitville lacks the geographical or architectural features that attract affluent families to a place. The village site is flat, with few trees, and therefore offers little charm of location. Nor is there the ambience of vintage houses with intrinsic beauty. Although the village has a city water system and municipal gas, it lacks a sewage system. Each house has an individual septic system, and some are so old that not even toilet paper can be deposited in them. A retired man commented, "There is no incentive for working people or better-class people to come here." Prairieview, equidistant from Central City but with locational ambience and convenience, grew by 50% each decade between 1980 and 2000 as affluent newcomers arrived, while Splitville's population continued to decline (tables 8 and 18).

People in Splitville think that others regard their village as marginal, located as it is on the county line. Furthermore, they say that because the village is defined as peripheral, the county neglects it: "We pay our taxes but can't get our roads plowed or the sheriff to come to town. We feel forgotten. I have no hope that things will ever get better," explained a middle-aged mother who is active on the school board. One problem is a lack of police protection, according to a farmer. "The undesirable people move out here because they will not be bothered by the police. . . . Those people don't want any trouble. What else would bring them here?" A couple who consider Splitville a peaceful place to live agree that the "criminal types" are being ignored by county officials: "You can live in Splitville and nobody knows you exist." One newcomer confirmed moving to Splitville to get away from the police: "They all got to know me up there [in Central City]," he said.

A mail carrier and his wife, three-decade village residents, raised eight children in Splitville; they are all college graduates, but none live in Splitville now. The parents have consistently been civically engaged: "You have to like joining the fire department, and the Lions and working at fish fries. You have to get involved." He thinks poor people were always a presence in town and that "every town has its town drunk." What caused the Splitville decline, he thinks, is a lack of jobs locally, especially for the poor. "You used to be able to get jobs near town, but now you need to go on aid. . . . It's heartbreaking to see a small town go downhill."

COMMUNITY CHANGE

Working-Poor Newcomers

The influx of low-income newcomers is strongly related to a real estate entrepreneur's purchase of village homes and lots that had been seized by the county for back taxes. Established residents blame the absentee landlord, who "rents to poor people," for the newcomers who are "ruining the community." Although several of her four village properties are among those in worst repair, the entrepreneur makes no improvements. She rents homes for only $100 to $150 per month, with an option to purchase by contract. (The median rent for village housing is $175 per month, according to the 1990 census.) Low-income families can buy her properties because a contract sale requires no down payment. Additional resentment toward this absentee landlord developed when the village board offered to purchase her properties with the intent of tearing them down and she set too high a price. Her "village busting" has transformed the village by attracting lower-income newcomers. An elderly woman explained, "It used to be that townspeople had money and the farmers did not. Now, the farmers have money and the townspeople don't. We don't have any rich people in town."

When newcomers began to trickle in during the 1970s, Splitville became more stratified. Categorization of village residents into the two factions that emerged was made inductively between the newcomers and the Old Guard (the newcomers' term for oldtimers). The oldtimers' criteria for an upstanding resident were used to categorize households, because this group firmly rules the village (Tornatore 1993). Although neither faction explicitly uses the word *class*, each group's designations of the other imply stratification. The oldtimers ($n = 30$) differentiate themselves socially from newcomers ($n = 25$), whom the oldtimers label as "those on welfare." Newcomers call themselves poor and feel that they are treated as "white trash" by the "rich" oldtimers, who, except for the single wealthy family, are not affluent. Seventeen oldtimer households whom the researcher interviewed had lived in Splitville since before 1960, or more than thirty years. Another thirteen households interviewed were relative newcomers who maintained their property according to oldtimer standards (outlined below). When the village factional conflict developed, this group acted as unaligned bystanders (Kantor and Lehr

1985). By remaining silent witnesses and keeping up their property, such uninvolved newcomers tacitly support those in power and were therefore counted as oldtimers.

The oldtimers and the newcomers do not differ significantly in their levels of education or income or in their occupations. Seventy-three percent of the oldtimers and 72% of the newcomers attended or graduated from high school (Tornatore 1993). The oldtimers, however, whose ages were between 56 and 65 years, are significantly older than the newcomers, who range in age from 36 to 45 years. The oldtimers tend to be lifelong village residents. Though more old-timers are home owners, both they and the newcomers have high levels of home ownership—97% and 80%, respectively. Two-thirds of the sample have household incomes of less than $20,000. Sixty percent of the oldtimers and 76% of the newcomers earn less than $20,000 a year. Their incomes of less than 1.5 times the official 1990 poverty level (which for a family of four at the time of the study was $12,675 and for near poverty was $19,012) situate them among the working-poor (Tickamyer 1992; Bureau of the Census 1990b). The reasons for the two factions' working-poor status are different, however. For the oldtimers as a group, low income is linked with advanced age (the group includes eight elderly widows) or retirement. Three-quarters of the newcomers live near poverty level despite being in dual-earner families. The newcomers typify rural poor families nationally: they are white home owners who are employed and who live as two-parent families (Levitan and Shapiro 1987; Duncan 1992).

Village retirees often are connected to agriculture as retired farmers or former tenant farmers or hired hands (Tornatore 1993). If not involved in agriculture, the oldtimers hold blue-collar jobs such as janitor or railroad worker (59%). Compared to the oldtimers, the newcomers as a group are younger, have lived in the village a relatively short time, and are more likely to be renters; most of them are unskilled workers (table 19) (Salamon and Tornatore 1994).

The newcomers are not urbanites seeking cheap rural housing; most were born in rural places. They say they prefer small towns because small towns' advantages—low-cost housing, a safe environment, and white neighbors—together help them to stabilize their lives. Of Splitville's twenty-five newcomer households, only three are highly transient urban transplants, "run out" of other places—the profile assumed by the oldtimers. An arrival account for several newcomer households was echoed by various oldtimers. In one case, the mayor of a nearby vibrant community decided to sell a property

Table 19 Splitville Employment Profile

YEAR	PERCENT COMPLETING HIGH SCHOOL OR HIGHER	MEAN TRAVEL TIME TO WORK (MINUTES)	PERCENT OVER 16 IN LABOR FORCE	PERCENT EMPLOYED IN AGRI-CULTURE	PERCENT EMPLOYED IN PROFES-SIONAL SERVICES	PERCENT EMPLOYED IN MANU-FACTURING
1980	41.5	31.8	42.7	10.5	19.7	10.5
1990	54.4	29.1	57.7	2.7	16.0	11.0
2000	69.9	33.0	63.2	4.5[a]	16.4[a]	10.4[a]

Sources: Bureau of the Census 1980a, 1990a, 2002.

[a] Due to major revisions in the 2000 census classification of jobs by industry, these data are not exactly comparable with the 1980 and 1990 data.

that housed such a family. He offered to help them buy a home in Splitville. Thus, the first "welfare family" was "kicked out" of this mayor's community, according to the oldtimers. Newcomers who rent several other deteriorated properties were similarly described as having been "kicked out" of other towns in the same county.

Prior to their move to Splitville, most newcomer families moved often (mean 5.7 times) from one rural town to another. Owning even a rundown Splitville home thus improved the position of the previously mobile newcomers. Not all are on welfare, as assumed by the oldtimers. Only three (12%) of the twenty-five newcomer households are self-identified as on welfare, and one receives Social Security; a single family has produced a second generation of welfare recipients. Eight (32%) newcomer households have one or two members working at blue-collar factory jobs, as unskilled laborers, or as self-employed craftsmen. Eleven newcomers (44%), with incomes at or below the poverty line, can be classified as persistently working-poor; six of them work in the informal economy only—unreported and outside the formal labor force (Tornatore 1993). Their irregular work patterns are scorned by an oldtimer man: "It breaks you down when you go to work and they're sittin' on their porch with a can of beer and wave as you go by." Four additional households (three headed by a female and one by a male) are sustained by support from members of oldtimer families, as subsidized residents. A divorced, mentally unstable, or unemployed sibling or child can be installed in a grandmother's home after her death, at little cost to kin. Subsidized relatives tend to be lumped as a group with the undesirable newcomers by the oldtimers.

Apart from being poorer than the oldtimers, newcomers regard themselves as kinder and more tolerant and see possessions as irrelevant to being a good person. A young woman reported that two of the newcomer families "have been very good to me since I moved in six weeks ago." Indeed, the researcher found as she carried out her interviews that newcomers (and farmers), more often than the oldtimers, offered her hospitality, such as a beverage. Such differential practices fundamentally shaped the village transformation caused by the lower-income newcomers (Salamon and Tornatore 1994).

Space and Place

At the time of the study, 12% of the village houses stood empty and in poor condition. Splitville properties deteriorated to a substandard condition as its many elderly owners on limited incomes (30% of the current population) became infirm. An oldtimer who keeps up his home assessed the situation: "People grew old and died . . . and some old people don't have the money to take care of the house." One elderly lifelong Splitville resident sounded an oldtimer theme of concern: "The town's gotten worse because the houses are getting more rundown." Splitville property taxes are low, averaging only several hundred dollars annually. Despite low taxes, some properties were abandoned by their absentee owners (in some cases heirs) who were unable to sell or unwilling to pay even small assessments. A surplus pool of deteriorated and vacant housing developed as a consequence.

Splitville's glut of cheap, substandard rural homes contributed to the low level of property values; the county tax rolls typically listed village homes in the $10,000 to $20,000 range (in 1990 the median home value reported by the census was $27,500), but many properties are worth less (table 18). For example, a small house in poor condition sold in 1988 for $3,000. Houses offered for sale stay on the market a long time. For more than a year, no bids were received on a home listed at $45,000, and it was finally rented to poor newcomers. An oldtimer commented, "It'll never sell at that price. Not here." According to a retired man still living in his first home, properties tend to be purchased on contract: "The only way you can sell is with no down payment. The people interested don't have the income or savings to afford a down payment or a substantial monthly payment." One young family explained the purchase of a deceased relative's home: "It was cheap; it was a rat-trap." Unless a family can afford a car, living in Splitville is impossible. In the entire village, only one elderly widow is without a car. Thus, Splitville is a magnet for the working-poor who own transportation but have limited financial resources for housing.

Poor newcomers are attracted to Splitville by its affordable housing. A retired farmer, commenting on the village transformation, stated, "There's been a drastic change in the last 20 years. Poor bought property." Once 6 lower-income households were established during the 1970s, members of their kinship or friendship networks followed in a chain migration. The influx increased to a total of 19 households during the 1980s. Their impact accelerated with the arrival of 4 additional families in 1989 alone. Newcomer households ($n = 25$) by 1989 occupied one-third of the village housing. If the newcomers maintain residential stability and increase at the same rate, they can be expected to eventually dominate the village, thereby achieving full succession (McKenzie 1967).

The oldtimers and the newcomers have differing perspectives about the responsibilities of community membership. The oldtimers, regardless of how they earned a living, share attitudes about the meaning of property and suspicion of those whose view of property differs from theirs. Property upkeep represents ownership pride and place-identification with the town to the oldtimers. For them, good citizenship is defined as maintaining painted and repaired exteriors, mowed lawns, and a neat appearance of one's home. A retired widow expressed the basic resentment about newcomers, "They don't keep their places up like they should. To keep a town going, you need people who are interested in the town. They aren't."

After newcomer families moved in, the village appearance changed. Although the decayed housing stock was not created by the newcomers, homes that had become run down under the ownership of elderly oldtimers remained dilapidated after acquisition by the working-poor, whose small incomes were stretched to make the home purchase. Furthermore, under newcomer occupation, the homes, especially along the main road, developed a more disorderly appearance. Objects not normally found around village yards, such as inoperative cars, toys, and garbage, now present a daily provocation. Without knowledge of the newcomers' family background, the oldtimers judged them according to their property maintenance, and the verdict was dismal. It is difficult for the oldtimers to fathom why the home owners among the newcomers are worse offenders than five newcomer families who are renters, because renters are more likely to be transient.

The oldtimers value a home for status enhancement, and they claim village space for the utilitarian aim of maintaining higher property values. Newcomers consider their homes to be a workplace used for survival; they claim village space for economic productivity (Low 2000). Although the oldtimers might use their home for a side business such as lawn mower or watch repair, they feel that the neatness of a home and business is proof of a good craftsman. Spare parts should not be stored on the front lawn, according to oldtimer norms, and one's cars should be kept in good working condition.

Vehicles beyond the requisite one per household adult are termed "junk" by the oldtimers. Four newcomer families had at one time a combined total of more than thirty nonfunctioning automobiles parked in their yards, along curbs, and in a vacant lot—filling the lot. These automobiles greatly irritated the oldtimers. A truck-driver home owner commented: "Six or seven years ago, the junk cars started moving in. They buy a car and run it until it stops, then push it in the back yard." The newcomers rationalize acquiring spare vehicles because their older cars frequently break down (Fitchen 1981). Repair of old cars is also a source of supplemental income in the informal economy. An owner of multiple cars remarked on many his unregistered vehicles: "I wasn't going to sell them [the cars]. I don't have no licenses for all of them because I don't use them all at once. I'm not going to tie up that money." In defense of his many unregistered and unattractive old cars, a newcomer appealed to the village board saying that cars are his livelihood. "One man's junk is another man's treasure," he testified.

Another source of friction has to do with responsible garbage disposal. The newcomers do not have regular trash service. Rather than paying for weekly pickups, newcomers accumulate trash for weeks before they make a "run to the dump." Irritation over the resulting piles of garbage was expressed by a former village board member: "A couple families throw garbage, including old diapers, out on the lawn and leave it." Garbage, like old cars, is an expression of the newcomers' taken-for-granted concrete, informal practices of home, neighboring, and family that reflect their social background (Bourdieu 1984; Lamont and Fournier 1992).

As the entrenched political structure, the oldtimers can employ formal power to enforce their definition of respectable property use. A newcomer resentful of oldtimer pressures to conform to middle-class property standards remarked: "The [village] board is tryin' to make me live by their standards. They're sweeping my porch." Several newcomers echoed an idealized view of private property rights expressed by another first-time home owner–newcomer: "If it's my property, I can do anything I want with it. I can build a wall on there if I wanted to and they couldn't tell me what to do!" Another commented, "I pay my taxes. It's my property. I can do what I want." The bystander newcomers ($n = 13$) are more concerned with outward appearances than inward ones, to the extent that they fix up

home exteriors before the interiors. Although this minority had re-
sided in Splitville only a few years, it sided with the oldtimers when
the board finally organized a bureaucratic initiative to clean up the
village.

The housing market shapes newcomer and oldtimer attitudes
about housing in opposite ways. The oldtimers maintain that good
citizens have an obligation to tend their homes and yards because
each home affects community property values, home sales, and thus
the greater good embodied in the tax base. But lowered property
values do not concern newcomer owners of decayed homes that they
are unlikely to sell. In fact, lower property values make the housing
more accessible to working-poor newcomers.

Interconnectedness

Despite its small size, Splitville was not a highly connected community even before the newcomer influx. Adversarial relations had prevailed between the village and the nearby farmers. A prominent oldtimer seethes about the local farmers: "[They] pulled themselves out
of the town to avoid taxes." The last year a retired farmer moved
to town was 1974. Few farmers attend church in Splitville. A prosperous farmer whose land is adjacent to the village "petitioned out"
(changed annexation) in the 1950s over a conflict about the city water
system on his land. Commented one farmer, "I wouldn't invest a
penny in the town." Another farmer said, "I like living here—far
enough out of town. . . . the town has gotten worse . . . steady downhill . . . people don't take care of what they have." A typical farmer
described his limited engagement with the town: "I'm drawn to
Splitville by the bank, the elevator, and the post office. A lot of us
go to the restaurant first thing in the morning." Complained a newcomer about the long-term conflict: "If [the farmers had] stayed true
to the town, it wouldn't have died."

The relations between the farmers and the village are strained
and adversarial, but the attitude of the oldtimers toward the lower-
income newcomers is outright hostility. For example, the oldtimers
consider the working-poor to be socially beneath them, a perspective
expressed by a young man who was raised in the village: "The only
people that buy houses or rent are low-income grits. [As property
values go down], the people that live here go down."

Newcomers were already a presence in Splitville by the mid-
1970s, but the oldtimers did not become galvanized into action until
the late 1980s, when the influx was finally perceived as a threat to
their control (McKenzie 1967). A tightly networked core of younger,

kin-connected, oldtimer families organized to "clean up the town." First they ousted the existing village board and then aggressively enacted ordinances targeted at property upkeep, superfluous cars, and garbage accumulation. One new ordinance made it illegal to store unregistered cars within the village. Even a newcomer could appreciate the new ordinances: "It makes the town look better, with no junk vehicles with weeds growing around." Another ordinance permitted the board to have garbage picked up and then to bill the recalcitrant violator. An atmosphere of trust might have facilitated cooperation in those practices that the oldtimers believed would enhance community well-being (Coleman 1988). As newcomers saw it, however, the oldtimers' acts benefited only the oldtimers themselves and the status quo, at the expense of trust and the well-being of all community members (Coleman 1990; Logan and Molotch 1987; Putnam 2000).

Although Splitville has fewer than 200 residents, the new board resorted to a formal, bureaucratic strategy of threatening the most recalcitrant newcomers (about ten households) with legal action, rather than making use of the informal, face-to-face interactions associated with an agrarian community. "If people have a problem, they don't talk to the person. They go to the board and the board sends a letter," complained a newcomer. Facing the bureaucratic initiative, the newcomers defended themselves with the weapons that are available to those with little vested in the existing system. A young male newcomer said: "They aggravate me, so I wanted to aggravate them." As the oldtimers struck out by aggressively enforcing property ordinances, the newcomers struck back by attacking oldtimer property: slashing tires, damaging landscaping, smashing a garage door. An extreme example of methodical and destructive vandalism targeted the home of a particularly vocal oldtimer family; after being away for a weekend, they returned home to find wholesale destruction of their appliances, walls, and furniture (Salamon and Tornatore 1994). The oldtimers' initiative to clean up the village, opposed by the newcomers' response of vandalism, made the village a highly contested territory. Basic trust and civility were absent as the two groups struggled to control public spaces, village power, and resources (Fernandez 1990).

Newcomers see the board's actions as punitive and claim that the new ordinances are unevenly enforced. A man commented, "The corn can be way over your head, but the grass can only be six inches high." Another newcomer argues that despite ordinance violations by oldtimer residents, only he must frequently move his vehicles: "These are the people [the board members] who have a car in their

back yard and they go and complain about somebody else's car. . . .
The town tells us how many cars we can have and shit like that. . . .
They just do things to hassle us." It cannot be an accident that although they were aware of the priority placed by the oldtimers on
village appearances, several newcomer home owners left their home
exteriors unrepaired but restored the interiors. (By not improving
the outside, they also avoided a tax increase.) A newcomer bought
a house on contract for twelve thousand dollars and reported that
the board demanded that he make many repairs before occupation
would be permitted. He declared, "Fine, I'll just close it up and let
it sit there 'til it falls down." The house stands vacant, a condemned
eyesore. He said angrily, "They think they're above the law. If they
start on me, I'm gonna get them right back. I want them to leave me
and the other people [newcomers] alone." One unemployed mother
summed up newcomer attitudes toward the board's actions: "[The
village clean-up] is a joke. A farce. It's a way to get at people to force
'em to leave. It's more harassment than anything." To the newcomers, the board's initiative is retribution for their audacity in buying
homes and using the property according to a lifestyle dictated by
their beliefs and practices.

Newcomers also complain that, in addition to the clean-up initiative, the oldtimers monitor their activities and constantly summon
county inspectors. When asked who had visited lately to check on
potential violations, a home owner said, "The gas company, looking
for leaks, which there weren't none. The Department of Health and
Welfare. They were told we were dumping raw sewage. The fire marshal, repeatedly. He was here just the other day. I told him I was
expectin' him." Officials agree that they are summoned far too frequently. An elderly oldtimer widow is sensitive about inspectors'
reactions when she makes a complaint: "Oh, it's someone from
Splitville calling again" was the usual response, she related. Splitville
depends on the county for police protection. The oldtimers resort
regularly to the sheriff's department to stop late-night noise on
weekends, irritated by what they consider irresponsible social behavior. "They don't need to sleep at night since they don't work during
the day," an oldtimer remarked. As newcomers see it, they receive
legal harassment but not legal protection—for example, from speed-
ers endangering children on the state road.

The daily struggle has eroded any semblance of a sense of community that existed, causing neighbors to avoid contact. A newcomer
mother commented that "people don't interact. They just don't com-
municate." Likewise, an elderly widow said, "I don't know anybody

across the pavement [state highway]. . . . We just pretty well keep to ourselves." Another newcomer commented on the lack of empathy or generosity on both sides: "Splitville is a splintered community. There's no community spirit . . . No willingness to help out." Newcomers are perceptive about their effect on the entrenched oldtimers. Commented a poor newcomer, "I think these people in Splitville are afraid of change. . . . I'm new; they don't want new. . . . Splitville people themselves are killing it. They try to run out people they think are undesirable—poor people like us." A middle-aged newcomer recounted the process that divided the community by factions: "The new blood came in and the Old Guard refused to give way."

Rapid transformation of the village by newcomers brought a breakdown of informal social controls, normally based on familiarity and an assumption of order (Engel 1984; Greider, Krannich, and Berry 1991; Lewis and Weigert 1985). The disintegration of any community interconnectedness that survived before the transformation was the result.

Social Resources

Most oldtimers who were interviewed were at one time or are now civically engaged in Splitville. For example, several present village board members are from one prominent family, which has a tradition of involvement. The father of this large family was a village policeman and served on the board; he belongs to the Lions Club. The mother used to run the Cub Scouts and the Girl Scouts when their children were small. No Cub Scout troop exists today. She commented: "We couldn't get anybody interested to take over. Couldn't get the parents involved. . . . The Cub Scouts used to have a meeting for parents once a month and they wouldn't even show up. . . . People just don't want to get involved. . . . There is nothing for the kids to do. That could be why they get into mischief."

One newcomer couple, better educated and with a higher income than most, moved to Splitville after inheriting a home from a deceased grandparent. They report starting a village improvement committee that operated for five years during the 1980s. According to the husband, the group "tried to bring back village pride" by planting flowers, building a park, and starting a Founder's Day celebration. They were particularly attentive to the elderly by holding Christmas and Thanksgiving dinners and bingo nights. The group disbanded, according to him, as a result of arguments among the members. A beautician explained, "Everybody found out the whole thing was work and they quit." The beautician also said that older residents had helped with the festivals, "We could'na done it without 'em." Thus, oldtimers come through with volunteerism if younger people provide some organization. Because the oldtimers are becoming elderly or are dying, any civic engagement that existed in Splitville declined or could not be sustained after the newcomers' arrival.

On the whole, the lower-income newcomers are not civically engaged, whether by general preference or in order to avoid the oldtimers. Some working-poor newcomers help one another and the village in tangible and intangible ways, however. A newcomer is a volunteer fireman, and another highly visible, lower-income newcomer served on the village board until he and other board members were ousted. To a certain extent, the participation of rural residents sustains any village volunteer activities that exist. One involved farmer estimated that the volunteer fire department is half rural, the Lions service club (which founded the café and built the park) is three-quarters rural, and the one surviving church has a congregation made up primarily of people from the countryside.

Despite the strained village relations, the elderly oldtimers maintain concern for each other and provide neighborly support. The organizer mentioned above feels that informally Splitville is a "close-knit community. Everybody helps each other out. The older people can't do physical stuff, but they will watch your house or pick up your paper. . . . everybody knows what you are doing." Women call on an elderly neighbor who falls ill, or check on elderly people by phone. When a frail woman did not answer the phone, her friend called a neighbor to look in on her, though she is a relatively recent (ten-year) resident and not particularly well liked. Commented the oldtimer woman who made the call, "Splitville takes care of its own," referring to her connected community.

Instead of generating community social resources in the form of trust, civic engagement seems only to embitter Splitville residents. When reflecting on civic service, people repeatedly said that their time, energy, and ideas were rarely appreciated and usually criticized. For example, one man served on the village board for several years and then was voted out. "People are sick and tired of fighting and don't care what happens anymore. . . . I'm glad I'm off the board because what went on so upset me that it was affecting my life and marriage." A woman who served on the board for six years described it this way: "All they want to do is fight." Community members have a certain cynicism about Splitville and express anger toward the elite who they think control the community. A dual-earner couple who have improved their property commented that "all the village board members are related and nothing gets done unless it benefits someone from their families. If it doesn't benefit them, you can forget about it." Several call Splitville a "Peyton Place," observing the divorces, several common-law couples, and one newcomer with a criminal record of burglary, theft, and drug offenses.

Another casualty of the conflict between the oldtimers and the newcomers is goodwill. A young housewife said about the village: "It's changed; no doubt about that. . . . There's more distance between everybody. Before, people could walk across the yard without someone calling the police on 'em. There is less trust in the community." Rather than making Splitville a better place to live, the clean-up campaign had the unintended result of causing some oldtimers to be intimidated about their home territory. Elderly residents, in particular, do not feel safe in the tiny hamlet where they have lived a lifetime. When an interview lasted until dusk, an elderly widow insisted on driving the student field worker to her car, parked two blocks away, because "I wouldn't walk outside after dark, no." The level of distrust was evident in an oldtimer man's reaction to a minor transgression by the researcher: she hastily parked in his driveway in order to catch his newcomer neighbor, who was about to leave. When she returned to her car a few minutes later, the man shouted, "Get the hell out of here before I call the law." Rather than asking her to move her car, he threatened her with legal action once he associated her with the newcomer camp.

Vandalism, as opposed to outright crime, characterizes what has spoiled the agrarian-community sense of security for most residents. One man recalled that he never locked his doors before he went into the service (ten to fifteen years before). Now, the couple lock their doors if they are leaving for more than half an hour. One day his car broke down two miles from town. When he came back for it later that afternoon, the windshield wipers were broken, the side-view mirror was bent, and a tire was flat. He, like other Splitville residents, attributes vandalism to one of the "welfare families," although they lack proof.

An oldtimer man manages the city water system and has the responsibility of shutting off the water if a household does not pay its bills for several months; he does so aggressively. His neighbors say that a newcomer family tore up his flower beds after he shut off their water. The couple who told this story argue that vandalism in Splitville differs from that in a city. Only in such a small town would one know where the person responsible for shutting off water lives. The contested territory has become so personalized that the water-system manager and a village board member, both targets of organized vandalism, have moved away. But newcomers as a group complain that only they are treated poorly—that the board worries more about petty issues such as old cars than about real problems like frequent boil orders for the water system (to purify drinking water).

As the two groups clashed about previously taken-for-granted, middle-class norms, primarily regarding property upkeep, the village social order gradually deteriorated. From the newcomers' perspective, the oldtimers are unwilling to accept a more heterogeneous village.

Cross-Age Relations

Residents have little good to say about life in this small, contested village. Tolerance in any form is a scarce commodity, given that tolerance requires commitment and an investment of oneself (Schwartz 1987). An elderly widow describes the social processes in the village: "There is a meanness here. It's not the kids, it's their parents. . . . The people who've lived here are as good as gold. It's the people that come in here from other towns that are the problem." Village children, however, have become pawns in the conflict over which group controls the village territory. Newcomer children regularly harass drivers of passing cars by pretending to throw a ball toward the vehicle, spitting, or making defiant gestures. A second-generation newcomer mother commented on her children's behavior toward the oldtimers: "I tell my kids to ignore them. They [her children] probably say somethin' more. They won't put up with what I did. My kids are wise. They tell 'em where to get off."

Meanness is also evident in the attitude of the oldtimers toward youth. People say that rather than civilly discussing differences or problems, several elderly women in particular quickly resort to calling the sheriff about children's noise or behavior. Families who are reported often to the authorities "hold a grudge and teach their kids to hold a grudge," commented a woman who was explaining how village encounters seem to fester. From the working-poor newcomers' perspective, the oldtimers, whom they consider wealthy, are selfish. According to one man, "The old people are keeping their money to themselves instead of using it to improve the community." He sees no inconsistency in expecting others to be more generous than he. "I don't get along with the town." He has junk autos in his yard and allows his children to spit at and make aggressive gestures at every car that travels his street. He has to admit, however, that some oldtimers are good people. One raised money for his son when the child needed medical care. But a good deed does not seem to offset what he regards as the vindictiveness of authorities toward his kind. People in Splitville consider themselves to be victims, a sentiment not conducive to trust or constructive civic engagement (Kemmis 1995). An adult son of a newcomer family thinks the village oldtimers do not care about children. "The ones that [have children] have had trouble with the law. . . . It's my personal opinion that they should leave the cars alone [broken down cars parked on people's property] and let the kids work on them."

The oldtimers, though of humble origins, had children who achieved upward mobility. An example is the mail carrier who raised eight college graduates, products of the local schools. Now, however, Splitville has a poor reputation within its consolidated school district. There is a definite stigma associated with coming from Splitville, and children from the village bear the brunt of the stigma. A retired farmer from Prairie Gem, a nearby agrarian community also in the school district, said in 1978, "Splitville never was much and it's getting worse." "All Splitville is, is slums and public aid," commented another Prairie Gem farmer. "The place is god-awful. . . . out of the population of 200, more than 100 are on welfare and those were run out of Central City by the law" and "90% of the kids are dirty" are comments by farmers made more than a decade before our study, indicating that the newcomer influx was correlated with stigma from the outset (Salamon 1992). A farm woman who is also the school district nurse admitted that a negative bias is attached to the hometown. "Sometimes people's actions are explained by just simply saying 'They're from Splitville.'"

Newcomers are aware of their bad reputation in the consolidated school district. A well-educated, sympathetic newcomer sees a certain insidious oldtimer prejudice toward working-poor children, in particular. "In the Little League and other sports the 'sabra' people [born in Splitville] are the ones that play," he said. A poor newcomer father recalled the heartbreak of seeing his son join Little League but spend his time on the bench because only the children of oldtimer families played. Similar processes occur in the school district, in his experience. "My daughter worked hard to get on the honor roll, and now she'll always be there, because she was once. . . . The thing your dad does [his occupation] determines your grades." From his perspective, the school district stigmatizes the lower-income students: "The teachers are inbred. . . . They either attended school there or their husband did. Their attitudes are formed." One newcomer father related the discrimination his son experienced at school: "He had the name of [family name] so he didn't get good grades." A young newcomer parent remembered when she attended the consolidated high school, "If you were considered poor you were . . . white trash. . . . That's what they called us. . . . If we had friends [in the new school], we weren't allowed to go visit in their homes."

Stigma works as a self-fulfilling prophecy for the poor children (Fitchen 1981, 1991). A disproportionate number of the children from working-poor families are in special education classes. It is not surprising that the three families with the most consistent record of using welfare are also those from which not a single child (five in one family, eight in another, and three in the other) has graduated from high school (Tornatore 1993). One dropout explained why she quit school: "I'm not learnin' anything. I'm not doin' anything." Another said, "I was workin' full-time, or not full-time, but it was better than sittin' in a classroom."

The consolidated school district is one that has invested heavily in agricultural education for the children from farms, a continually declining group. Apparently vocational training for nonfarmers has not been deemed important for human capital investment. An adult son of a lower-income but stable newcomer family does not feel that the education he received from the consolidated school district served him well. "Schools should have more classes in auto maintenance and house wiring instead of so many years of English."

Although the working-poor newcomers have improved their life chances by obtaining security from owned housing in Splitville, parents have not succeeded in improving their children's lot in life. One woman is an unwed mother at sixteen and a second-generation welfare recipient, a pattern that does not bode well for the third generation. Another young mother hopes her children will do better: "I want my kids to have something to look forward to. I want them to know they *are* somebody, that they can do what they want with their life." Once youth feel stigmatized, it is difficult for them to break out of poverty (Fitchen 1991; MacTavish 2001). Unlike the oldtimers, who as children of tenant farmers or hired laborers were able to educate their children and watch them leave and achieve a better life, this generation of youth seems destined to stay and over time create a rural enclave of similarly poor people who live by barter and welfare (Harvey 1993). Sadly, the evidence that a stigma has been internalized is in a newcomer youth's self-image: "We can't do nothin'; we're poor people" (Tornatore 1993).

REFLECTIONS

As a result of the Splitville rift, the integration of most newcomers is highly unlikely. Rather, as the oldtimers die off or move out, it can be expected that the population balance will shift and the newcomers will gradually assume village control. A newcomer who was particularly vehement about the struggle predicted: "We're gonna have to outwait them [the oldtimers]. They know it and it makes them mad. They know I will go and spit on their graves. This is cruel to say, but I want my kids to come back and build this town up when these sons-of-bitches die. I don't want them to do it while the Old Guard is still alive—so they [the oldtimers] won't profit out of it."

Despite the antagonism between the oldtimers and the newcomers, in general their views suggest shared concerns about Splitville. Both factions prefer small communities, home ownership, safe streets, and a vibrant main street. Furthermore, newcomers can provide a future for a village that, despite their influx, has experienced a population decline in every decade since 1970 (table 18). "The town will die if they keep trying to run us out," said a newcomer who has a clear perception of demographic realities. Another newcomer, a veteran of the village board, recognizes that the community's conflict prevents the cooperation that it needs: "I kinda wanted to see the community grow. But the more I tried to get involved, the more red tape. They didn't want nobody to come in and change the town." Although people in each faction say, as did an unemployed newcomer, "If they leave me alone, I'll leave them alone," the village remains an actively contested territory where residents feel that their neighbor is the enemy.

Community life is so disorderly that the regional newspaper ran a 2001 commentary headlined: "Someone needs to restore peace and order in Splitville." Referring to the anarchy during monthly village board meetings, the commentator sympathized with the mayor, who for just $600 a year endures constant insults and threats over alley paving and lot lines, which began long before he took office in 2001. Central to the turmoil is that the village has committed to a new standpipe and water distribution system improvement but cannot come to an agreement about how to pay for its $100,000-plus share of the work. One newcomer, who plasters his auto repair shop with antimayor signs, knows that the disputes and rumors are bad for the village: "It's getting to the point now here it's just neighbor versus neighbor," he said. As the commentator notes, there does not seem to be much worth fighting about in Splitville, but the conflicts continue (area newspaper, Oct. 13).

Communities such as Smallville and Splitville have always had social differentiation, but the citizens have shared agrarian links. The hope for upward mobility or the potential for local employment has muted possible resentment among the lower strata toward those above them. In contrast, the working-poor newcomers who transformed Splitville never expect employment by the oldtimers, and thus agrarian-community norms that exert pressures for conformity, such as family reputation or future favors needed, are ineffective. Because the working-poor buy homes, signaling a commitment to stay, these families pose a particular threat to the oldtimers, who control the village and operate according to a different set of priorities about property and social behavior (Tornatore 1993). Perhaps the oldtimers unreasonably expect middle-class property practices from newcomers who, like the inner-city poor, have a legacy of neighborhoods with deteriorated housing. The Splitville newcomers also inherit from the oldtimers a village with fewer opportunities for employment or social mobility than it has offered in the past. Thus, the struggle between village status groups is motivated by nonmaterialistic issues of cultural ideas, respect, and dignity (Hatch 1989).

Because of the hostility that is present, Splitville represents perhaps a worst-case contested-territory scenario for a postagrarian community. The newcomers, who, as we saw, were highly mobile before home ownership made their lives more stable, hold an idealized view of community, believing that privacy and respect should temper interactions. The oldtimers, who witnessed the further decline of the village with the influx, do not trust the newcomers; they do not believe that newcomers hold ideals that will benefit community well-being. The newcomers feel betrayed by the oldtimers, yet their common status as the target for the clean-up initiative has not unified them. Despite being negatively stereotyped by the oldtimers, those who are gainfully employed and not using alcohol look down on those who drink and are on welfare. Thus far, the newcomers lack the sense of ownership of Splitville that would motivate them to invest socially in it. The oldtimers, at the same time, seem less interested in saving the community than in preserving their own net worth. What has occurred in Splitville represents a lost opportunity in the transforming rural countryside. The death of a sense of community seems to have been hastened, rather than reversed, via the transformation by newcomers. The Splitville story demonstrates that the relative attitudes and expectations of newcomers and old-timers toward property—personal and public—are of paramount importance in postagrarian communities that become purely residential. Property appearance and value are, of course, suburban priorities.

PART III

The Postagrarian Countryside

[E]ach day, several thousand more acres of our countryside are eaten by the bulldozers, covered by pavement, dotted with suburbanites who have killed the thing they thought they came to find. . . .

The semisuburbanized and suburbanized messes we create in this way become despised by their own inhabitants tomorrow. These thin dispersions lack any reasonable degree of innate vitality, staying power, or inherent usefulness as settlements. Few of them, and these only the most expensive as a rule, hold their attraction much longer than a generation; then they begin to decay in the pattern of city gray areas. . . .

. . . An all too familiar kind of mind is obviously at work here: a mind seeing only disorder where a most intricate and unique order exists; the same kind of mind that sees only disorder in the life of city streets, and itches to erase it, standardize it, suburbanize it. . . .

It may be romantic to search for the salves of society's ills in slow-moving rustic surroundings, or among innocent unspoiled provincials, if such exist, but it is a waste of time. Does anyone suppose that, in real life, answers to any of the great questions that worry us today are going to come out of homogeneous settlements?

Jane Jacobs, *The Death and Life of Great American Cities*

9 WHITHER THE RURAL HEARTLAND?

My local newspaper recently reported a rural midwestern trend that is touted as the latest economic salvation for communities: financial incentives to draw new home buyers (fig. 8). The smokestack-chasing to gain industrial jobs that characterized previous decades is being abandoned for marketing a town as a package that delivers "small-town life" to urban, middle-class families. Mayors, pessimistic about ever generating local jobs, argue that new residents can revitalize a main street, much as the boosters of Bunkerton reasoned. But a rural revival using town real estate as a growth machine is a strategy fraught with problems, as several case studies highlight. The sense that a town is a special place is a casualty of transformation into a sleeper town—the suburbanization process. Communities that have sustained a more diverse economy have preserved themselves as organic places in which the agrarian web of social interdependencies is maintained (Kunstler 1993). Developers in reality market suburban rather than small-town life with subdivisions adjacent to, not in, old towns.

Rural hinterlands retain a powerful lure for Americans, and small-town mayors understand that. Therefore, the reverse migration, the movement of people into small towns rather than out of them, is likely to continue unabated. The postagrarian landscape, resembling a landlocked archipelago, can be expected to become more densely peopled. In the Midwest east of the Mississippi, archipelago island-towns (such as Villa Grove, fig. 8) are typically within an hour's commute from places like Central City, where the jobs are. Thus, numerous midwestern rural regions share the conditions that triggered the transformation of the Central City commuting zone. Because mayors and other small-town boosters buy into the idea that

Rural towns seek crop of homes

■ **Officials using incentives, marketing to attract residents**

VILLA GROVE (AP) — In an idle farm field on the north edge of this one-stoplight town, Mayor Ron Hunt is sowing the seeds of a rural revival.

Where once crops sprouted from this field in east-central Illinois, Hunt sees single-family homes for the young families he wants to lure here. He also envisions condominiums for local widows and the retired, new businesses and a sports complex.

Hunt says the setting is bucolic, the schools are excellent and have plenty of empty desks, and the land is cheap. In fact, the town is offering $10,000 grants to people who buy a plot and build a house within a year.

"I think people are tired of the rat race. They want a nice, quiet place to live," Hunt says. "For young families ... this puts them in a new home."

Using financial incentives and simple marketing campaigns that promote idyllic small-town life, rural towns throughout Illinois are attempting to reshape themselves by attracting new residents. Hunt and other nascent town planners appear to have tapped into something — despite the fact these towns often lack some of the basic services that young families need and sit miles from the nearest cities. Villa Grove is about 20 miles south of Champaign-Urbana with little more than farmland between the two.

"I think people are willing to drive an extra 10 or 15 minutes to live in these places," said Norman Walzer, the director of the Illinois Institute for Rural Affairs at Western Illinois University. "You can get the equivalent space for maybe half the price and I think people have begun to accept that payoff."

Jack Piper was concerned about the departure of young families and the depressed property values in his hometown of Ohio, Illinois, so he spearheaded a successful redevelopment project there. He now runs his own development company from his home and helps other towns, including Villa Grove, do the same.

"Every town used to look for a widget factory to create jobs, but we didn't know how to do that," he said of his experience in Ohio. "We kind of came up with this idea, 'What if we offer incentives to families rather than factories?'"

New projects are on the drawing board or in progress in places such as Wood Hull, Oblong, Meridosia, Table Grove and Paw Paw.

One tool Piper used in Ohio, and is using in Villa Grove and elsewhere, is to have land that is targeted for development declared a Tax Increment Financing district. This allows towns to secure loans for infrastructure improvements and pump property taxes from new homes into a fund to be used to pay off the loans and for more improvements and further development.

While some towns offer financial incentives, other recruitment efforts involve simply getting the word out. In Taylorville, the school board has mailed pamphlets to households in nearby Springfield and Decatur in an attempt to lure families with young children to fill the local schools.

"There are so many communities that need it and want it," Piper said. "Big-time developers were never going to come to these towns."

Hunt said the response to Villa Grove's proposed Pheasant Pointe subdivision has been enthusiastic and he has experienced little opposition from locals in the town of 2,700.

"At night you can leave your front door open. You can go for a walk and not get mugged or harassed," he said. "There's just a terrific amount of interest in what we're doing."

But some longtime locals aren't convinced.

"I think he's blowing smoke," said Charles Bassett, who has lived in Villa Grove off and on for more than three decades. "He's trying to make a big city out of a one-horse town."

Bassett, a retiree, said he'd like to see the town address the concerns of the current populace, such as the chronic flooding of the Embarras River, which splits Villa Grove.

Some of the Illinois cities that could be affected by the departure of stable families have also raised concerns. School and city administrators in Decatur and Springfield, for example, have accused Taylorville of subtly attempting to lure only a certain type of student and family — namely ones who can afford to pick up and move, leaving behind the poorest families.

But Walzer said he believes this trend is ruled by pocketbook concerns alone — these small towns need infusions of capital, and people in turn are always seeking affordable, attractive places to live.

But he admits that the rebirth of such small towns can be startling to longtime residents.

"You have people who have lived there all their lives and suddenly their tax bills are so much higher. They want their children to stay in town, but they can't afford a $200,000 home," he said. "These people are really being priced out of their homes. I think that's one of the effects."

New residents may also want to raise taxes to pay for a new library or better municipal services, he said.

But proponents point out that an increase in property taxes simply means an increase in property values.

"That's a pretty good trade," Hunt said.

"For these little towns it ain't a matter of options, it's a matter of life and death," Piper added. "The old saying is, grow or die."

Figure 8 Becoming a bedroom community, the newest small town survival strategy. This article appeared in *The News-Gazette*, April 3, 2000. Reprinted with permission of the Associated Press.

any growth is good, their towns are vulnerable to growth-machine entrepreneurs. Exurban development of the rural landscape appears unstoppable for a small town once a growth machine starts to operate (Daniels and Bowers 1997; Olson and Lyson 1999). What the doomsayers had right about the dying of small towns is that unique identity erodes as suburbanization occurs. Because newcomers bring social as well as material baggage, whether they settle in new subdivisions or older homes, their taken-for-granted beliefs and practices alter the landscape and the social ties forged by the original community.

We are learning that for small towns, just as for big cities, it is important to preserve a diversity of uses. The combination of commercial and residential activities makes a small town, like a city, resilient by providing a textured, vital life to residents (Jacobs 1992). Coherent, organic small communities are those that sustain some productive work, shopping, different classes of residents, well-used public spaces, and houses clustered on streets with sidewalks. Such features combine to create a high-density town, one that teems with life. When small towns are captured as real estate ventures and development modeled on suburban ideals of privacy, exclusivity, and automobile convenience, the residents become more mobile, the streets become empty, and the public spaces are neglected in old areas and absent in new ones. Without vital public spaces for a communal focus, a place loses some integrity. Oldtimers are overwhelmed by the challenges of sustaining the positive attributes of an agrarian community in the face of a massive suburban onslaught.

Agrarian towns were places where people both worked and lived; farmers shopped there, churched and schooled their families there, and moved into town to retire. The arrival of newcomers, although under the same circumstances of regional restructuring, triggered differing reverberations in specific rural Illinois communities. The original town size, the town's economic type, its local culture, and the type of newcomer arriving have emerged as the critical indicators of how an agrarian community is altered by an influx. The towns that have deviated the least from their previous character after a newcomer influx have been larger and have had a diversified economy, one not solely dependent on agriculture. Such towns attracted newcomers that shared lifestyle and community norms with oldtimers. Corntown, Arbordale, and, to a lesser extent, Bunkerton fit these criteria: a population of more than 2,500 and an economy diversified by small industry or governmental services. Newcomers attracted to these towns had social class and culture akin to those of the oldtimers. They chose to settle because these towns offered both local jobs and affordable housing. Smallville, of course, represents a community type predicted to die, but its great store of social resources gives it a fighting chance for survival as a densely connected sleeper town, albeit for diminishing numbers of people committed to life there. It has little to attract newcomers. Smallville, Corntown, and Bunkerton show how traditional agrarian practices serve a community well in meeting new challenges.

Prairieview is healthy according to any economic indicator, and it represents the future for towns courting affluent middle-class urbanites. Through the 1980s and 1990s, median incomes and home values increased as the population doubled (table 8). Because a small core of landowners and businesspeople bought into growth-machine dynamics, agrarian community practices were overwhelmed. Newcomers have little good to say about the oldtimers. Yet it was the oldtimers' community commitment that produced the select schools and well-tended infrastructure that lured the newcomers. Newcomers engage in community activities narrowly, only in those institutions from which they see direct personal benefit—the schools or a church. Newcomers enjoy Prairieview's rural ambience and the safety and security that its size and homogeneity provide, but not those qualities that made it so special to oldtimers. Children of the "subdivision people" know that their affluent parents intend to move on after extracting full value for them from the local institutional commodities.

When a town serves only as a residence space, the inhabitants do not look to the town to provide a unique place identity or social status, as oldtimers did. After Prairieview oldtimers are gone (such as the one who in his letter blessed the transformation; see chapter 1), the memory of the community's agrarian identity will survive only in photos on the local newspaper's wall. Postagrarian Prairieview has evolved into a place for mobile, upscale commuters and is virtually indistinguishable from towns that serve the same purpose in the Chicago suburban ring. The Prairieview story confirms that suburbanization has extended beyond the ring surrounding larger cities to exurbia; it now incorporates the rural heartland.

At the bottom end of the regional-community economic hierarchy lies Splitville, which was transformed, like Prairieview, into a homogeneous neighborhood sleeper town. The working-poor newcomers, aside from their financial situation, resemble the upscale Prairieview newcomers in their attitude toward the community—uncommitted, critical, and ungenerous. Newcomers value their homes, but they do not value the town as a special place. Unlike Prairieview newcomers, however, Splitville newcomers do not plan to move on; they can barely afford Splitville's shabby circumstances. They have not grown to care enough about the village to adopt the social and property norms of the Splitville oldtimers.

Because the rural poor are pushed out of upscaled towns into affordable ones like Splitville (or into a trailer park), upscale Prairieview exists at the expense of oldtimers in marginal, shabby towns. Owing to the single founding family's tight hold on local land, businesses, and finances, Splitville never functioned as a responsive democracy. Rather than appealing to the aspirations of newcomers, the village board treated them as criminals, a strategy that heightened the incivility that had caused the board to act in the first place. Each group, newcomers and oldtimers, considers itself the victim of the other, a position unlikely to evoke the good citizenship that might alter the downward trend (Kemmis 1995). Under these circumstances, residents are splintered and alienated rather than united by attachment to place. Splitville therefore represents a rural midwestern "forgotten place" that regional prosperity is passing by. Conceivably, with time, given its peripheral location and the poverty of its newcomers, Splitville will become the persistent rural slum of the Central City commuting zone (Duncan 1999; Falk and Lyson 1993). Its population continues to decline (table 18).

The towns that experienced the greatest divergence from past agrarian traits were still farming-dependent when newcomers began to arrive. Prairieview and Splitville, both of small size, experienced reshaping by newcomers who, unlike the oldtimers, expected to live but not find jobs there. These towns were transformed into virtual bedroom towns by newcomers who differed greatly from the oldtimers socially, culturally, and, in Prairieview especially, economically (Bourdieu 1984; Lamont and Fournier 1992). The consequence of this scenario was a strong negative impact on public spaces, the social system, and the community identity, from the perspective of oldtimers. Thus, whether richer or poorer than the oldtimers, newcomers wrought a similar transformation in sleeper towns.

Corntown is successfully preserving what locals value about an old town, despite receiving a minority settled-out migrant group as newcomers. Although at first apprehensive and even hostile toward the Mexicano newcomers, Corntown eventually integrated them into the community. It is clear that Corntown was willing to be inclusive toward newcomers who sought full integration and oldtimer status through home ownership, civic engagement, and even intermarriage. Smallville, on a much more modest scale, achieved the same ends with its few newcomers, some of whom were well off but most of whom were poor. Arbordale and Bunkerton have only partially incorporated newcomers who differ by ethnicity and class, respectively. The newcomers in both towns are unobtrusive, and the business elites continue to dominate the towns.

To varying degrees, Smallville, Corntown, Bunkerton, and Arbordale as communities have prevailed in ways that oldtimers value. Local people draw on admirable strengths and resiliency to sustain a sense of community by keeping on and not giving up, while facing challenges either courted by themselves or imposed on them by newcomers. Change is dealt with by the social processes that have been used to face continual change over the last century. The pace of change is accelerating in rural America, but these densely connected and resourceful towns demonstrate what it takes to continually renew a community.

POSTAGRARIAN COMMUNITY SOCIAL PROCESSES

A sense of community, or what symbolizes community to residents, resides in how local space is shared, the strength of social connections, the quality of social resources, and the relationship of cross-age groups, especially adults with youth. Community theorists from the 1960s through the 1980s worried about "the community question"—the consequences for a sense of community of such factors as economic restructuring, population growth and mobility, and suburbanization (Wellman 1979). Community was lost, according to classic theorists such as Tonnies, when agrarian or gemeinschaft-like relations were transformed into urban or gesellschaft-like relations. No, said others such as Wirth, Fischer, or Gans, community was robust; it could be saved because neighborhoods in cities or suburbs functioned as supportively as agrarian communities did. They argued that people sustain community by fashioning it anew, because a sense of community is desired or even needed by everyone. Recently some scholars have been celebrating community liberated from the bounds of geography by technology: the telephone and now E-mail and the Internet free social life from proximity. Technology can unite far-flung kin, friends, or even virtual friends in communities untethered from propinquity (Smith and Kollock 1999; Wellman and Gulia 1999).

Some thinkers question why, despite having being liberated from place, we as a nation still search for some idealized equivalent to an agrarian community where one is known, attached, nurtured, and can sustain a coherent identity. Community from this perspective is a good thing, although it has social costs. But community, they judge, is needed by people to gain fulfillment and to extract the best from life (Bellah et al. 1985; Fowler 1991; Oldenburg 1999; Putnam 2000; Wuthnow 1998). The sense of community that people desire seems to resemble that of an old town with an agrarian culture.

What do our postagrarian towns tell us about whether or how community is sustained in the context of rapid change? Are newcomers and oldtimers finding in postagrarian towns what they need or seek in the context of community life?

Space and Place

A farming community has organic coherence because its residents have strong ties to the land that defines the place. This agrarian attachment to land as a part of place differs from the characteristic postagrarian attachment to land as personal property or investment, the type of interest in land exhibited by Prairieview subdivision new-comers. For land in the form of space to undergird community at-tachment, ownership of some land must be shared by the entire community, as it is in Smallville, where communal investment in main-street businesses was mobilized as a strategy to sustain essen-tial public spaces.

Town public land and spaces provide a symbol of permanence for the community group, one that is not conveyed by other, more ephemeral shared institutions such as a high school sports team. Pub-lic town spaces—a café, a bar, a bowling alley, or a softball field—are arenas essential to developing and sustaining a sense of community. Informal public spaces allow cultural norms to be enacted or renego-tiated and make it possible to forge the social bonds that connect a community. Community members must regularly work through issues informally in order to build the understandings that are used to mobilize, should the need arise. Only through repetitive informal interactions do people forge the shared meanings that foster a sense of community. When a place is cherished for its uniqueness, people are more committed to sustaining the place—as are the residents of Smallville.

If a sense of community is to be created, public spaces must be provided for all and must be accessible to all. Suburban communities notoriously lack public spaces such as parks or a downtown, because developers prioritize the private property investor. Suburbanites fo-cus their social lives elsewhere; they may seldom want the regular face-to-face interactions in informal settings that weave the connec-tions underlying a small-town community's social fabric. Suburban communities, which are often focused on appearances, are notori-ously intolerant of public space use, particularly by adolescents. In a postagrarian community being transformed by a growth machine, existing public community spaces may suffer from neglect or from usurpation for commercial purposes. Thus there is a public-space challenge for youth who live in postagrarian towns that are primarily residential. Postagrarian communities are best at providing privacy and autonomy; agrarian communities opt for maximizing togeth-erness.

When town changes wrought by a newcomer influx are contested, the disputes are played out in town public spaces. In Splitville and, to a certain extent, Bunkerton, public spaces are where oldtimers and newcomers vie to control the community physical and social resources. The subdivision people of Prairieview are spatially alien-ated from the original heart of the town. They have not contested public spaces because the growth-machine developers have acted in their behalf. In Prairieview the space-control battle was quickly lost by the oldtimers, who, being elderly and less affluent than the newcomers, had fewer resources at their disposal. The oldtimers not only lost the main street to gentrified boutiques, but they also had to share their beloved park with a sewage treatment facility, built to serve the newcomer influx. Prairieview youth have no place to gather where they are tolerated. Their complaints about lacking such space echo those of suburban youth. Even the churches are moving to the edge of town, nearer to the subdivisions. Postagrarian Prairieview has become a suburban place lacking a center or authentic public spaces where newcomers and oldtimers regularly meet informally.

Although newcomers are a minority in Splitville and Bunkerton, public spaces in both towns are highly contested. These space disputes highlight how in postagrarian communities the appearance of public spaces takes priority over the social connections supported there. Bunkerton is moving toward suburbanization by no longer tolerating youth who "drag main" or hang out on the main street. Agrarian community concessions to youth have been abandoned in Bunkerton's dedication to business growth. A recent poll of adolescents, to the town's chagrin, found that youth considered Bunkerton a distinctly unwelcoming place.

Newcomers, being less affluent and lacking middle-class property norms, aroused the most belligerent reaction in Splitville by their contesting town public and private space. Forceful legal actions directed against the newcomers had the unintended consequence of triggering revenge toward oldtimers' property and space. The oldtimers thought they could "save" the town with an aggressive cleanup campaign, but the warring factions together destroyed any sense of community. Social connections were fragmented and, even more important, any semblance of security or trust about place eroded. Although Prairieview and Splitville (and, to a lesser degree, Bunkerton) differ in size and affluence, the political and social ramifications of being exploited by a growth machine for the extraction of wealth have wrought a similar spatial consequence—isolating residents in their homes.

In Arbordale, Splitville, and Bunkerton, which have been run in the past by elite or business families, newcomers are either actively discouraged from becoming civically engaged in activities that might result in ceding control of public spaces, or at least they are not encouraged in that direction. Democratic vitality is not as evident in these transformed places as it is in the more egalitarian communities of Smallville and Corntown, where people say that everyone is "pretty much alike" and where public spaces belong to and are used by residents of all ages. The provision and use of public spaces, then, reflects the sense of community shared among town residents.

What does town space in a postagrarian archipelago look like? Whether public spaces are highly contested or not, public streets or parks in suburbanized postagrarian towns usually are vacant. That is, when certain categories of community members are made to feel unwelcome in public spaces, the feeling seems to be contagious. A hallmark of a postagrarian community successfully forged by joint actions of newcomers and oldtimers is that public spaces have vitality because they are used by all residents, young and old. Such spaces—the main street, parks, or schools—become the crucible for the collective processes that create a shared good life based on an attachment to place and a strong sense of community identity.

Interconnectedness

Community integration does not happen just because people live in proximity. Newcomers and oldtimers live side by side in Prairieview and Splitville, but neither town can be called interconnected. Occasional cooperation is important to creating a community linked by strong horizontal networks, but the repetitive, ordinary daily social encounters during which people learn about one another in diverse settings are what build the shared norms and trust and overlapping social networks that are crucial to establishing an organic, highly connected social system. In agrarian towns, strong connections form among residents who acknowledge that they share community and responsibility for a place. Smallville and Corntown, in particular, are towns where some or all of the people regularly interact. Their strong sense of community was constructed through such connections (Arensberg 1972, 1981; Williams 1988).

The case study communities represent differing social strategies used by oldtimers and newcomers to deal with one another; the connective outcomes for community differ correspondingly. Each strategy must be envisioned in the context of a town territory shared by both groups. Each group brings different qualities to the encounters. The relative size of the groups makes a difference. *Resistance*, in the form of avoidance, rejection, or hostility, is one strategy. The community outcome if either group resists connections is avoidance (Prairieview) or hostility (Splitville). *Acceptance* is a strategy in which neither camp tries very hard to engage (Bunkerton and Arbordale). Its outcome is accommodation. The connections are weak, but they do exist, in contrast to resistance encounters. *Incorporation* (Smallville and Corntown) can produce cooperation, engagement, or tolerance. Incorporation seemed to occur when the newcomers constituted a relatively small proportion of the total town population. In the towns where newcomers threatened to outnumber oldtimers, or did outnumber them, each group is more resistant to forming connections. Of course, if a large newcomer invasion results in succession, the newcomers need not be concerned about whether the oldtimers accept or reject them, or vice versa, as in Prairieview (McKenzie 1923, 1967). Connections thus are not only a question of newcomer resolve or oldtimer willingness to construct a new community. Both sides must participate for a densely connected, richly resourced postagrarian community to emerge from the encounter process. Forging an interconnected community made up of newcomers and oldtimers requires that both sides desire that social end and use strategies to achieve it.

Certain newcomer attributes seem to be crucial to whether a strongly connected postagrarian community is generated through incorporation. Transformed communities become interconnected when the newcomers are rural people, have the same economic circumstances as the oldtimers, and have realistic expectations about small-town life and culture. (Such people resonate with the traits caricatured in the "You Might Be from a Small Town If . . ." E-mail list quoted in chapter 1.) For oldtimers, a best-case scenario for a newcomer influx exists when the newcomers are similar to them, like the town, and want their children to live there as adults.

Newcomers who differ in class from oldtimers seem to consider a weakly connected postagrarian community as their best-case scenario. They prefer being left alone, but this is a priority that comes at the expense of community. If residents live in a place but avoid informal interactions with their neighbors, the overlapping social networks that horizontally link a well-connected community never form. Thus, unless both newcomers and oldtimers seek the habitual interactions that are fundamental to developing norms and networks, an interconnected community cannot emerge. In the suburbanizing towns (Prairieview, Bunkerton, Splitville), newcomers keep to themselves, and their residence pattern reinforces avoidance. In Arbordale, the Mexicanos are not linked with the Anglo community but are densely connected themselves through their church and by their ethnic identity.

The small towns that recruit urbanites as an economic development strategy (fig. 8) are potentially creating connective challenges for themselves. If the newcomers recruited are from small towns originally, the task will be easier. But a town cannot expect that urban newcomers will become active participants just because they choose to live in a place. If urban newcomers live in subdivisions outside the original town limits, their incorporation is least likely. Such a town plan almost ensures that newcomer and oldtimer paths will seldom cross and that informal interactions will be rare.

Social Resources

Those who quest for community are seeking an intrinsic good—a social resource. A much-heralded structural resource related to a sense of community—social capital—is thought to make life flow smoothly or better for those who have access to that resource. Most of those who describe this resource cannot explain how a community creates social capital; they just know it when they see it. That is, we are often given a description of a community instead of a recipe for creating community.

Recent research shows that altruism for the group is related to its stability. When members' reputations and behaviors are predictable, group contributions can be accounted for and indirect reciprocity assumed (Nowak and Sigmund 2000; Wedekind and Milinski 2000). Strong connections emerge when trust is derived from knowing people and being able to count on them. An agrarian community intrinsically has such stability and trust; those elements are not nearly so likely to be found in mobile suburbs, where residence is fluid and reputations anonymous. Furthermore, community stability fosters participatory and democratic decision-making, the hallmark of the agrarian towns. Participation is easiest to manage when relationships are comfortable and committed (Michael M. Bell, personal communication, 2000). Unless there is an effort to help residents become comfortable and committed, a postagrarian social system will not produce the altruism that seems fundamental to a sense of community.

Robert Booth Fowler has thought philosophically about what people are seeking when they say they want community and about what a sense of community means. He argues: "For its denizens community must be seen, chosen, and experienced. . . . A common life is crucial, but it is not sufficient. A shared life, self-consciously accepted is required" (1991, 4). Our six case studies represent a wide range of what people label as community. Those who live in a vibrant and interconnected place recognize that theirs is genuine community. Conversely, those who do not live in genuine community are aware of that fact. According to Fowler, it is not enough for community to be chosen—for Prairieview and Splitville were chosen, by well-off and poor newcomers, respectively. In these postagrarian towns, residents' lives are fragmented and loosely connected. Interactions via the Internet may be more intensive than those with neighbors, by choice or default (Baumgartner 1988; Wellman and Gulia 1999). Mexicano newcomers chose Corntown because they valued the very qualities that the oldtimers valued in the town, and the newcomers and the oldtimers shared economic status. The town was selected because of the unique social qualities that the newcomers saw in Corntown, particularly its trust and egalitarianism. Now the newcomers cooperate to generate community social resources with the oldtimers.

For Fowler, community is a self-consciously accepted shared life; it does not occur spontaneously. Community exists where people are pragmatic and realistic, rather than idealistic, about what is possible. Smallville people complain all the time about their old town. The mayor showed me an anonymous letter that criticized the maintenance of the main street. "I get those all the time," he said with a chuckle. But the mayor just pockets such notes, sloughing off the vent as part of his volunteer job.

What is important is that Smallville residents are committed enough to community to complain, to worry, to argue about decisions—they are engaged citizens. They continually build community at the main-street restaurant's "Liars' Table," hashing over issues. The decisions made are ones that most residents are willing to go along with, although no one may be entirely satisfied. Community building is not a neat process, or an efficient process, but it is a process that generates social capital. Community building does not alienate citizens; resourceful towns continue to engage people (Kemmis 1995). Community is not generated in Splitville because no one works at it or cares enough; newcomers and oldtimers have become set against each other.

Trust is fundamental to rich community social resources. Trust cannot be bought, demanded, or obligated; it must be slowly built by people who are engaged with their neighbors in small and large ways. Newcomers to small towns can become trusted if they participate in the community and demonstrate commitment to more than their personal financial investment. Trust requires extending some generosity to others in the form of tolerance, especially toward youth. Oldtimers like the Prairieview letter writer (chapter 1) caution newcomers that community is an organic thing: "Prairieview is a great community. I say to the Young Guard: Treat her well and give her lots of tender loving care, and I'm sure she will give to you many good feelings as you lead Prairieview." Social resources are generated by such dedication and the willingness to pass the baton to the next generation in a timely fashion.

Cross-Age Relations and Youth

Youth (adolescents) are the "crop" raised by a small town. How a town treats youth—as weeds or as seed corn—is closely related to the priorities citizens hold for their community. Good places have a "community effect" on the development of youth as much as poor inner-city places do. In a town's youth, we see whether the community is successfully socializing citizens who will continue to value the place as being special and engage in activities to sustain it. Youth who develop successfully reflect a resourceful, interconnected community whose social fabric is woven with trust, tolerance, and norms of civic engagement (Elder and Conger 2000; Furstenberg et al. 1999).

Smallville, as an agrarian community, uses its rich social resources to nurture children and youth. It is a good place to grow up because everyone is concerned about all the dimensions of the youth's lives. Parents are not solely responsible for their son or daughter's well-being, and youth have respected rights to town public spaces. In Corntown, a fortuitous set of culture brokers (the high school principal, a high school counselor, and a Catholic priest) worked with the settled-out migrant families, a self-selected group of Mexicanos with tenacity, independence, and energy. Actions by key culture brokers fostered the eventual incorporation of the Mexicanos and the successful development of all town youth.

In Arbordale the culture brokers are neither as evident nor as committed; and, of course, power is not diffusely distributed, as it is in Corntown. Nonetheless, key authority figures such as the police chief, the librarian, the junior high principal, and the Mexicano Catholic community worker show tolerance regarding youth gathing in public spaces—a park, the town square, and the library, for example. Together they have contributed to the attachment of Mexicano youth to the community and to small-town life.

Prairieview resembles a suburban town in its patterns of civic engagement, housing practices, and privatizing of child rearing. Youth in suburbanized postagrarian towns belong only to their parents. Adolescents are socialized with the expectation that they will leave, rather than that they will become attached to the community. Youth are not expected to contribute to the town, except as members of the high school band or teams. They are responsible only for their personal development, as students of the high school, not as members of the community. Consequently, cross-age relations are weak; generations are segregated, and each is internally focused. Youth are not considered the place's future, and therefore community investment in the form of tolerance is less generous or even-handed (Baumgartner 1988; Kenny 2000; Schwartz 1987).

Schools help to maintain an agrarian town's unique place identity by linking family histories with the history of a central institution. Tolerance of adolescents is a hallmark of agrarian towns and a casualty of suburbanization into postagrarian nontowns. Postagrarian towns would do well to mimic the distinctive features of agrarian communities: tolerance, adult-structured environments and community watchfulness over youth, and schools reflecting these town qualities, because they produce the positive community effect of successful youth development. An agrarian community effect works for Mexicano migrant children, who, nationally, are among those most likely to be at risk.

A sense of community is linked to the interaction among the core dimensions of space, connectedness, social resources, and cross-age relations. Each dimension reinforces the others to shape various degrees of community in a town, from a one with a strong, unique identity to a generic suburban nontown. Community that emerges from this reinforcing process is more than the sum of the four crucial dimensions that define it.

History, Culture, and Community Identity

A distinctive community identity, we know, helps generate the place attachment that makes people care about their locality (Low and Altman 1992). Community culture is an aspect of local identity (see chapter 1) and is pivotal to whether a place is connected and rich in social resources. In my research for *Prairie Patrimony*, I found that even before the 1980s surge of newcomers began transforming Illinois farming communities, those communities were distinctively organized because their local cultures differed in fundamental ways. Despite experiencing the same economic and social circumstances and sharing the same physical environment (soils, weather, and region), villages only a few miles apart visibly and culturally differed, according to the ethnic origin of the population. That is, village vigor is a barometer of a community's cohesiveness, attachment, and commitment to the maintenance of a sense of community with a collective identity (Salamon 1992).

Even two communities in the same school district—Prairie Gem, described in *Prairie Patrimony*, and Splitville—that share location and the core institution of a school have, for ethnic or historical reasons, vastly differing cultures. Prairie Gem works cooperatively as a community, but Splitville apparently never did. Similarly, Smallville differs from Bigville, only six miles away, by having a rich store of social resources and strong connections in the form of overlapping social networks. Because such agrarian towns maintain vitality and have well-kept homes, they are appealing to upscale newcomers. If an agrarian community is located in a scenic area, it has more lure for developers. What worked in the past to maintain an agrarian identity thus may be what is now most attractive to newcomers, even though they do not share the culture that made it possible.

In *Prairie Patrimony* I focused on ethnicity as a fundamental source of community culture. Other factors, described in this book, also account for a distinctive culture that determines how a community deals with change, such as a newcomer influx. History tells us, for example, whether a community is able to mobilize itself for the common good. If a community has well-established traditions of supporting school activities, caring for its dependent citizens, and organizing celebrations, cooperativeness and trust will infuse the local culture. Splitville is a town whose conflicted history makes cooperation difficult, even when circumstances demand it. Community commitment and loyalty are critical components of a vital local culture. If people see their community as a special, good place, they are more likely to take action to maintain it.

Postagrarian communities have to make extra efforts to produce rituals that bring together newcomers and oldtimers in a celebration of their shared community. These communities cannot depend on high school football and basketball games to unite them. The newcomers are not invested in the schools as deeply as the oldtimers have been. Other rituals, such as festivals or farmer's markets, must be used to build a community identity and the attachment that creates loyalty and commitment among citizens (Aronoff 1993; Kemmis 1995; Lavenda 1997; Prosterman 1995).

THE EMERGING SOCIAL FABRIC OF THE HEARTLAND

Rural midwestern towns have changed over the past twenty years. Some old towns mourn the passing of agrarian norms, but others embrace change as inevitable. As rural places have transformed from agrarian communities into regional neighborhoods for small cities, towns have become internally more homogeneous by class. At the same time postagrarian towns now differ more from nearby places, also homogeneous by class, with which they formerly shared much. What is being lost is the rich diversity of small towns: internally it came from a mix of classes, and externally robust cultural distinctions differentiated the communities in a region. What were genuine hometowns are becoming indistinguishable nontowns.

In transformed towns such as Prairieview, Splitville, and potentially Arbordale and Bunkerton, it is likely that the oldtimers, for the first time, will experience minority status (culturally and even ethnically) in their original old town. As a newcomer influx rolls over the agrarian community, the oldtimers' common history of doing things in certain ways will no longer shape community behavior, especially if the oldtimers are aging. An entirely new shared history must be cultivated if a sense of a unique community is to emerge.

The towns of Prairieview, Bunkerton, and Splitville were used as a growth machine, and that was what brought the newcomers. In Prairieview and Bunkerton, growth was defined as good, with locals buying into the booster goal. This boosterism is a new incarnation of a phenomenon that began in the nineteenth century, a prioritizing of capitalistic goals that was seen especially in old small towns even then. With few zoning controls, in part because farmers and rural people resisted them, the free market has had its way in the communities. Prairieview and Bunkerton have become suburbs of Central City, and the shabby Splitville housing stock absorbs the detritus and flotsam of the rural population displaced by the suburbanization process. In this way relatively independent towns in the regional archipelago have become interrelated, albeit indirectly.

Agrarian towns had social differences, but the elite was permeable if worthy newcomers or middle-class residents accumulated wealth or had style (Adams 1994; Duncan 1999). Now emerging in the rural Midwest is a town stratification that can be expected increasingly to chart the life chances of residents. Prairieview exemplifies the most affluent stratum, followed by Bunkerton, which is lower-middle-class and upper blue-collar. The people of both towns are primarily employed in the new economy, outside of their own towns. Corntown and Arbordale definitely are working-class, although Arbordale's small elite has sustained itself until now with robust agribusinesses. Smallville is on a decline, economically and, because it has an aging population, demographically. At the bottom of the town hierarchy is Splitville, now dominated by the rural working-poor.

As a consequence of the more pronounced, stratified rural social fabric, there are more barriers to social mobility—geographic as well as social—than existed previously in the rural Midwest. In the Central City archipelago (one in all likelihood being replicated outside small cities throughout rural America), rural growth machines in the hinterlands are transforming unique places into economically homogeneous, suburbanized sleeper towns. Now more than in the past, the nontown place where you live identifies your class position (see also appendix A).

Just as local governments began to question the wisdom of smokestack-chasing to obtain jobs, any jobs, towns may now want to question the recruiting done by a rural growth machine that treats community and land simply as real estate commodities. Boosterism is inherently a small-town business ideal, but the whole community is drafted to serve the aim that ultimately benefits the few. The booster assumption is that once newcomers are attracted to live in a town, they will also shop there, gain oldtimer-like loyalty, and contribute their resources to the common good. Perhaps what happened to Prairieview or Bunkerton should cause oldtimers to rethink whether they want to uncritically embrace a rural growth machine (see fig. 8). As a way to mobilize people, boosterism works well, but the process has produced broad residential changes that have transformed what locals valued about community. Jobs were one thing, but urban newcomers who do not buy into small community connections and jointly generated social resources are another. When newcomers begin to outnumber oldtimers, the community as an organic entity becomes fragile. Reservoirs of social capital that have served the community for generations drain away if suburban priorities emerge or if newcomers do not produce the levels of civic engagement taken for granted by oldtimers.

Can agrarian community ideals of egalitarianism, commitment, connectedness, trust, and cooperation be sustained under the new conditions of a transformed postagrarian social fabric? Only Corntown and Smallville (with few newcomers) have moved into the postagrarian era with sustained agrarian norms of trust, engagement, loyalty, and tolerance for youth. What those residents love about their towns is the distinctive local culture and the public spaces. Their willingness to cooperate has sustained the communities. The challenge for the postagrarian, suburbanized communities is that newcomers, if they buy into the local beliefs about trust and a commitment to children, must become as engaged as the oldtimers who have constructed the sense of community that attracts them. The new-comers of Bunkerton and Arbordale show some signs of being so engaged.

Because newcomers lead fragmented lives, postagrarian communities are postmodern; only one dimension of family life—residence—is experienced locally. Fragmented lives reduce the likelihood that frequent interactions will occur, interactions that create a shared history, norms of reciprocity, and the place attachment fundamental to agrarian communities. It is doubtful that urban newcomers even are aware of this unspoken but unifying social order (Bloom 2000). For these reasons, postagrarian, postmodern places lack widely shared norms other than an intense focus on the nuclear family, privacy, consumerism, privilege, and moral minimalism (Baumgartner 1988; Kenny 2000). Their mobility and privacy mean that newcomers do not have a history, a family reputation; effective social control traditionally depended on the coercive power of family reputation. In this respect, postagrarian rural communities exhibit a society-wide decline of institutions based on family as the central element of social organization. Replacing those institutions are others based on reason, run by bureaucracy, and driven by the market (Coleman 1993). Just as the agrarian community is a distinctive social environment, so is the postmodern, postagrarian community. Like true suburbanites, families in postagrarian town subdivisions live in a place where they are not embedded socially but which they seem to prefer, while always longing for a real community with high property values.

The connectedness that made people cherish agrarian hometowns as special places emerged as an unintended consequence when people were committed enough to pull the community through changes wrought by the ups and downs of the wider society. The way change was managed integrated the town in a configuration that retained what people valued, and the community forged thereby in turn sustained the residents. Youth, the product of these agrarian communities, reflect the trust and commitment that exists. Dedication to the youth as future citizens and to maintaining the public spaces that enhance a unique identity motivated civic engagement in agrarian communities. The youth in small towns, like the canaries in a mine shaft, are predictors: how they fare developmentally will prophesy clearly about the well-being of a postagrarian community.

The forces that built community and produced successful development for youth—those taken-for-granted features of an agrarian community—have become more challenging to sustain in the context of strong growth-machine pressures on the postagrarian social fabric of rural America. A history of dealing with exodus rather than influx of residents has not prepared old towns for the onslaught of suburbanization. Small towns have survived by being resilient, and that sort of strength should enable the communities to face the new changes. Their challenge is to sustain a real community by not transforming into a nontown, a place holding little meaning for those who live there.

The development of the postagrarian social fabric represented by our six towns raises challenging questions for planners and policymakers. How should those who are interested in a vital rural America invest their resources—in people or in places? Up to now that investment has focused on places, whether through growth-machine processes, road building, or downtown beautification. The towns that have better sustained a sense of community, however, are those where people working together have made the difference. Small-town communities have a culture worth nurturing and protecting. We can see that small-town resources, connections, and commitment contribute to the successful development of youth. Outbreaks of high school violence in places recently suburbanized have shown us that the destruction of small town culture does away with some of what is good about us as a nation.

APPENDIX A

THE REGIONAL SUBURBANIZATION NEIGHBORHOOD HYPOTHESIS

With Matteo B. Marini

This appendix uses standard economic criteria to test the *neighborhood hypothesis*, a hypothesis about rural regional transformation arrived at inductively from the six qualitative community studies. Our goal is to characterize the emergent regional relationship between small towns and small cities in the postagrarian rural Midwest. The neighborhood hypothesis to be tested is this:

> Each small town that is altered by newcomers becomes more homogeneous within its boundaries as it becomes more differentiated from other towns in the rural landscape, functioning as if it were a neighborhood—where like lives near like—of the small city that anchors the commuting zone.

Testing the hypothesis allows us to answer such questions as, Is social stratification becoming located spatially, as town-neighborhoods, in relation to the small city? Have class differences become more pronounced among the set of communities since the 1980s? Do the changes visible in rural Illinois correspond with the evidence typically used to assess community well-being? Before testing the neighborhood hypothesis, we must explore what it means to be a "neighborhood" in the rural countryside within commuting distance of a small city.

THE NEIGHBORHOOD CONCEPT

Residential neighborhoods are typically what city dwellers consider to be their community: where they know people personally and have some expectation for reciprocity in times of need, as discussed in chapter 1 (Fischer 1982). Small cities such as those in central Illinois (Decatur, Bloomington-Normal, Champaign-Urbana, Danville, and Springfield) (see fig. 1), have distinctive neighborhoods but also serve as the source of big-city amenities for the surrounding small towns. Chapter 2 describes a gradual absorption of most activities of rural people from towns into the city, so that rural places are used only for residence.

Our argument is that the emergent postagrarian landscape is not a simple continuum of rural to urban but a spatial structure with economic and social differentiation among the small towns. Such towns were more alike even as recently as a decade ago. Community differentiation, in the form of economic specialization, has been iden- tified in North Dakota, for example, as a consequence of deliberate corporate policy decisions of local business and political leaders (Tauxe 1993). Differentiation in central Illinois, and indeed in the Midwest, however, results from the imperative of small-town resi- dential choices made by newcomers. These people keep their towns firmly in the small city's orbit by their daily commute. Thus, the differentiation is residential, and the towns are emerging as distinc- tive "neighborhoods," with population specialization. The effect is that increased social stratification is becoming located spatially, so that geography reinforces class distinctions more than it once did.

One way of looking at the differentiation and specialization pro- cess is termed *metropolitanization* of the nonmetro areas (Elliott and Perry 1996). Another perspective describes a *bifurcation* process, in which some rural towns are becoming wealthy from the arrival of relatively affluent, probably urban-based, newcomers, while other towns, which historically have housed the rural poor in significant numbers, are becoming marginalized and even excluded from the benefits that new wealth brings (Bradshaw 1993). Yet another view regards the emergent countryside, the fastest growing entity in rural America, as loosely linked nonplaces, without a center or clear boundaries (Herbers 1986). None of these conceptions, however, adequately describe the settlement relationships in the emerging midwestern rural landscape in which small towns that were previ- ously more heterogeneous become more homogeneous after the arrival of newcomers, while simultaneously being drawn more tightly into a central place. A new metaphor is needed to describe the emerging rural countryside: a commuting zone in which small towns function as noncontiguous urban neighborhoods for a small city anchoring the zone. This metaphor describes the neighborhood hypothesis.

THE SOCIOECONOMIC PROFILE OF THE CASE STUDY COMMUNITIES

Our test of the neighborhood hypothesis with census data has three levels: level 1 provides a snapshot of the six case study towns' structural characteristics at one point in time, 1990 (when the studies were done); level 2 looks at the contextual changes occurring in the labor market between 1980 and 1998, assuming that the towns reflect broader regional changes taking place at the county level; and level 3 examines town changes during the same span of time (1980 to 2000) in order to verify the neighborhood hypothesis. These three comparisons incorporate major indicators that economists typically use to evaluate community performance over time.

Level 1: Within-Community Characteristics

In table A1, the six communities are ordered by population size. According to 1990 census figures, the set of communities clusters into two types. Corntown, Bunkerton, and Prairieview, whose populations fall in the census category of "places between 2,500 and 9,999," are considered towns. The second group, Arbordale, Splitville, and Smallville, with populations below 2,500, are considered villages. (Although Smallville is not in the central Illinois commuting zone, it represents a type of town found there.) These clusters do not mean, however, that size is more important than other factors to the neighborhood effect.

When the focus shifts to the occupations reported by residents, according to the three most significant sectors—agriculture, manufacturing, and professional service—the towns cluster differently, as can be seen in table A1. Of course, many rural individuals have more than one occupation, combining self-employment that is home based with a job in the labor force (Barlett 1986). For example, we found in the communities hairstyling, cake decorating, and sewing businesses, operated by women, and automobile repair, blade sharpening, and furniture refinishing businesses, operated by men. The pattern of residents' labor force participation reflects the social and economic structure of the town (table A1). Smallville has the second

Table A1 Community Demographic and Economic Characteristics at Time of Field Studies (ca. 1990)

	CORN-TOWN	BUNKER-TON	PRAIRIE-VIEW	ARBOR-DALE	SMALL-VILLE	SPLIT-VILLE	U.S.
Population	5,900	4,300	3,100	1,300	500	180	249 million
Employed in agriculture (%)	1	1	2	17	9	3	2
Employed in manufacturing (%)	38	19	13	25	26	11	24
Employed in professional service (%)	13	24	33	15	19	16	20
Education (% high school graduates)	69	74	89	63	78	54	78
Median age	31.0	32.8	29.9	33.3	41.7	32.2	32.8
Receiving Social Security (%)	34.5	33.7	18.9	38.5	42.7	38.8	15.9
Receiving public assistance (%)	6.4	5.1	2.4	5.8	7.9	2.9	15.26
Median household income ($)	22,262	23,770	39,085	22,365	16,635	22,083	29,943
Income inequality within community[a]	0.40	0.37	0.28	0.40	0.40	0.31	0.43

Sources: Bureau of the Census 1990a, 1990b.
Note: Numbers have been rounded.
[a] Gini Coefficient (0–1).

largest number of residents employed in agriculture, supporting its use as the agrarian benchmark community. Corntown and Arbordale, characterized as blue-collar communities, have more residents involved in the manufacturing sector. From an economic point of view, these manufacturing towns represent a step forward with diversification of the local economy beyond agriculture. Bunkerton and Prairieview represent further diversification, given the majority of residents involved in the service sector. Splitville confirms the marginal nature of its economy, being underrepresented in each of the three main sectors and having the lowest proportion of residents participating in the labor force. Much self-employment and seasonal agricultural work, such as detasseling corn, was reported by Splitville residents.

The educational levels of residents reinforce the economic profile described in the case studies: Prairieview has the largest proportion of residents with a high school or greater education, and their children score higher than the national average on standardized tests. Smallville and Bunkerton follow, with educational levels at about the national average. Corntown, Arbordale, and Splitville cluster, with values below the national educational level. Splitville ranks very low, confirming the profile of a marginal community that emerged in the case study. In general, the educational achievements in the six communities correlate with the economic profiles of the communities depicted here and in chapter 2. The towns whose workers are incorporated into the professional sector (Prairieview and Bunkerton) have better-educated populations than the blue-collar towns (Corntown and Arbordale) and the marginal village (Splitville). The anomaly of Smallville, the agrarian village ranking high on educational level, confirms the high priority it places on education, evidenced by taxing itself heavily to retain its two school districts, the smallest in Illinois, until the mid-1990s.

Educational achievement is closely correlated with economic well-being in our set of towns. Corntown, Bunkerton, Arbordale, and Splitville have about the same median income, a shared position that is lower than the national median income but not lower than the rural median income of $21,365 for places with populations 2,500 to 9,999 (Bureau of the Census 1990a). Prairieview has a 25% higher median income than the national average. At the bottom of the ladder, Smallville's median income is 40% lower than the national average. Smallville's low position is better understood when we note that the median age of its residents is one-quarter higher than that in the other towns and the national median age and that 42.7% of the town receive Social Security benefits. These factors are indicative of an elderly population (table A1). Excluding aging Smallville, Splitville occupies the lowest position according to the criteria of family income.

The distribution of income among community residents is considered (last row, table A1) in order to assess the degree of income inequality within each community. The Gini Coefficient was used to measure the degree of income concentration among residents. The value of the indicator varies between 0 and 1. It tends to be 0 when income is equally distributed, and it would tend toward 1 if all the town income was concentrated in one family (Gardner 1988). The concentration of income shows little variation among the six towns, and each resembles the national distribution level of 0.43. Prairieview and Splitville, however, have a lower Gini Coefficient, indicating more homogeneity of income among residents. The fact that these two towns score at the opposite ends of the income range (excluding the elderly Smallville) significantly supports the neighborhood hypothesis. Indeed, these two places are at the extremes of the social ladder whether income, education, or the qualitative case study is taken into account. That these polar opposites are also internally

Table A2 Job Variation Reported at County Level, 1980 to 1998 (%)

	PRAIRIEVIEW AND SPLITVILLE COUNTY	BUNKERTON COUNTY	CORNTOWN COUNTY	ARBORDALE COUNTY	SMALLVILLE COUNTY
Total	+23	−3	−6	+6	−6
Primary[a]	−4	−21	−26	−40	−20
Secondary[b]	+65	−20	−34	+6	−25
Tertiary[c]	+43	+9	+15	+27	+6
Governmental[d]	−12	+5	−7	0	−9

Source: U.S. Department of Commerce 2000.

[a] Primary sector: farming, forestry, fishing, and mining.

[b] Secondary sector: manufacturing and construction.

[c] Tertiary sector: transportation, public utilities, trade, finance, and other professional services.

[d] Governmental sector: federal, state, and local; civilian and military.

the most homogeneous in terms of income distribution confirms our assertion that a spatially visible social differentiation is occurring among a regionally linked group of rural communities.

Level 2: Changes in the County Context

According to the neighborhood hypothesis, community-level change is affected by trends in the particular regional commuting zone. If the regional level is important for interpreting community-level change, the trends for the five counties in which the set of towns is located should indicate which forces are shaping the towns' futures. We evaluate these changes by utilizing county-level employment data for 1980 and 1998, shown in table A2. These data reflect actual jobs reported by businesses, plants, or services to the U.S. Department of Commerce, rather than the occupations reported by town residents in the national census. Thus, these data represent a fairly accurate estimate of labor demand (rather than labor supply) and therefore an estimate of economic-level structural trends.

The only county to grow significantly in jobs between 1980 and 1998 is the one in which Prairieview and Splitville are located; it is also the site of Central City, which serves as the anchor for the commuting zone (table A2). The rate of growth is a remarkable +23%; the other counties lost jobs in the same decade at a rate of −3% to −6%. The job growth in the Prairieview and Splitville county is concentrated mainly in the secondary sector (manufacturing and construction), indicative of the attractive power of that county in the region. The job losses in three of the five counties are concentrated in the primary and secondary sectors, paralleling the crisis in traditional industries throughout the nation during the decade (Galston 1993). Nonetheless, counterbalancing signs of growth in the tertiary sector are evident in those three counties; in the Bunkerton county, where Bunkerton is the county seat, there is also growth in the governmental sector.

Level 3: Differentiation in the Postagrarian Countryside

We now assess the effects of such county-level changes on the community level, using basic indicators of well-being also employed in table A1: population, family median income, and income distribution among families. Whereas the former analysis examined the static situation in 1990, our focus now shifts to the dynamic changes that occurred between 1980 and 2000 in the set of towns. This analysis allows us to test the neighborhood hypothesis more thoroughly and to describe the distinctive community identities emerging in the postagrarian countryside.

When we look at population change (table A3), it is evident that there are winners and losers in the postagrarian countryside. Prairieview clearly has gained the most in population (+145%), while Splitville has lost 25% of its original population. Smallville and Corntown are also losers (−10% and −8%, respectively); Arbordale and Bunkerton have gained (+27% and +7%, respectively). Arbordale's growth is accounted for by an influx of Mexicanos.

The presence of a winner (Prairieview) and a loser (Splitville) in the same county supports the neighborhood hypothesis. Economic growth in Central City (as evidenced from the rapid growth in jobs, table A2) apparently created a need for an upscale suburban place such as Prairieview while simultaneously emptying such marginal, more remote places as Splitville. Maintaining Splitville's population even at that low level, however, was achieved only as lower-income people moved in during the late 1980s and early 1990s, attracted by the low-cost surplus housing that resulted from the outmigration of the young and the gradual dying off of retirees. Population loss in Corntown is linked to the loss of manufacturing jobs in town and at the county level. As described in chapter 6, Corntown lost a major canning factory, and that loss was compounded by the loss of a major industrial plant in the county seat.

Shifting to household income variation, table A3 shows that during the last two decades the median incomes of the six study towns did not lose ground (+138%) compared to the median income of the United States as a whole (+133%). This comparison, however, masks a polarization among the six communities, an outcome that supports the neighborhood hypothesis. Prairieview's and Arbordale's median incomes rose respectively by 178% and 168%, but

Table A3 Changes in Population and Income among the Communities (between 1980 and 2000)

		PRAIRIEVIEW	SPLITVILLE	BUNKERTON
Population	1980	2,000	200	4,200
	2000	4,900	150	4,500
	1980–2000 (% change)	+145	−25	+7
Median household income (current $)	1980	20,680	15,662	15,953
	2000	57,574	31,875	37,804
	1980–2000 (% change)	+178	+103	+137
Income inequality[a] within the community	1980	0.37	0.53	0.43
	2000	0.24	0.28	0.33
	1980–2000 (% change)	−35	−47	−23
Income inequality[b] across all communities	1980			
	2000			
	1980–2000 (% change)			

Source: Data from U.S. Census Bureau 1980, 2002.
[a] Gini coefficient (0–1).
[b] Variation coefficient (0–1).

Splitville's, Corntown's, and Smallville's median incomes fell behind the national gains. Prairieview's unsurprising income rise is related to the suburbanization process. Arbordale's rise, however, results from the Mexicano immigration to that area and, probably more importantly, from expectations for jobs in a proposed, controversial third Chicago-area regional airport to be built in a nearby county. Bunkerton's median income maintains the national pace, perhaps owing to its dependence on the governmental sector.

The final indicator is the income inequality within each town during the past twenty years. Historically, the towns were more alike as a group and more diverse within themselves. But according to the neighborhood hypothesis a homogenization within the towns and a differentiation among the towns should have taken place between 1980 and 2000. Whether the process of internal homogenization occurred is tested by the percent variation of the Gini Coefficient within each town. A decrease of the Gini Coefficient would imply homogenization of household incomes within each town, and indeed this is what the data show. At the national as well as the community level the Gini Coefficient decreased between 1980 and 2000 (see table A3).

An increase in the variability of per capita income among the communities, however, would imply a process of differentiation among

CORNTOWN	ARBORDALE	SMALLVILLE	ACROSS THE SIX COMMUNITIES	U.S.
6,500	1,100	440		226,100,000
6,000	1,400	400		281,422,000
−8	+27	−10		+24
15,045	13,392	12,414	15,524	17,785
31,947	35,852	26,458	36,918	41,433
+112	+168	+113	+138	+133
0.45	0.48	0.48		0.42
0.40	0.38	0.46		0.34
−11	−21	−4		−19
			0.17	
			0.27	
			+59	

the towns. Indeed, the variation coefficient did increase from 0.17 to 0.27 over the period. As discussed above, Prairieview and Arbordale became richer, while Splitville, Smallville, and Corntown became relatively poorer. In general, those communities with a more diversified local economy were better off. Clearly, towns with such economies can maintain a wider distribution of income than places that were or became basically bedroom communities.

FORCES DRIVING URBAN NEIGHBORHOODIZATION IN A RURAL COMMUTING ZONE

Small midwestern cities during the 1980s and 1990s were magnets for regional jobs, services, and national superstores. These cities clearly depend on the rural countryside to generate both customers and employees. It has not been small-city political policy to preempt the small towns, but as service and medical centers developed, an absorption of everything but residential functions from towns to small cities occurred. Agrarian community members attempt to resist the trend by patronizing local businesses and services, if possible. Central City, serving as a magnet for the four counties represented by five of the six towns, had a population change from about 100,000 in 1990 to about 104,000 in 2000, a change that does not reflect its robust job and business gains (Bureau of Economic and Business Research 1992, 1999). But each of the transformed residential "neighborhood towns" has emerged with a new function in the regional archipelago anchored by Central City (Alonso 1993). Now more than previously, demographic shifts in Central City's commuting zone—in towns like Prairieview and Splitville—must be explained by events occurring at a regional level. Central City and the surrounding towns are inextricably linked.

As the case studies show, the towns developed into Central City neighborhoods because of a newcomer influx. Only in the upscale town of Prairieview, and perhaps in Bunkerton, can change be attributed to urban dispersion, that is, outmigration from Central City (Elliot and Perry 1996). Arbordale and Corntown grew or changed as newcomers from Texas or Mexico settled in those towns, and the changes in Splitville can be traced, apparently, to the relocation of the working-poor from other rural towns. No single migration pattern explains the change.

Within the commuting zone, a hierarchy of towns has developed in which there are winners and losers. The regional postagrarian midwestern pattern is clearly distinct, however, from the bifurcation pattern emerging in California (Bradshaw 1993). Bifurcation in the Midwest is inhibited because in the past many towns had diversified economies that combined agriculture and manufacturing with services, and these diversified towns have maintained a middle position. Thus, midwestern towns have not followed the California pattern of clustering at the top and the bottom of the income range (Cronon 1991). Interestingly, Corntown and Arbordale, which absorbed minority newcomers, are firmly entrenched in the middle, whereas in California minority communities tend to be poor and disadvantaged. Midwestern towns emerging as economic "losers" are white, working-poor, or aging, as exemplified by Splitville and Smallville. The orbit of a small midwestern city probably cannot support more than one upscale rural community such as Prairieview. A similar example is presented by Kalona, Iowa, a town that lies about a twenty-mile commute south of Iowa City. Kalona has been transformed into an upscale suburban community by commuters from Iowa City who have bought up property formerly owned by Mennonites and Amish farmers (Calvin L. Beale, personal communication, 1996). The homogenization of towns at each end of the income spectrum augurs poorly for broad persistence of the diversified and more egalitarian agrarian community form.

It is evident from the community case studies that we must increasingly consider small-town change in a regional context. Change within the small setting is now, more than before, linked to changes in the urban regional center, owing to residential preferences. As long as gasoline is relatively cheap, these processes, driven by people's willingness to commute, can be expected to continue reshaping the rural Midwest.

APPENDIX B

COMMUNITY SAMPLE
CHARACTERISTICS AND
STUDY METHODS

My interest in rural communities evolved from writing a previous book about farm families (Salamon 1992). As I concluded that manuscript, I saw a correspondence between an ethnic farmer group's commitment to maintaining a community and the kind of town that anchored the group (Salamon 1987, 1989). Finding that Illinois towns differed in culture and vitality despite being located in the same region, being of similar size, and having outwardly homogeneous populations motivated a gradual shift in my studies of rural communities (Salamon 1995). My approach departs from that of the classic rural and small-town study that seems to keep community impersonally at arm's length (see, e.g., Goldschmidt 1978; Vidich and Bensman 1958). Rather than studying community from the top down by, for example, using the local power structure as a focal point, I study from the bottom up to capture community from the family stance. In this respect my approach resembles research that highlights the interface between family and community by capturing a sense of place or attachment or the effect of context on interpersonal relationships (see, e.g., Baumgartner 1988; Erikson 1976; Schwartz 1987; Williams 1988). Following the lead of these latter researchers, I construct a community culture as it emerges from the aggregation of individual households interviewed and observed. No community-level analysis of governmental institutions, for example, is presented, although governance is explored through local family encounters. Questions asked by my research include how community is experienced in ordinary ways in a neighborhood or in town public spaces (or when such spaces are absent), how cross-age interactions shape the lives of adolescents, and how newcomers and old-timers interact.

As in *Prairie Patrimony* (Salamon 1992), my goal is a community ethnography, but my research strategy differs from the year-long residence in the field that many anthropologists still favor. Living for a year in a place affords the leisure of interacting with and observing people on a redundant basis, learning the rhythm and reason of their lives by experiencing it. I had to innovate because I was working with students whose applied professional goals led them to seek a master's degree (in a unit that did not offer a Ph.D. degree until relatively recently). Two of the five field assistants were at the master's level when working with me; however, they went on to complete a doctorate elsewhere, one in family studies and one in anthropology. Another, Stacey Williams, would have pursued the Ph.D. after completing her master's had I not introduced her to my younger son, whom she eventually married. The members of the workshop class were all Ph.D. candidates.

Thus, my team method for community ethnography was invented out of necessity. Team ethnography carries both advantages and limitations. We do not have the luxury of extended field time (as I would prefer) because master's students must complete their data collection, analysis, and thesis in approximately a year's time. They learn qualitative research strategies as they carry them out. Close supervision of the process is required, and preferred, by such field assistants. I typically visit the community with the research assistant at the outset. We meet with a key community member, such as a village administrator or a minister (the occupation of the person varies by community). That individual helps us to gain entry and lets others know that we are officially recognized. In one community we had to obtain a vendor permit to do the household survey. A short description of the study is placed strategically in the local (usually weekly) newspaper to advertise our activities to the community. As a faculty member in the College of Agricultural, Consumer, and Environmental Sciences at a land-grant university, I fortunately can rely on county University of Illinois Extension expertise. Extension people know their county well, typically live there, and serve as background informants. In some cases they provided introductions to

Table B1 Sample Household Characteristics

COMMUNITY (STUDY DATE, SAMPLE SIZE)	MEDIAN AGE	MEDIAN EDUCATION	MEDIAN INCOME ($)	OWN HOME (%)	EMPLOYED IN AGRI- CULTURE (%)
Smallville (1988, N = 41)	36–45	Vocational education	20,001– 40,000	82.9	19.5
Prairieview (1995, N = 52)	36–45	Some college	40,001– 60,000	96.2	3.8
Bunkerton (1991–92, N = 52)	36–45	Some college	20,001– 40,000	86.0	0.0
Corntown (1991–92, N = 25)	36–45	Some high school	20,001– 40,000	71.0	0.0
Arbordale (1994–95, N = 15)	26–35	Some high school	20,001– 40,000	93.0	33.3
Splitville (1989–90, N = 72)	36–45	High school	10,001– 20,000	84.7	9.7

families. I have also used introductions from students in my classes (in Smallville) or other personal contacts developed over the years to gain initial entry into a community. We benefited greatly from the generous hospitality of midwestern small-town folk, who are exceedingly open about sharing their lives (Salamon 1995).

Each community ethnographic case study is constructed from data obtained with multiple methods that include a household survey, follow-up interviews with a representative group of households, and varying types of participant observation. Fieldwork is augmented by census data, newspaper archives, and key community-figure interviews. Because each study originated independently, it is important to note, the data are not uniform across all communities. For example, aside from some key informant interviews, people of Mexican origin were the subjects in Corntown and Arbordale. Yet enough topics were consistently examined in each setting to allow for cross-community comparisons. Table B1 shows the sample household demographic characteristics, and table B2 shows connections linking household and community, by comparing the six communities across a set of common variables. The community sample descriptions presented follow the chronological sequence of the studies. Consolata Kabonesa, using some preliminary work by Grace Malindi, conducted the frequency analyses for tables B1 and B2.

I chose each community and the subsample of households that were studied intensively, met some families, and guided what was asked and which issues were pursued. In the acknowledgments I indicate what each of my fieldwork collaborators did. My research strat-

EMPLOYED IN PROFESSIONAL SERVICES (%)	EMPLOYED IN MANUFACTURING (%)	WORKING FULL-TIME (%)	WORKING PART-TIME (%)	RETIRED (%)	ON PUBLIC ASSISTANCE (%)	SELF-EMPLOYED (%)
49.0	2.4	70.0	14.6	0.0	0.0	0.0
52.8	13.5	76.9	1.9	17.3	3.8	0.0
50.0	8.0	58.0	12.0	18.0	2.0	16.0
8.0	40.0	56.0	16.0	16.0	8.0	0.0
47.0	7.0	67.0	7.0	7.0	13.0	0.0
18.0	11.1	38.9	9.7	30.6	5.6	18.1

egy, especially the initial door-to-door survey, essentially depends on capturing a cross section of community households. The overview obtained from a household survey, in particular, facilitates strategically focused follow-up interviews with and observations of representative families. During the course of the studies, field workers ate at local cafés, attended local festivals, and talked with people they met casually on the street. Most crucial to the research process are weekly discussions as the work unfolds. I read all field notes, and the team discusses the interviews and observations. This process provides an ongoing mechanism for joint analysis of our findings. We continually refine our working hypotheses as new data are collected, and we test them with the families being studied (Denzin 1989; Patton 1990).

Aside from the survey instrument completed with household members in their home, all data are recorded from memory as soon as possible after a visit is completed. (The only exception was that the Arbordale field worker used a tape recorder.) My student assistants are trained to record field notes in quotation form whenever possible. They always worry about missing something, but several factors ensure the faithful capturing of what happens. First, people tend to repeat themselves, particularly if what they say is important to them. Second, one's memory and observational skills improve rapidly in the field. Field workers learn to make key-word notations on the survey instrument or in small notebooks in the privacy of the bathroom or their car, to remind them of what has occurred. Some-

Table B2 Connections between Sample Households and the Community

CONNECTION TYPE	SMALL- VILLE $N = 41$	PRAIRIE- VIEW $N = 52$	BUNKER- TON $N = 52$	CORN- TOWN $N = 25$[a]	ARBOR- DALE $N = 15$[a]	SPLIT- VILLE $N = 72$
Ethnicity (%)						
American, English, Welsh, or Scottish	65.9	71.1	66.0	0.0	0.0	58.3
Irish	2.4	3.8	4.0	0.0	0.0	11.1
German or Dutch	22.0	13.4	14.0	0.0	0.0	22.2
Swedish	2.4	0.0	14.0	0.0	0.0	2.8
Mexicano	0.0	0.0	0.0	100.0	100.0	0.0
Religious affiliation (%)						
Catholic	2.4	15.4	8.0	90.0	93.0	9.7
Mainstream Protestant	87.7	65.3	62.0	0.0	0.0	66.6
Evangelical	7.3	3.8	2.0	0.0	0.0	5.6
Attend church in community (%)	65.5	53.8	73.7	96.0	93.0	33.3
Born in community (%)	56.1	36.6	40.0	4.0	26.0	30.6
Have relatives in community (%)	68.3[b]	34.6	55.3	84.0	100.0	37.5
Participation in civic activities (%)						
Educational	75.7	48.1	74.0	12.0	13.0	45.8
Local government	14.6	5.8	18.0	8.0	0	15.3
Service organization	29.3	9.6	26.0	24.0	0	20.8
Religious	80.5	46.2	64.0	44.0	27.0	31.9

[a] Mexicanos only.
[b] Siblings only.

times a comment is particularly insightful, and we find that speakers do not seem to mind being asked, "Would you mind if I write that down? It is so well put." That helps to get an accurate quotation. The quotations used in the case studies are the words of one person out of at least three who expressed the same sentiments in different contexts. I chose the quotation that was the most representative. That is to say, the quotations incorporated in the book are those that best crystallize patterns observed more widely. I found that a particularly useful technique was to ask everyone about the same pressing community issue, such as saving the local school, the retention of a program for latchkey children, a recent hard-fought election, or whether teenage gangs were developing. This technique provides a strategic focus—an analytical window—that allows cultural change (before and after the event) or the enduring structure of community meaning and identity to be traced (Ohnuki-Tierney 1990; Fernandez 1990). By obtaining multiple perspectives on the same event, we also avoid becoming biased by one category of people or by one interpretation of community meaning.

THE CASE STUDY COMMUNITIES

Smallville

Smallville was chosen to represent the community effects of rapid economic restructuring in agriculture that occurred as a result of the early-1980s farm crisis. Located in western Illinois, in a county considered to be one of those in the state hardest hit by the crisis, Smallville was farming-dominated and highly cohesive, according to local University of Illinois Extension specialists. The community's valiant effort to maintain the smallest school district in the state, despite great pressure to consolidate with nearby towns, evidenced strong loyalties. I came to see Smallville as an archetypical agrarian community and therefore an appropriate benchmark with which change in the other five postagrarian communities could be compared.

A controlled comparison field study of two neighboring towns was carried out by Karen Davis-Brown between June and October 1988 in a west-central Illinois county of less than 20,000 in population. As a full-time research associate, she lived in the county during the five-month study. The goal was to compare the effects of the farm crisis on community functioning in two different places. The criteria for selecting the paired communities were proximity (they are six miles apart), similar size, high elderly population (around 25%), similar resources such as farmland soils, and similar distance (about fifty miles) from a metro area. Bigville has a combined village and countryside population of approximately 1,500, and Smallville has a population of approximately 700 in the combined village and countryside. Although Bigville is twice as large as Smallville, its small size of 1,500 means that Bigville citizens, like Smallville's, can know everyone in the community (Salamon and Davis-Brown 1990; Salamon 1996).

A snowball sample was used, but in conjunction with a matrix designed to ensure that interviews captured a comparable cross section of households in both communities. Males and females in each of three age groups (20–35, 35–60, and over 61 years) were selected to capture a community profile of occupational and class variation. These occupations were similar in structure, for example, social service worker, businessperson, religious leader, clerical or other white-collar worker, laborer or craftsperson, homemaker, unemployed person or one on public aid, and farmer. One-quarter of the 44-household sample in Bigville and almost one-third of the Smallville 41-household sample represent interviews conducted jointly with a husband and wife. In Smallville the sample constitutes 19% of the 216 total village households, according to the 1990 census. An additional set of approximately 10 interviews was conducted with county-level professionals working with senior citizens, at the community college and the local newspaper, with churches, with individuals working for the Farmer's Home Administration and for the county public aid administration, and with a local historian.

Rose Marie Zabel, a research assistant, and Cathey Huddelston, a graduate student, compared the two cross-sectional samples along every standard dimension (age, education, income, etc.) and found no statistically significant difference between them in either demographic characteristics or human capital. Furthermore, using discriminate analysis, we found the samples almost indistinguishable for religious affiliation, level of community involvement, occupation, ethnic diversity (Smallville is slightly more German), and embeddedness in kinship networks. The only statistically significant difference we found is that Smallville people were more likely to consider themselves as close-knit and caring about one another (χ^2 9.97609, 1 df p = .001), whereas Bigville folks saw themselves as less so. Smallville thus is an example of a strongly connected agrarian community that represents the ideal characteristics of this type.

Splitville

I was inspired to look at the low-income residential community, Splitville, during my membership on the W. K. Kellogg National Rural Studies Committee (NRSC), chaired by Emery Castle, and by the Rural Sociological Society Task Force on Persistent Rural Poverty (initiated by NRSC member Gene Summers), which renewed rural sociologists' concern for persistently poor rural people (1993). NRSC seminars examining rural poverty motivated a revisiting of my field notes, written ten years previously, describing a farming community I call Prairie Gem (Salamon 1992). In retrospect, I realized that my focus on farmers had given me tunnel vision for these middle-class subjects and their view of other people. I located in my notes comments by a farm woman that Splitville, which was in the Prairie Gem consolidated school district, was "never very much and it's gotten worse." I phoned a contact in the village bank to ask whether the poor families remained in Splitville, now a decade later. "They're still here," reported my informant with disgust. Thus, the impact of poor newcomers on the smallest community of the set became the study focus.

The data were obtained from nine months of fieldwork (1989–90) when Jane B. Tornatore carried out the study for her master's thesis project (Tornatore 1993; Salamon and Tornatore 1994). Tornatore never lived in the village. After two summer months of being in the village daily to carry out the household survey, she continued to visit frequently during the seven following months. The study's question was "What is the impact on a farming community of a low-income newcomer influx?" Because the village is so small, she knocked on every door and also contacted households in the two miles of countryside immediately surrounding the village. The two-mile radius was chosen after asking several townspeople and farmers to show on a plat map what they considered the Splitville village boundaries to be. The sample of 55 village households constitutes 80% of the 78 inhabited houses; the residents of 14 households refused participation or were unavailable; the remaining 9 households were vacant. (Our impression, based on the appearance of the homes, is that the 14 nonvacant households in which no one was interviewed contained suspicious, elderly home owners.) Another 17 households (38%) of the 45 inhabited dwellings in the countryside were interviewed (5 houses were vacant). Four households refused to be interviewed. Of the 17 interviewed, 7 were the homes of farmers, 1 the home of a farmhand, and nonfarmers lived in the remaining 9. The other 24 countryside households were not interviewed owing to time constraints and because the village emerged as the focus of the study. The survey interviews were semistructured, conducted with one or more of the household adults, and typically lasted from one to four hours. The information obtained included household and work histories, residence history, social network, and community participation and perceptions. Participant observation and more extensive interviews were carried out with a willing subsample of 12 village families in an average of four visits. In addition, Tornatore attended a senior citizen's group and the village board meetings and occasionally lunched at the village café.

County tax records were used to determine the history of home ownership and the real estate market for the village. Transfers of property deeds from 1975 to 1990 and tax redemption records from 1976 to 1990 were examined. This time period coincides with a spurt of newcomers to Splitville. Tax redemption records show that of the 115 total land tracts in the village, some tracts were sold a total of 53 times to reclaim county taxes during the thirteen-year period. Of the properties sold, 9 had tax deeds issued to the buyer, 2 were forfeited to the state, and 2 were bought by the township. Back taxes were paid by owners in arrears on the remaining tracts and ownership thereby maintained. Because the number claimed for back taxes exceeded the number of newcomer households, it is clear that oldtimers (or their heirs) also experienced financial problems over the period (Tornatore 1993). Such data pointed up that newcomers and oldtimers did not differ across the demographic indicators (such as education or income) that typically account for socioeconomic divergence. Rather, the two groups differed primarily in their property attitudes.

Corntown

Several years later my newcomer-oldtimer interest shifted to the settling of people of Mexican origin in small midwestern communities. That trend, labeled the browning of the rural Midwest, was elsewhere emerging in conjunction with the rapid industrialization of beef and pork processing (Fink 1998; Stull, Broadway, and Griffith 1995; Thu and Durrenberger 1998). (Throughout this discussion, as in the text, I use the term *Mexicanos* to cover a diversity of groups including Mexican Americans from Texas or Illinois and Mexican immigrants. When U.S. census data are cited, the term *Hispanics* is used to reflect the census usage.) The two towns Corntown and Arbordale (studied 1991–92 and 1994–95, respectively) were intriguing because Mexicanos had begun settling more than thirty years previously, initially attracted by jobs in local agribusinesses connected with vegetable crops rather than animal production and meat processing. Corntown, a blue-collar town, had been the topic of an anthropology colleague's doctoral dissertation some twenty years before, which provided unique baseline data for comparison of change (Williams 1975).

A two-part ethnographic field study of Corntown, the largest town in the set, was conducted by Stacey Williams in 1991–92 for her master's thesis project. The goal of the study was to determine how settled-out migrants have adapted to the community as a follow-up to Brett Williams's study, which had found a great deal of hostility toward migrant workers (1975). Mexicano households were contacted initially by phone after selecting every Hispanic surname in the local telephone listings. Subsequently, several households were contacted via a snowball referral process. Several households were never contacted despite repeated tries, but only one household actually declined to participate. The 25 interviewed households represent 108 individuals of the approximately 270 Hispanics in Corntown reported in the 1990 census. The total sample represents 40% of the Mexicano population. A single household contained an extended family with one member an in-marrying European American. Because the household of six identified with the Corntown Mexicanos, all of its members were counted among that minority. Special effort was made to include households of varying income levels located in neighborhoods throughout the community, so that a representative cross section of Corntown's Mexicano population was obtained. Semistructured interviews were conducted in each family's home with at least one household adult (typically with other family members present) and were completed within one to three hours. Information obtained included data on family and social network composition; the backgrounds of household members; perceptions of and participation in the community; and occupational, educational, and residential histories. Participant observations of family life included sharing meals with families and witnessing cross-household visitation and parent-child interactions.

All interviews were conducted by Stacey Williams, whose working knowledge of the Spanish language was fair to moderate. Except for one Mexicano household interview performed exclusively in Spanish and another in both Spanish and English, all interviews were conducted in English. The study's initial phase also included interviews with seven Anglo community leaders and school personnel over the nine-month period. Interviews with community leaders and school personnel were conducted in their offices. The combined Mexicano and Anglo interviews, totaling 32, represent 1% of the 2,300 Corntown households (Bureau of the Census 1990a).

As a consequence of findings from the study's first phase, the second phase targeted Corntown Mexicano youth (ages 13 to 21). This phase included interviews with 18 youth (7 males and 11 females), conducted over seven months in 1992. The adolescents either are members of families surveyed in the initial phase or were introduced to Williams by such families. All youth contacted agreed to participate (full parental consent was obtained for underage respondents). The original survey was revised and amended to reflect the concerns of youth. With the youth, particular attention was paid to school and academic achievement, parent-child dynamics, and questions of ethnic identity. Extensive scholastic data were gathered at the Corntown high school, whose principal graciously opened academic records (which were used with parental consent).

Corntown's Mexicano population diverges in several 1990 census categories from the town's overall population. Although only 27% of Corntown's population is under 18 years of age, almost half of its Hispanics are under 18. Similarly, less than 1% of Corntown

Hispanics are over 65 years of age, whereas 17% of the general town population fit this category. The high school completion rate for all Corntown residents over 25 years of age is 40%; the rate for Hispanics is 26%. In contrast, Hispanic households on the whole appear economically more successful than those of the overall town population. Almost one-third (32%) of all incomes in Corntown are above $35,000; only 18.7% of the households have incomes above $50,000. In comparison, 100% of Hispanic incomes cluster above $35,000, with more than three-quarters higher than $50,000. Our sample household incomes resulted from two or more adults working, however. Despite this difference, Hispanic-owned homes have a lower median value ($27,013) than the overall Corntown median home value ($33,000) (Bureau of the Census 1990a). Thus, Hispanic home owners are living in more modest housing.

Although other family members contributed to the interviews with the 25 Mexicano households in phase 1, the adult head of household present was considered the primary informant. This group included 11 women, 4 men, and 10 married couples. Fifty-four percent of the group were between the ages of 36 and 55 (22% below 36, and 25% above 55). All but a single adult were parents, of whom all but two divorced mothers and two widows were remarried. Of the four female-headed households, only one included children under the age of 18. The mean number of Mexicanos per household was 4.6, in contrast to 2.63 persons per household overall. Compared to the overall Corntown Hispanic population, the sample Mexicano households were more likely to own their homes (71% compared to 57%), somewhat more likely to fall below the poverty level (14% compared to 7%), and slightly more likely to be unemployed (3% compared to 0%). We know that our sample contains several Mexicano families, more recently settled-out migrants who arrived after the 1990 census, who are poorer than those who have lived in Corntown a longer time.

Ninety percent of the sample reported membership in the local Catholic church. Forty percent of the Mexicanos worked in manufacturing or construction, as did 43% of Corntown residents overall. More than 82% of the respondents were born in Mexico or the south Texas border region. A majority (87.5%) of the Texas-born respondents hail from the same general region, referred to as the McAllen-Pharr-Edinburg Metropolitan Statistical Area (Bureau of the Census 1990a). This shared place of origin reveals the families' linkages to the Texas-Illinois migrant labor stream and a chain-migration pattern. Accordingly, 75% of the sample had been migrant workers or belong to migrant extended families.

Bunkerton

Twenty years ago I carried out an ethnographic field study of a farm community, then pseudonymously called Svedberg in honor of its Swedish heritage (Gengenbacher 1980; Salamon, Gengenbacher, and Penas 1986). My interest in Svedberg farmers narrowed the original study to only one group in a more diverse town. In recognition of the diminished importance of Swedish ethnicity and farming to the community, I now call it Bunkerton to highlight the working-class and lower-middle-class character of the town. What motivated the follow-up community study (1991–92) was the closing of a nearby military base, an increasingly common restructuring event in rural America. Bunkerton had long served as the bedroom community for the military and civilian employees of the base. The economic impact on Bunkerton of the base closing was steady and drawn out, with the final act delayed for almost a decade. I was interested in how the Bunkerton business community mobilized to recruit jobs and new residents, with the aim of restoring the town to its former economically and socially robust status.

Its size (Bunkerton is the second-largest town of the set) precluded our knocking on every door. One neighborhood close to the center of town, with a mixture of new and old houses, was selected for study. All interviews were conducted in homes by Cynthia Loula, a graduate research assistant, over eight months during 1991 and 1992. There was a high degree of suspicion in the town, apparently owing to aggressive religious soliciting that was going on at the same time. Initially, door-to-door contacts were used, but they met with little success. Families living in the targeted neighborhood then were randomly selected from the telephone directory and called. Although the telephone method was more effective than door-to-door contacts, the refusal rate approximated 60%. Most of the sample was obtained by telephone; however, when participants provided introductions to neighbors or kin, the snowball method of identifying households enlarged the sample and the area slightly. The majority (86%) of the 50 interviews were from households clustered in a neighborhood consisting of six roughly parallel streets and the streets connecting them in a five-block area that was within a few blocks of the main street. The remaining households are located near but not contiguous to the core area. The interviews averaged about 60 to 90 minutes, and follow-up intensive interviews were conducted with four individuals. Aside from three males and six married couples, the interviews were with women. The ages of the participants ranged from 15 to 88 years. Additional background interviews included interviews with the ministers of the four largest churches and with the high school principal and two teachers, one from the high school and the other from an elementary school. Cathey Huddelston did the statistical analysis of the sample.

In conjunction with the neighborhood ethnography carried out by Loula, an associated study (directed by a colleague, Maureen Perry-Jenkins), which examined dual-earner Bunkerton blue-collar families, broadened the coverage of households. The goal of this second study was to understand the effect on marriages and children of having both of their rural, blue-collar, small-town parents in the workforce. This sample consisted of 63 families, all with a target child living at home who was under the age of 14 and over the age of 7. Data were collected for this study during spring and fall 1993 (see Perry-Jenkins and Salamon 2002). The combined sample of 103 households from the two studies constitutes about 7% of the 1,650 households in Bunkerton.

About half of the dual-earner households contacted in the second study fell within the boundaries of the targeted neighborhood sample; however, all respondents lived in fairly close proximity in this small town. Of the families in the second study, 44 were households in which both parents were employed full time outside the home in working-class occupations. Nineteen were single-parent households; in those cases the parent was employed full time. Families were recruited through the local middle school and via a roster of all students and telephone numbers provided by the principal. All listed families were called and, if they fit the study's criteria, asked to participate. Data were obtained from in-home interviews with mothers, fathers (where applicable), and the target child. The focus was on work, social networks, social support, psychological well-being, and aspects of the marital relationship, using standard psychological measures. In addition, parents filled out a questionnaire describing their perceptions of their neighborhood and community as a place to live (Perry-Jenkins and Salamon 2002). Field assistants were trained to record in a field-note log observations and comments about home and family heard during the data collection.

After both studies were completed, I continued to follow Bunkerton political and social events through the regional newspaper.

Bunkerton, because of its size and its function as the county seat, is often in the news. Much of the newspaper material about the issue of youth hanging out on the main street came from this follow-up research.

Arbordale

My intent in targeting the working-class community of Arbordale was to compare the impacts of a similar number of Mexicano newcomers on towns of differing size. Corntown is twice as large as Arbordale. In 1990 Hispanics made up 5% of the Corntown population, while in Arbordale about the same number constituted almost 25% of the population. I was curious to know whether a minority group's experiences differed directly in relation to how large a proportion of the total population they formed, in accord with findings elsewhere (Lieberson 1980). That is, would about the same size group of a minority in a smaller community create more feelings of hostility or, among oldtimers, a sense of being threatened? Thus, the focus was on what happens to a village when a large proportion of the families are Mexicano newcomers and the population balance transforms it from an agrarian to a postagrarian and ethnically mixed community. A particular concern was adolescent experiences and whether ethnicity affected embracement of a typical small-town ideology (Hummon 1990).

Introduction to the community was through Ben Mueller, with the University of Illinois Extension, who was connected professionally with several prominent Arbordale Mexicano families. The fieldwork was carried out by Patricia Howard, a graduate research assistant and doctoral candidate in the Department of Anthropology during 1994 and 1995. Chain or snowball referrals were used to obtain the sample of 15 Mexicano households, from which 13 adults and 11 youth (ages 13 to 21) were interviewed. Five long-term Anglo residents were interviewed in their capacity as business owners or as professionals whose services brought them into contact with Mexicano residents. In particular, the owner of the main agribusiness employing Mexicano workers spoke with us at length. The 15 Mexicano households and 5 Anglo interviews combined represent 4.2% of the total of 470 households but the 15 represent 25% of the Hispanic households reported for Arbordale in the 1990 census. Because our informants told us the numbers of Mexicano households were increasing, in 1995 Howard carried out a house-by-house windshield survey of the village with the assistance of a middle-aged Mexicano man who had lived in Arbordale more than twenty years. They counted 92 Mexicano households, which constitutes 32% of the town, an increase of 7% in only five years.

Mexicano households often include extended family and nonfamily members living together, pooling their resources. The Mexicano household sample in our study is representative of those reported for Hispanics in the 1990 census. However, as we discovered by doing our windshield household survey, it is difficult to say how representative the census survey is in light of our information about population growth. Single Mexicano males from Mexico, the only seasonal migrant workers in Arbordale, were underrepresented in the census data and not represented in our study. Interviews established that about 100 migrants are housed in Arbordale at the peak of the seasonal employment (down from a much larger number because of the mechanization of nursery production, according to the Anglo owner of the nursery business).

Face-to-face interviews were conducted using a survey questionnaire with a mixture of closed- and open-ended questions. Transcripts were made from taped interviews. The average time for an interview was two hours, with some people revisited to clarify information. Participant observation of the Mexicano community occurred when Howard was invited by residents to attend public events. A first communion and a Quinceañera were both observed in the local church, and a party was attended after the latter event. A community Mexican festival was observed in the town park (see fig. 6). Fieldwork was not conducted in Spanish because most of the youth were born in Illinois and thus are fluent English speakers. However, greater fluency in Spanish on the part of the field worker would have presented more opportunities to speak with their parents or grandparents, whose first language is Spanish. Several longtime Mexicano residents had little English proficiency.

About five years after the field study was completed, I learned of an ethnographic field study carried out in 1995 and 1996 as part of a University of Illinois College of Education dissertation that focused on Arbordale Mexicano students in the high school. The Godina dissertation (1998) is drawn on throughout the Arbordale case study and provides triangulation for trends identified by our study.

Prairieview

The study of this affluent residential community was stimulated by a 1994 article in the regional newspaper that compared 1990 with 1980 census town populations. This community near Central City, it reported, had doubled in size between the two censuses. Such a radical change made Prairieview an ideal subject for examining newcomer-oldtimer interactions, a continuing interest of mine since the Splitville study. In spring 1995 I taught a graduate course in qualitative methodology for which a community study was an appropriate focus. The transformation of Prairieview, a former farm community, into a location for upscale subdivisions populated by doctors, engineers, and other professionals who commute to several small cities about 15 to 30 minutes away, constituted the course's workshop component. Data were collected by a team of four University of Illinois doctoral-level graduate students, Patricia Howard (Anthropology), Bret Kloos (Community Psychology), and Consolata Kabonesa and Stephanie Schaefer (Human and Community Development), during spring semester 1994.

The students designed the household survey instrument and carried out the interviews. A total of 52 household representatives (usually an adult, but in some cases an adolescent) were interviewed at home to obtain a cross-sectional profile of town demographics, networks, citizen involvement, and attitudes. Questions were both guided open-ended and closed-ended. To construct a representative cross section of Prairieview, differing neighborhoods were targeted on two successive weekends. On the first weekend neighborhoods in the older part of town were visited, and on the second weekend new subdivision neighborhoods adjacent to the village were visited. In addition, the entire team interviewed the village administrator, and one or two team members interviewed ministers from five of the fourteen local churches. A local police officer, social workers from the elementary and junior and senior high schools, and the latchkey program director were also interviewed. Of the household representatives interviewed, 35% were 18 to 35 years of age, 48% were 36 to 65, and 17% were 66 or over. All were white. Most of the sample (78%) had been born elsewhere, and these households were disproportionately those in the younger age categories and were located in the newer subdivisions. The sample of households interviewed constitutes 5.2% of the total Prairieview households reported in the 1990 census. With the additional 10 interviews with village professionals (all local residents), the proportion of the community contacted reaches 6.2%.

Each student was required to write a final paper on a segment of the community that had piqued her or his interest while conducting the household interviews. To flesh out the topic, each student conducted some additional interviews or made a second visit with someone already surveyed to obtain richer data on the topic. The topics explored included the elderly (Howard), an after-school latchkey child care program funding crisis (Schaefer), the local churches (Kloos), and substance abuse among high school students (Kabonesa).

Some of the newcomer comments obtained by the students vilified a mobile home park nearby; these piqued my interest and eventually motivated a subsequent study of the effects of rural mobile-home-park residence on families and children. This latter study kept me involved in Prairieview through 1999. Interviews conducted for the park study, such as with the village manager and school district administrators, informed the case study with additional background materials.

REFERENCES

Adams, Jane. 1994. *The Transformation of Rural Life: Southern Illinois, 1890–1990*. Chapel Hill: University of North Carolina Press.

Alonso, William. 1993. "The Interpretation of Rural and Urban America." In *Population Change and the Future of Rural America: A Conference Proceedings*, edited by Linda L. Swanson and David L. Brown, 10–28. Staff Report no. AGES 9324, Economic Research Service. Washington, DC: U.S. Department of Agriculture.

Ammerman, Nancy Tatom. 1997. *Congregation and Community*. New Brunswick, NJ: Rutgers University Press.

Aponte, Robert, and Marcelo Siles. 1997. *Winds of Change: Hispanics in the Heartland and the Nation*. CIFRAS 5 (Statistical Brief). Julian Samora Research Institute, Michigan State University, East Lansing, MI.

Arensberg, Conrad M. 1972. "Culture as Behavior: Structure and Emergence." *Annual Review of Anthropology* 1:1–36.

———. 1981. "Cultural Holism through Interactional Systems." *American Anthropologist* 83, no. 3: 562–81.

Aronoff, Marilyn. 1993. "Collective Celebration as a Vehicle for Local Economic Development: A Michigan Case." *Human Organization* 52:368–79.

Atherton, Lewis. 1954. *Main Street on the Middle Border*. Bloomington: Indiana University Press.

Barlett, Peggy F. 1986. "Part-time Farming: Saving the Farm or Saving the Lifestyle?" *Rural Sociology* 51:289–313.

Barron, Hal S. 1997. *Mixed Harvest: The Second Great Transformation in the Rural North 1870–1930*. Chapel Hill: University of North Carolina Press.

Barth, Fredrik. 1969. *Ethnic Groups and Boundaries*. Boston: Little, Brown.

Baumgartner, Mary P. 1988. *The Moral Order of the Suburb*. New York: Oxford University Press.

Beale, Calvin L. 1989. "Significant Trends in the Demography of Farm People." *Proceedings of the Philadelphia Society for Promoting Agriculture 1987–88* (February): 36–39.

———. 1990. "The Revival of Population Growth in Nonmetropolitan

America." In *A Taste of the Country: A Collection of Calvin Beale's Writings*, edited by Peter A. Morrison, 137–52. University Park: Pennsylvania State University Press.

Beale, Calvin L., and Judith Kalbacher. 1989. "Farm Population Trends: Shrinkage, Shifts, and Fewer Heirs." *Farmline* 9:19.

Becker, Howard S. 1963. *Outsiders: Studies in the Sociology of Deviance*. New York: Free Press.

Bell, Michael M. 1994. *Childerley: Nature and Morality in a Country Village*. Chicago: University of Chicago Press.

Bellah, Robert, Richard Masden, William M. Sullivan, Ann Swidler, and Steven M. Tipton. 1985. *Habits of the Heart: Individualism and Commitment in American Life*. Berkeley: University of California Press.

Bender, Lloyd, ed. 1985. *The Diverse Social and Economic Structure of Non-metro America*. U.S. Department of Agriculture, Economic Research Service, Rural Development Research Report no. 49.

Benson, Peter L. 1997. *All Kids Are Our Kids: What Communities Must Do to Raise Caring and Responsible Children and Adolescents*. San Francisco: Jossey-Bass.

Billington, Ray. 1966. *America's Frontier Heritage*. New York: Holt, Rinehardt, and Winston.

Bloom, Stephen G. 2000. *Postville: A Clash of Cultures in Heartland America*. New York: Harcourt.

Blumenthal, Albert. 1932. *Small-Town Stuff*. Chicago: University of Chicago Press.

Bourdieu, Pierre. 1984. *Distinction: A Social Critique of the Judgement of Taste*. Translated by Richard Nice. Cambridge, MA: Harvard University Press.

Bradshaw, Ted K. 1993. "In the Shadow of Urban Growth: Bifurcation in Rural California Communities." In *Forgotten Places: Uneven Development in Rural America*, edited by Thomas A. Lyson and William W. Falk, 218–56. Lawrence: University Press of Kansas.

Brunner, Edmund de S., Gwendolyn S. Hughes, and Marjorie Patten. 1927. *American Agricultural Villages*. New York: George H. Doran.

Bryant, Brenda. 1985. *The Neighborhood Walk: Sources of Support in Middle Childhood*. Monographs of the Society for Research in Child Development, Serial no. 210, vol. 50, no. 3.

Bureau of Economic and Business Research. 1992. *1992 Illinois Statistical Abstract*. Champaign: University of Illinois College of Commerce and Business Administration.

Butler, Margaret A., and Calvin L. Beale. 1994. *Rural-Urban Continuum Codes for Metro and Nonmetro Counties, 1993*. Agriculture and Rural Economy Division, Economic Research Service, U.S. Department of Agriculture, Washington, DC.

Campion, Amy, and Gary Alan Fine. 1998. "*Main Street* on Main Street: Community Identity and the Reputation of Sinclair Lewis." *Sociological Quarterly* 39, no. 1: 79–99.

Castle, Emery N., ed. 1995. *The Changing American Countryside: Rural People and Places*. Lawrence: University Press of Kansas.

Cayton, Andrew R. L., and Peter S. Onuf. 1990. *The Midwest and the Nation:*

Rethinking the History of an American Region. Bloomington: Indiana University Press.

Chapa, Jorge, and Richard R. Valencia. 1993. "Latino Population Growth, Demographic Characteristics, and Educational Stagnation: An Examination of Recent Trends." *Hispanic Journal of Behavioral Sciences* 15:165–87.

Charles, Jeffrey A. 1993. *Service Clubs in American Society: Rotary, Kiwanis, and Lions.* Urbana: University of Illinois Press.

Chawla, Louise. 1992. "Childhood Place Attachments." In *Place Attachment,* edited by Setha M. Low and Irwin Altman, 63–86. New York: Plenum Press.

Childress, Herb. 1993. "No Loitering: Some Ideas about Small Town Teenage Hangouts." *Small Town* 23 (September–October): 20–25.

———. 2000. *Landscapes of Betrayal, Landscapes of Joy.* Albany: State University of New York Press.

Clifford, James, and George E. Marcus. 1986. *Writing Culture: The Poetics and Politics of Ethnography.* Berkeley: University of California Press.

Coleman, James S. 1988. "Social Capital in the Creation of Human Capital." *American Journal of Sociology* 94:S94–S120.

———. 1990. "Social Capital." In *Foundations of Social Theory,* by James S. Coleman, 300–321. Cambridge, MA: Harvard University Press.

———. 1993. "The Rational Reconstruction of Society." *American Sociological Review* 58:1–15.

Coleman, James S., and Thomas Hoffer. 1987. *Public and Private High Schools: The Impact of Communities.* New York: Basic Books.

Cook, Peggy J., and Karen L. Mizer. 1994. "The Revised ERS County Typology: An Overview." In *Rural Development Report 89,* Rural Economy Division, Economic Research Service, U.S. Department of Agriculture, Washington, DC.

Coontz, Stephanie. 1992. *The Way We Never Were: American Families and the Nostalgia Trap.* New York: Basic Books.

Cronon, William. 1991. *Nature's Metropolis: Chicago and the Great West.* New York: W. W. Norton.

Curti, Merle. 1959. *The Making of an American Community.* Stanford, CA: Stanford University Press.

Daniels, Thomas L., and Mark B. Lapping. 1987. "Small Town Triage: A Rural Settlement Policy for the American Midwest." *Journal of Rural Studies* 3, no. 3: 273–80.

Daniels, Tom, and Deborah Bowers. 1997. *Holding Our Ground: Protecting America's Farms and Farmland.* Washington, DC: Island Press.

Davis, John Emmeus. 1991. *Contested Ground: Collective Action and the Urban Neighborhood.* Ithaca, NY: Cornell University Press.

Denzin, Norman K. 1989. *The Research Act: A Theoretical Introduction to Sociological Methods.* 3d ed. Englewood Cliffs, NJ: Prentice Hall.

Duncan, Cynthia M. 1999. *Worlds Apart: Why Poverty Persists in Rural America.* New Haven, CT: Yale University Press.

———, ed. 1992. *Rural Poverty in America.* New York: Auburn House.

Elder, Glen H., Jr., and Rand D. Conger. 2000. *Children of the Land: Adversity and Success in Rural America.* Chicago: University of Chicago Press.

Elliot, James R., and Marc J. Perry. 1996. "Metropolitanizing Nonmetro Space:

Population Redistribution and Emergent Metropolitan Areas, 1965–90." *Rural Sociology* 61:497–512.

Engel, David M. 1984. "The Oven Bird's Song: Insiders, Outsiders, and Personal Injuries in an American Community." *Law and Society Review* 18:551–82.

Erikson, Kai T. 1976. *Everything in Its Path: Destruction of Community in the Buffalo Creek Flood.* New York: Simon and Schuster.

Etzioni, Amitai. 1993. *The Spirit of Community.* New York: Crown.

Falk, William, and Thomas A. Lyson, eds. 1993. *Forgotten Places: Uneven Development in Rural America.* Lawrence: University Press of Kansas.

Federal Writer's Project. 1983. *The WPA Guide to Illinois.* 2d ed., with introduction by Neil Harris and Michael Conzen. New York: Pantheon Books. First edition published in 1939.

Fernandez, James W. 1990. "Enclosures, Boundary Maintenance, and Its Representations over Time in Asturian Mountain Villages (Spain)." In *Culture through Time: Anthropological Approaches,* edited by Emiko Ohnuki-Tierney, 94–127. Stanford, CA: Stanford University Press.

Fink, Deborah A. 1986. *Open Country, Iowa: Rural Women, Tradition, and Change.* Albany: State University of New York Press.

———. 1998. *Cutting into the Meatpacking Line: Workers and Change in the Rural Midwest.* Chapel Hill: University of North Carolina Press.

Finnegan, William. 1996. "The New Americans." *New Yorker,* March 25, 52–71.

Fischer, Claude S. 1982. *To Dwell among Friends: Personal Networks in Town and City.* Chicago: University of Chicago Press.

———. 1991. "Ambivalent Communities: How Americans Understand Their Localities." In *America at Century's End,* edited by Alan Wolfe, 79–90. Berkeley: University of California Press.

Fishman, Robert. 1987. *Bourgeois Utopias.* New York: Basic Books.

Fitchen, Janet M. 1981. *Poverty in Rural America: A Case Study.* Boulder, CO: Westview Press.

———. 1991. *Endangered Spaces, Enduring Places.* Boulder, CO: Westview Press.

———. 1994. "Residential Mobility among the Rural Poor." *Rural Sociology* 59, no. 4: 416–36.

———. 1995. "Spatial Redistribution of Poverty through Migration of Poor People to Depressed Rural Communities." *Rural Sociology* 60, no. 2: 181–201.

Flora, Cornelia Butler, and Jan L. Flora. 1990. "Developing Entrepreneurial Rural Communities." *Sociological Practice* 8:197–207.

Flora, Jan L., Jeff Sharp, and Cornelia Flora. 1997. "Entrepreneurial Social Infrastructure and Locally Initiated Economic Development in the Nonmetropolitan United States." *Sociological Quarterly* 38:623–45.

Fowler, Robert Booth. 1991. *The Dance with Community: The Contemporary Debate in American Political Thought.* Lawrence: University Press of Kansas.

Francaviglia, Richard V. 1996. *Main Street Revisited: Time, Space, and Image Building in Small-Town America.* Iowa City: University of Iowa Press.

Freudenberg, William R. 1986. "The Density of Acquaintanceship: An Overlooked Variable in Community Research?" *American Journal of Sociology* 92:27–63.

Fuguitt, Glenn V., David L. Brown, and Calvin L. Beale. 1989. *Rural and Small Town America*. New York: Russell Sage Foundation.

Fuller, Wayne E. 1982. *The Old Country School: The Story of Rural Education in the Middle West*. Chicago: University of Chicago Press.

Furstenberg, Frank F., Jr., Thomas D. Cook, Jacquelynne Eccles, Glen H. Elder Jr., and Arnold Sameroff. 1999. *Managing to Make It: Urban Families and Adolescent Success*. Chicago: University of Chicago Press.

Gallaher, Arthur, Jr., and Harlan Padfield, eds. 1980. *The Dying Community*. Albuquerque: University of New Mexico Press.

Galston, William. 1993. "Rural America in the 1990's: Trends and Choices. In *Population Change and the Future of Rural America: A Conference Proceedings*, edited by Linda L. Swanson and David L. Brown, 10–22. Staff Report no. AGES 9324, Agriculture and Rural Economy Division, Economic Research Service, U.S. Department of Agriculture, Washington, DC.

Gans, Herbert J. 1961. "The Balanced Community: Homogeneity or Heterogeneity in Residential Areas?" *Journal of the American Institute of Planners* 27: 176–84.

———. 1967. *The Levittowners: Ways of Life and Politics in a New Suburban Community*. New York: Vintage Books.

Gardner, H. Stephen. 1988. *Comparative Economic Systems*. Chicago: Dryden Press.

Gengenbacher, Kathleen Marie. 1980. "Father-Son Joint Agricultural Operations and Continuity in a Midwestern Swedish-American Farm Community." Master's thesis, University of Illinois at Urbana-Champaign.

Gieryn, Thomas F. 2000. "A Space for Place in Sociology." *Annual Review of Sociology* 26:463–96.

Gilbert, Dennis L., and Josephy A. Kahl. 1993. *The American Class Structure: A Synthesis*. Belmont, CA: Wadsworth.

Gladwell, Malcolm. 2000. *The Tipping Point: How Little Things Can Make a Big Difference*. Boston: Little, Brown.

Godina, Heriberto. 1998. "Mexican American High-School Students and the Role of Literacy across Home-School-Community Settings." Ph.D. diss., University of Illinois at Urbana-Champaign.

Goffman, Erving. 1963. *Stigma: Notes on the Management of Spoiled Identity*. Englewood Cliffs, NJ: Prentice-Hall.

Goldschmidt, Walter. 1978. *As You Sow*. 2d ed. Montclair, NJ: Allanheld, Osmun.

Granovetter, Mark S. 1973. "The Strength of Weak Ties." *American Journal of Sociology* 78, no. 6: 1360–80.

Greenhouse, Carol J. 1986. *Praying for Justice: Faith, Order, and Community in an American Town*. Ithaca, NY: Cornell University Press.

Greenhouse, Carol J., Barbara Yngvesson, and David M. Engel. 1994. *Law and Community in Three American Towns*. Ithaca, NY: Cornell University Press.

Greider, Thomas, Richard S. Krannich, and E. Helen Berry. 1991. "Local Identity, Solidarity, and Trust in Changing Rural Communities." *Sociological Focus* 24:263–82.

Gruidl, John, and Norman Walzer. 1990. *A Profile of Conditions and Trends in*

Rural Illinois. Macomb: Illinois Institute for Rural Affairs, Western Illinois University.

Halle, David. 1993. *Inside Culture: Art and Class in the American Home.* Chicago: University of Chicago Press.

Harvey, David L. 1993. *Potter's Addition: Poverty, Family, and Kinship in a Heartland Community.* New York: Aldine de Gruyter.

Hasselmo, Neils. 1976. *Swedish America: An Introduction.* Minneapolis: Brings Press.

Hatch, Elvin. 1979. *Biography of a Small Town.* New York: Columbia University Press.

———. 1989. "Theories of Social Honor." *American Anthropologist* 91:341–53.

Herbers, John. 1986. *The New Heartland: America's Flight beyond the Suburbs and How It Is Changing Our Future.* New York: Times Books.

Hollingshead, August B. 1975. *Elmstown's Youth and Elmstown Revised.* 2d ed. New York: John Wiley and Sons. First edition published in 1949.

Hondagneu-Sotelo, Pierrette. 1994. *Gendered Transitions: Mexican Experiences of Immigration.* Berkeley: University of California Press.

Hudson, John C. 1985. *Plains Country Towns.* Minneapolis: University of Minnesota Press.

Hummon, David M. 1990. *Commonplaces: Community Ideology and Identity in American Culture.* Albany: State University of New York Press.

Illinois Department of Agriculture. 1996. *Annual Summary of Illinois Agricultural Statistics.* Bulletin 96-1. Springfield: Illinois Agricultural Statistics Service.

Illinois State Board of Education. 1990. *School Report Card, Elementary, Junior and Senior High Schools.* Springfield: Research Division, Illinois State Board of Education.

———. 1992. *Illinois School Report Card.* Springfield: Illinois State Board of Education.

Jackson, Kenneth T. 1985. *Crabgrass Frontier: The Suburbanization of the United States.* New York: Oxford University Press.

Jacobs, Jane. 1992. *The Life and Death of Great American Cities.* 1961; New York: Random House.

Johansen, Harley E., and Glenn V. Fuguitt. 1984. *The Changing Rural Village in America.* Cambridge, MA: Ballinger.

Johnson, Hildegard Binder. 1976. *Order upon the Land: The U.S. Rectangular Land Survey and the Upper Mississippi Country.* New York: Oxford University Press.

Johnson, Kenneth M., and Calvin L. Beale. 1998. "The Rural Rebound." *Wilson Quarterly* 22, no. 2: 16–27.

Kantor, David, and Willam Lehr. 1985. *Inside the Family.* San Francisco: Jossey-Bass.

Kasarda, John D., and Maurice Janowitz. 1974. "Community Attachment in Mass Society." *American Sociological Review* 39:328–39.

Kemmis, Daniel. 1995. *The Good City and the Good Life: Renewing the Sense of Community.* Boston: Houghton Mifflin.

Kenny, Lorraine Delia. 2000. *Daughters of Suburbia: Growing Up White, Middle Class, and Female.* New Brunswick, NJ: Rutgers University Press.

Killian, Molly S., and Timothy S. Parker. 1991. "Education and Local Employ-
ment Growth in a Change Economy." In *Education and Rural Economic
Development: Strategies for the 1990s*, chap. 4. Staff Report no. AGES 9153,
Economic Research Service, U.S. Department of Agriculture, Washington,
DC.

Komarovsky, Miriam. 1967. *Blue-Collar Marriage*. New York: Vintage Books.

Kornblum, William. 1974. *Blue Collar Community*. Chicago: University of Chicago Press.

Kottak, Conrad P. 1999. "The New Ecological Anthropology." *American Anthropologist* 101:23–35.

Kunstler, James Howard. 1993. *The Geography of Nowhere: The Rise and Decline of America's Man-Made Landscape*. New York: Simon and Schuster.

Lamont, Michele, and Marcel Fournier, eds. 1992. *Cultivating Differences: Symbolic Boundaries and the Making of Inequality*. Chicago: University of Chicago Press.

Lamphere, Louise. 1992. "Introduction: The Shaping of Diversity." In *Structuring Diversity: Ethnographic Perspectives on the New Immigration*, edited by
Louise Lamphere, 1–34. Chicago: University of Chicago Press.

Lavenda, Robert H. 1997. *Corn Fests and Water Carnivals: Celebrating Community in Minnesota*. Washington, DC: Smithsonian Institution Press.

Levitan, Sar A., and Isaac Shapiro. 1987. *Working but Poor: America's Contra-
diction*. Baltimore: Johns Hopkins University Press.

Lewis, David J., and Andrew Weigert. 1985. "Trust as Social Reality." *Social
Forces* 63, no. 4: 967–85.

Lewis, Pierce. 1995. "The Urban Invasion of Rural America: The Emergence of
the Galactic City." In *The Changing American Countryside*, edited by Emery
N. Castle, 39–62. Lawrence: University Press of Kansas.

Lieberson, Stanley. 1980. *A Piece of the Pie: Black and White Immigrants since
1890*. Berkeley: University of California Press.

Lippard, Lucy R. 1997. *The Lure of the Local: Senses of Place in a Multicentered
Society*. New York: New Press.

Logan, John R., and Harvey L. Molotch. 1987. *Urban Fortunes: The Political
Economy of Place*. Berkeley: University of California Press.

Logan, John R., and Glenna D. Spitze. 1994. "Family Neighbors." *American
Journal of Sociology* 100:453–76.

Low, Setha M. 2000. *On the Plaza: The Politics of Public Space and Culture*.
Austin: University of Texas Press.

Low, Setha M., and Irwin Altman, eds. 1992. *Place Attachment*. New York: Plenum Press.

Luloff, A. E., and Louis E. Swanson, eds. 1990. *American Rural Communities*.
Boulder, CO: Westview Press.

Lynd, Robert, and Helen Lynd. 1929. *Middletown: A Study in American Culture*.
New York: Harcourt and Brace.

———. 1937. *Middletown in Transition: A Study in Cultural Conflicts*. New
York: Harcourt and Brace.

MacTavish, Katherine. 2001. *Going Mobile in Rural America: The Community
Effect of Rural Trailer Parks on Child and Youth Development*. Ph.D. diss.,
University of Illinois at Urbana-Champaign.

MacTavish, Katherine, and Sonya Salamon. 2001. "Mobile Home Park on the Prairie: A New Rural Community Form." *Rural Sociology* 66, no. 4: 487–506.

McKenzie, Roderick Duncan. 1923. *The Neighborhood: A Study of Local Life in the City of Columbus, Ohio*. Chicago: University of Chicago Press.

———. 1967. "The Ecological Approach to the Study of the Human Community." In *The City*, edited by Robert E. Park and Ernest W. Burgess, 63–79. Chicago: University of Chicago Press.

Molnar, Jerry J., and G. Traxler. 1976. "People Left Behind: Transitions of the Rural Poor." *Southern Journal of Agricultural Economics* 23, no. 1: 75–83.

Monti, Daniel J. 1994. *Wannabe: Gangs in Suburbs and Schools*. Cambridge: Blackwell.

Naples, Nancy A. 1997. "A Feminist Revisiting of the Insider/Outsider Debate: The 'Outsider Phenomenon' in Rural Iowa." In *Reflexivity and Voice*, edited by Rosanna Hertz, 70–94. Thousand Oaks, CA: Sage.

National Center for Educational Statistics. 1992. *Dropout Rates in the United States, 1992*. U.S. Department of Education. Washington, DC: U.S. Government Printing Office.

Nisbet, Robert A. 1953. *The Quest for Community: A Study in the Ethics of Order and Freedom*. New York: Oxford University Press.

Nowak, Martin A., and Karl Sigmund. 2000. "Shrewd Investments." *Science* 288: 819–20.

Ohnuki-Tierney, Emiko. 1990. "Introduction: The Historicization of Anthropology." In *Culture through Time: Anthropological Approaches*, edited by Emiko Ohnuki-Tierney, 1–25. Stanford, CA: Stanford University Press.

Oldenburg, Ray. 1999. *The Great Good Place: Cafes, Coffee Shops, Bookstores, Bars, Hair Salons, and Other Hangouts at the Heart of Community*. 3d ed. New York: Marlowe.

Olson, Richard H., and Thomas A. Lyson, eds. 1999. *Under the Plow: The Conversion of Agricultural Landscapes*. Boulder, CO: Westview Press.

Ortner, Sherry B. 1984. "Theory in Anthropology since the Sixties." *Comparative Studies in Society and History* 26, no. 1: 126–66.

———. 1990. "Patterns of History: Cultural Schemas in the Foundings of Sherpa Religious Institutions." In *Culture through Time: Anthropological Approaches*, edited by Emiko Ohnuki-Tierney, 57–93. Stanford, CA: Stanford University Press.

———. 1991. "Reading America: Preliminary Notes on Class and Culture." In *Recapturing Anthropology: Working in the Present*, edited by Richard G. Fox, 163–89. Santa Fe, NM: School of American Research Press.

Palen, J. John. 1995. *The Suburbs*. New York: McGraw Hill.

Patton, Michael Quinn. 1990. *Qualitative Evaluation and Research Methods*. Newbury Park, CA: Sage.

Perry-Jenkins, Maureen, and Sonya Salamon. 2002. "Blue-Collar Kin and Community in Small-Town America." *Journal of Family Issues* 23, no. 8: 927–49.

Portes, Alejandro, and Julia Sensenbrenner. 1993. "Embeddedness and Immigration: Notes on the Social Determinants of Economic Action." *American Journal of Sociology* 98:1320–50.

Prosterman, Leslie. 1995. *Ordinary Life, Festival Days: Aesthetics in the Midwestern County Fair.* Washington, DC: Smithsonian Institution Press.

Putnam, Robert. 1993a. *Making Democracy Work: Civic Traditions in Modern Italy.* Princeton, NJ: Princeton University Press.

———. 1993b. "The Prosperous Community: Social Capital and Public Life." *American Prospect,* no. 13: 35–42.

———. 2000. *Bowling Alone: The Collapse and Revival of American Community.* New York: Simon and Schuster.

Reynolds, David R. 1995. "Rural Education: Decentering the Consolidation Debate." In *The Changing American Countryside,* edited by Emery N. Castle, 451–80. Lawrence: University Press of Kansas.

Riley, Matilda White, and Peter Uhlenberg, eds. 2000. "Essays on Age Integration." *Gerontologist* 42, no. 3: 261–308.

Riley, Robert. 1985. "Square to the Road, Hogs to the East." *Illinois Issues* 11, no. 7: 22–26.

Rimer, Sara. 1993. "Washing, Baking, and Lugging, Too: Frontier Women of the Flooded Plain." *New York Times,* August 5.

Ross, Andrew. 1999. *The Celebration Chronicles: Life, Liberty, and the Pursuit of Property Value in Disney's New Town.* New York: Ballantine.

Ross, Edward Alsworth. 1915. *Changing America: Studies in Contemporary Society.* Chautauqua, NY: Chautauqua Press.

Rubin, Lillian B. 1994. *Families on the Fault Line: America's Working Class Speaks about the Family, the Economy, Race, and Ethnicity.* New York: Harper Collins.

Rudel, Thomas K. 1989. *Situations and Strategies in American Land-Use Planning.* Cambridge: Cambridge University Press.

Rural Sociological Society Task Force on Persistent Rural Poverty. 1993. *Persistent Poverty in Rural America.* Boulder, CO: Westview Press.

Salamon, Sonya. 1984. "Ethnic Origin as Explanation for Local Land Ownership Patterns." *Research in Rural Sociology and Development* 1:161–86.

———. 1987. "Ethnic Determinants of Farm Community Character." In *Farm Work and Fieldwork: American Agriculture in Anthropological Perspective,* edited by Michael Chibnik, 167–88. Ithaca, NY: Cornell University Press.

———. 1989. "What Makes Rural Communities Tick?" *Rural Development Perspectives* 5, no. 3: 19–24.

———. 1992. *Prairie Patrimony: Family, Farming, and Community in the Midwest.* Chapel Hill: University of North Carolina Press.

———. 1995. "The Rural People of the Midwest." In *The Changing American Countryside,* edited by Emery N. Castle, 352–65. Lawrence: University Press of Kansas.

———. 1996. "Social Infrastructure: The Case Study." In *Rural Development Research: A Foundation for Policy,* edited by Thomas D. Rowley, David W. Sears, Glenn L. Nelson, J. Norman Reid, and Mervin J. Yetley, 197–212. Westport, CT: Greenwood.

Salamon, Sonya, and Karen Davis-Brown. 1990. "Rural Communities in Transition." In *Proceedings of the W. K. Kellogg National Rural Studies Committee,* edited by Emery Castle and Barbara Baldwin, 31–42. Corvallis: Western Rural Development Center, Oregon State University.

Salamon, Sonya, Richard L. Farnsworth, and Jody A. Rendziak. 1998. "Is Locally Led Conservation Planning Working? A Farm Town Case Study." *Rural Sociology* 63:214–34.

Salamon, Sonya, Kathleen M. Gengenbacher, and Dwight J. Penas. 1986. "Family Factors Affecting the Intergenerational Succession to Farming." *Human Organization* 45, no. 1: 24–33.

Salamon, Sonya, and Jane B. Tornatore. 1994. "Territory Contested through Property in a Midwestern Post-Agricultural Community." *Rural Sociology* 59, no. 4: 636–54.

Schellenberg, James A. 1981. "County Seat Wars: Historical Observations." *American Studies* 22, no. 2: 81–95.

Schwartz, Gary. 1987. *Beyond Conformity or Rebellion*. Chicago: University of Chicago Press.

Siu, Paul C. P. 1952. "The Sojourner." *American Journal of Sociology* 58:34–44.

———. 1987. *The Chinese Laundryman: A Study of Social Isolation*. Edited by John Kuo Wei Tchen. New York: New York University Press.

Smith, Marc A., and Peter Kollock, eds. 1999. *Communities in Cyberspace*. New York: Routledge.

Smith, Page. 1966. *As a City upon a Hill: The Town in American History*. New York: Knopf.

Sofranko, Andrew J. 1992. "The Lore and Reality of Small Towns." *Illinois Research* 34, no. 3: 4–8.

Sokolow, Alvin D. 1981. "Local Politics and the Turnabout Migration: Newcomer-Oldtimer Relations in Small Communities." In *Population Redistribution in the Midwest*, edited by Curt Roseman, Andrew J. Sofranko, and J. Williams, 169–90. Ames: North Central Regional Center for Rural Development, Iowa State University.

Sorensen, Ann A., and J. Dixon Esseks. 1998. *Living on the Edge: The Costs and Risks of Scatter Development*. DeKalb, IL: American Farmland Trust.

Spain, Daphne. 1993. "Been-Heres versus Come-Heres: Negotiating Conflicting Community Identities." *Journal of the American Planning Association* 59: 156–71.

Stewart. James B. 1993. "Annals of Disaster: Battle on the Sny." *New Yorker*, August 3, 30–40.

Stull, Donald D., Michael J. Broadway, and David Griffith, eds. 1995. *Anyway You Cut It: Meat-Processing and Small-Town America*. Lawrence: University Press of Kansas.

Suttles, Gerald D. 1972. *The Social Construction of Communities*. Chicago: University of Chicago Press.

Tauxe, Caroline S. 1993. *Farms, Mines, and Main Streets: Uneven Development in a Dakota County*. Philadelphia: Temple University Press.

Terry, Don. 1995. "Town Takes a Hard Line on Street Gang's Symbols." *New York Times*, February 7.

Thu, Kendall M., and E. Paul Durrenberger, eds. 1998. *Pigs, Profits, and Rural Communities*. Albany: State University of New York Press.

Tickamyer, Ann R. 1992. "The Working Poor in Rural Labor Markets: The Example of the Southeastern United States." In *Rural Poverty in America*, edited by Cynthia M. Duncan, 201–11. New York: Auburn House.

Tickamyer, Ann R., and Janet Bokemeier. 1988. "Sex Differences in Labor Market Experiences." *Rural Sociology* 53:166–89.

Tilly, Charles. 1973. "Do Communities Act?" *Sociological Inquiry* 43, nos. 3–4: 209–40.

Tolbert, Charles M., Thomas A. Lyson, and Michael D. Irwin. 1998. "Local Capitalism, Civic Engagement, and Socioeconomic Well-Being." *Social Forces* 77: 401–28.

Tonnies, Ferdinand. 1957. *Community and Society.* Translated and edited by Charles P. Loomis. Originally published in 1887 as *Gemeinschaft and Gesellschaft.* East Lansing: Michigan State University Press.

Tornatore, Jane B. 1993. "Invasion and Social Reproduction in a Rural Midwestern Village: A Precarious Future." Master's thesis, University of Illinois at Urbana-Champaign.

Turner, Frederick. 1998. "The Landscape of Disturbance." *Wilson Quarterly* 22, no. 2: 37–41.

Urry, John. 1995. *Consuming Places.* London: Routledge.

U.S. Bureau of the Census. 1950. *Characteristics of the Population: Census of the Population.* Washington, DC.

———. 1960. *Census of Population and Housing.* General Social and Economic Characteristics. Washington, DC.

———. 1970. *Census of the Population: Characteristics of the Population.* Washington, DC.

———. 1980a. *Census of Population and Housing 1980.* Summary Tape Files 1A and 3A. Unpublished microfiche data on characteristics of places of less than 2,500 population. On deposit at the Illinois State Data Center, Springfield.

———. 1980b. *Population Census of 1980.* General Housing Characteristics. Washington, DC.

———. 1980c. *Population Census of 1980.* General Social and Economic Characteristics. Washington, DC.

———. 1990a. *1990 Census of Population and Housing.* Summary Tape File 3A. http://www. census.gov/cdrom/lookup.

———. 1990b. *Money, Income, and Poverty Status in the United States, 1989: Advanced Data from March 1990.* Current Population Survey no. 168:60. Washington, DC.

———. 1990c. *Summary Population and Housing Characteristics.* C3.224/3, 1990 CPH-2-1. Washington, DC.

———. 1991a. *The Hispanic Population in the United States.* Washington, DC.

———. 1991b. *Population Profile of the United States 1991: Current Population Reports.* Series P-23, no. 173. Washington, DC.

———. 1999. *Statistical Abstract of the United States.* Tables 617, 613. Washington, DC.

———. 2001. *Census of Population 2000.* http://www.census.gov/census2000/states/il.html.

———. 2002. *Census of Population 2000.* http://censtats.census.gov.pub/Profiles.shtml.

U.S. Department of Agriculture (USDA). 1982. *Census of Agriculture.* Washington, DC: Government Printing Office.

———. 1997. *Census of Agriculture.* Washington, DC: Government Printing Office.

U.S. Department of Commerce. 2000. Bureau of Economic Analysis. *Regional Economic Information System* (REIS) CD-ROM, 1969–98, Employment Files.

Van Maanen, John, ed. 1995. *Representation in Ethnography*. Thousand Oaks, CA: Sage.

Van Slyck, Abigail A. 1995. *Free to All: Carnegie Libraries and American Culture, 1890–1920*. Chicago: University of Chicago Press.

Varenne, Herve. 1977. *Americans Together: Structured Diversity in a Midwestern American Town*. New York: Teachers College Press.

Vidich, Arthur, and J. Bensman. 1958. *Small Town in Mass Society*. Princeton, NJ: Princeton University Press.

Warren, Roland L. 1978. *The Community in America*. 3d ed. Lanham, MD: University Press of America.

Wedekind, Claus, and Manfred Milinski. 2000. "Cooperation through Image Scoring in Humans." *Science* 288:850–52.

Wellman, Barry. 1979. "The Community Question: The Intimate Networks of East Yorkers." *American Journal of Sociology* 84:1201–31.

Wellman, Barry, and Milena Gulia. 1999. "Net-Surfers Don't Ride Alone: Virtual Communities as Communities." In *Networks in the Global Village: Life in Contemporary Communities*, edited by Barry Wellman, 331–66. Boulder, CO: Westview Press.

Williams, Brett. 1975. "The Trip Takes Us: Chicano Migrants on the Prairie." Ph.D. diss., University of Illinois at Urbana-Champaign.

———. 1979. "Migrants on the Prairie: Untangling Everyday Life." In *The Chicano Experience*, edited by June Macklin and S. West, 83–110. Boulder, CO: Westview Press.

———. 1984. "Why Migrant Women Make Their Husbands Tamales." In *Ethnic and Regional Foodways in the United States*, edited by Linda Keller Brown and Kay Mussell, 113–26. Knoxville: University of Tennessee Press.

———. 1988. *Upscaling Downtown: Stalled Gentrification in Washington, D.C.* Ithaca, NY: Cornell University Press.

Williams, Stacey. 1996. "Familia y Communidad: Social Capital and Mexican-American Educational Attainment in a Midwestern Town." Master's thesis, University of Illinois at Urbana-Champaign.

Willits, Fern K., Donald M. Crider, and Richard B. Funk. 1988. "Small Town Youth Relate Their Recreational Preferences." *Small Town* 18, no. 4: 14–18.

Wilson, John, and Thomas Janoski. 1995. "The Contribution of Religion to Volunteer Work." *Sociology of Religion* 56:137–52.

Wilson, Tamar Diana. 1994. "What Determines Where Transnational Labor Migrants Go? Modifications in Migration Theories." *Human Organization* 53: 269–78.

Wright, Harry. 1988. "Study of Fourteen Communities in a Western Illinois County." Unpublished document in Salamon's file.

Wuthnow, Robert. 1994. *God and Mammon in America*. New York: Free Press.

———. 1998. *Loose Connections: Joining Together in America's Fragmented Communities*. Cambridge, MA: Harvard University Press.

Zavella, Patricia. 1994. "Reflections on Diversity among Chicanas." In *Race*, edited by Steven Gregory and Roger Sanjek, 199–212. New Brunswick, NJ: Rutgers University Press.

INDEX

abandoned housing: contract purchases or rentals of, 53; county takes for back taxes, 49; shabby residential town, 49; Splitville, 160

adolescent gangs: Arbordale, 151–52; Corntown, 152

adolescent mall rats, 38

adolescent pregnancy, Arbordale, 151

affluent residential town, economic type, 44–47

aging population: shabby residential town, 49; Smallville, 73; trait of agrarian town, 41

agrarian community or town: authentic hometowns, 10; community culture in, 4, 5, 13, 18, 23, 179, 181, 183; community effect of, 190; cross-age relations, strength of, 12, 19, 20, 21–22; definition of, 5; differential community change of, 179; diverse economy and, 177; as an economic type, 41–44; and exurban sprawl, 8; farmers in, 23–24, 36; generation of social capital by, 18; grid railroad town layout of, 12; identity and attachment to land, 181, 182–83; interconnectedness and networks in, 5, 14–15, 185; land use change in, 12, 51; public spaces with change, 179; resembles *gemeinschaft*, 14; resist neighborhoodization, 205; resources prevent growth machine, 54; similarity to shabby residential town, 44; social resources and trust, 18, 187; stranger in, 23; subtle tapestry of cultures among, 10; tolerance of youth in, 13, 18, 19, 20, 109, 190; transformation and effects of, 4, 5, 6, 191–92; volunteerism as social resource, 17

agrarian vs. postagrarian communities: church membership, 16; community building, 16; cross-age relations, 19–22; extent of "communityness," 11; interconnectedness in, 14–17; social resources, 17–19; space and place, 12–14

agribusiness: Arbordale economy dependent on, 132; technology changes cut jobs, 145

agriculture, Illinois economy dependent on, 36

altruism, related to group stability, 187

Arbordale: accommodation of newcomers, 185, 192; adolescent gangs in, 151–52; agribusiness economy, 132, 134; Anglo cultural brokers, 141–42, 146, 147–48; Anglo oldtimers, 139–40; Carnegie library in, 134; census designation as village, 199; community setting, 132–36; controlled by elite families, 134; deviated little from past with transformation, 134, 179; educational profile, 200–201; employment pattern, 200; high school rituals in, 145–46; income distribution, 201; magnet town for Mexicanos, 25, 150; median income rise, 204–5; as mixed-economy town, 48; mosaic of small worlds, 139–40; newcomer engagement in, 181, 184, 193; nursery businesses, 134–35; postagrarian stratifica-